MODERN TAROT

ALSO BY MICHELLE TEA

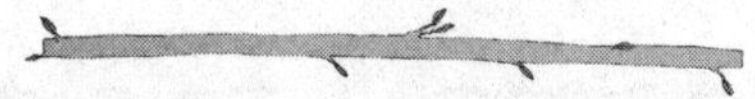

The Beautiful

Mermaid in Chelsea Creek

Girl at the Bottom of the Sea

Castle on the River Vistula

Black Wave

How to Grow Up: A Memoir

Valencia

Without a Net: The Female Experience of Growing Up Working Class

Rent Girl

Girl at the Bottom of the Sea

Rose of No Man's Land

The Chelsea Whistle

The Passionate Mistakes and Intricate Corruption of One Girl in America

MODERN TAROT

CONNECTING WITH YOUR HIGHER SELF THROUGH THE WISDOM OF THE CARDS

Michelle Tea

ILLUSTRATED BY AMANDA VERWEY

HARPERELIXIR
An Imprint of HarperCollins*Publishers*

HarperCollins books may be purchased for educational, business, or sales promotional use. For information, please email the Special Markets Department at SPsales@harpercollins.com.

FIRST EDITION

Library of Congress Cataloging-in-Publication Data is available upon request.

ISBN 978–0–06–268240–6

17 18 19 20 21 LSC 10 9 8 7 6 5 4 3 2 1

For the Witches who do not know they are Witches,
And for the ones who do.

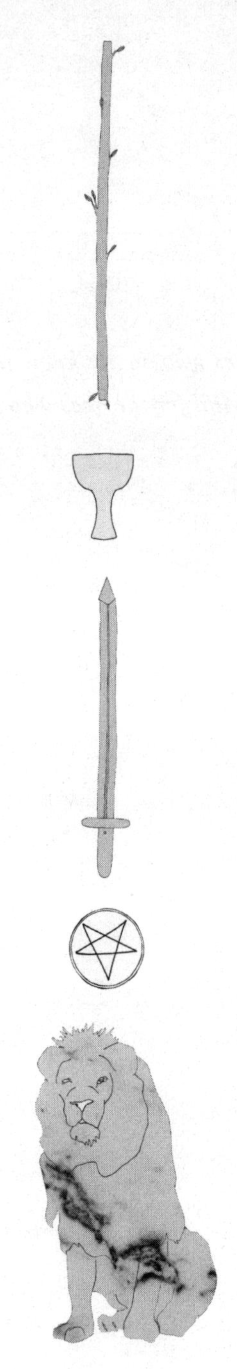

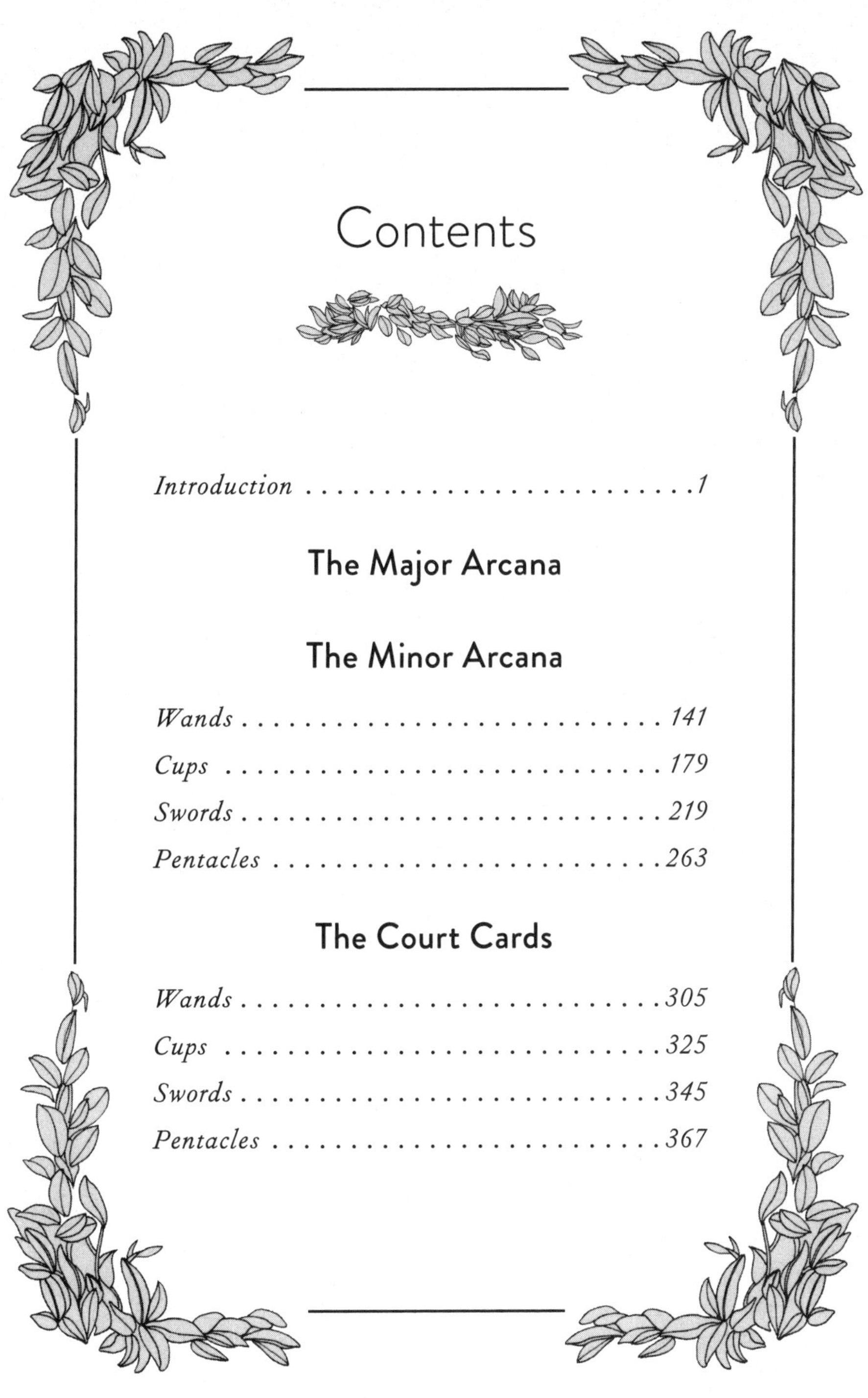

Contents

MODERN TAROT

Introduction

I've been reading tarot cards since I was fifteen years old, when Danny Frizi, a then-closeted gay boy who loved Axl Rose *so much* that he spent his extracurricular time listening to "Sweet Child O'Mine" on his headphones and weeping, gave me my first deck. He had an afterschool job at Barnes & Noble and swiped a Rider-Waite deck for me, a great starting deck, the classic tarot that most other decks riff on. I thought it was great that Danny gave it to me because I'd heard a superstition that you weren't supposed to buy your own tarot cards, they were meant to be gifts.

I treated my deck of cards as reverently as I'd heard you ought to. I wrapped them in silk (I think it was silk, it might have been polyester) and tucked them under my pillow, thereby ruining many a night of sleep. I learned the deck by practicing on my witchy, Goth friends, teenagers who accompanied me to New England spell boutiques like Arsenic and Old Lace, where the walls were stacked with jars of herbs, and on pilgrimages to Salem, Massachusetts, to explore the many occult shops and bookstores. As I continued to read cards, and have my own read by my friends, I was in a growing state of awe at their intuitive accuracy, the way the small stories encapsulated in each illustration knit together into a wider narrative that made sense, sometimes poetic, sometimes chillingly pointed. I didn't know *how* the Tarot worked its magic, but I didn't feel the need to, either. There are many mysteries in the world, and I was thrilled to have a relationship with this one.

As I grew older and moved out into the wider world I became acquainted with the variety of tarot cards that are available. The Thoth Deck, designed by the drug-addled mystic Aleister Crowley, gave strong readings. So did Daughters of the Moon, a lesbian feminist deck, purple and circular with a single optional male card. The Secret Dakini Oracle came to me via a street reader in Tucson, Arizona, and its collaged imagery, both playful and nightmarish, is a cosmic riddle. When I made my way to San Francisco in my early twenties, my first "job" was reading tarot cards on Haight Street. Still sensitive to so many tarot-related superstitions, I didn't charge for my readings but solicited "donations." I recall receiving a rock from a hippie (not a crystal, mind you, but a rock) and a single American Spirit from a street kid. I also got great advice about getting food stamps, which kept me fed as I tried to find my place so far from home.

Eventually I was plucked from the streets and into a Haight Street boutique called Love, which sold incense and essential oils and lovely candles I aspired to afford. I charged a fixed, modest price for my readings, and in the more professional environment I grew more focused and learned more about the craft. I recall one client, brooding and sulky, practically tossing her ten-dollar bill at me. I spread the cards across the floor, but oddly they made no sense. I could not connect their stories together into a larger, helpful narrative. "I'm sorry," I sputtered, returning the ten-dollar bill to the girl. "I don't know what's going on, but I just can't make sense of this."

"I knew this was bullshit," she replied, smiling for the first time, bitterly vindicated. She left me in the wake of her bad vibes, and something important was revealed to me: If the person receiving the reading doesn't actually believe in the Tarot, the Tarot doesn't work, like a fairy whose existence has to be affirmed for her to survive. Tarot readings are an exchange of trusting energy between the reader and the seeker, and if that faithful collaboration is missing—in my experience—the magic does not happen.

Further study into the Tarot, in particular the connection between the Tarot and the Kabbalah beefed up my skills so that I was able to give a decent reading with a deck of playing cards, or even a deck of Uno cards, substituting colors for suits and working my knowledge of the properties of each number. This might sound silly, but it increased my respect for the underlying numerical system of the Tarot, as well as the undeniable magic that occurs when two people come together to earnestly practice divination.

Due to space and time limitations my professional tarot practice has died down, but I still seek the wisdom of the cards regularly, and often use them to assist friends in need. It is also *very* hard for me to pass up a deck of tarot cards, which means in the thirty years I've been practicing I have built up quite a collection. They live in my Sagittarian grandfather's old suitcase, stuck with now-vintage stickers from all the places he traveled to, so many decks I can't latch it closed. Buddhist decks and Greek mythology decks, pornographic Italian decks and UFO decks. Charlie Brown decks, cat decks, old fortune-telling decks and older French decks, queer decks, and voodoo decks. Each one is a beautiful world, familiar yet altered by the creator's impressions

and inspirations. After studying them for all these years it seemed time to put my own spin on them.

The Tarot is an ancient story system, a pack of cards that tell a multitude of tales depending on the ways in which they're placed alongside one another. Pull the High Priestess, the Page of Coins, and the World, and it tells the story of an individual seeking a higher purpose through the material world, someone who is just beginning a path of knowledge but whose deep inspiration and devotion will take her very far. Lay the Eight of Cups next to the Tower next to the King of Coins and I see a person in mourning because they had to abandon something—a person, place, or thing—that was close to their heart but very, very destructive. In the end they will be stronger and whole for making this difficult choice. The trick to being able to deduce this is to know the cards well and allow yourself to link their stories together and—and this is really important—trusting that you are reading the cards clearly. It could, if you're nervous, be pretty easy to look at that last spread of cards and then say, "Oh, um, actually, it could also mean that walking away from this situation might bring the Tower down and ruin your life. I'm not sure! Thanks for coming!" Tarot speaks to our intuition, to our guts. More and more scientific research points to the right-on power of our "guts" to make quick, intuitive, and correct decisions (it's not actually our intestines sending you these powerful hunches, but two bits of our brains, the ancient Amygdala and the tiny, hidden yet emotionally powerful Insula). I believe this is the part of our selves that we engage when we read cards. Often, when I am reading for another, I hunch my head over the cards and quickly link the stories, not checking in with the

seeker or even looking at them. I don't want anything to distract me from my initial read! Going with my gut, I tell the story as I see it, and only when I reach the end do I check in with the seeker to see if anything I laid on them made a lick of sense. More often than not they are looking at me with a dazed expression, nodding their head as if in a trance. Sometimes, though, a certain claim doesn't make sense. When that happens I dig deeper into the meaning of the cards, feeling about for alternate reads or twists that feel correct to the seeker. It's important to note that I am not a "psychic," you don't have to have "psychic powers" to read tarot, and that reading tarot will not *give you* psychic powers (though it will likely strengthen your intuition and your faith in it). The Tarot doesn't shoot me random factoids about the person I'm reading. What it does is, through the use of vibrant, detailed imagery, engage my creativity and intuition and allow me to see a story, a pattern, and use that to help the seeker make sense of where they're at and where they're headed. A tarot reading isn't like a visit with a Hollywood witch who looks into her swirling crystal ball and tells you you're going to die. It's more like a really good therapy session with a preternaturally insightful therapist.

My personal take on the Tarot, as you will see, is a bit more plainspoken and down-to-earth than many of the guides that are out there. I believe wholeheartedly in the Tarot (duh), but my teenaged reverence is tempered with the fact that some of the cards are made, say, in a game factory. They hold mysteries, but we hold mysteries, too, and it's the coming together that creates the helpful uncanny. By working with the Tarot, we learn more about ourselves and perhaps more about some of humanity's big themes—

love, heartache, betrayal, friendship, triumph, despair. When you have a regular relationship with the Tarot—say, picking a card a day, doing regular tarot-guided check-ins with yourself—you have a tool to dig under the surfaces you present not just to the world but to yourself: the ways we hide from ourselves, lie to ourselves, engage in denial, the Tarot cuts through these with a single undeniable image. Alternately, it can bust up our pity-party with an illuminating image of joy to remind us that regardless of how we feel right now we've got it pretty fucking good. The result of this is balance, an honest picture of our lives and its swirl of sorrow and pleasure. It helps us not take ourselves too seriously. It consoles us—how validating to get a card of a weeping person while in the throes of a miserable breakup!—and it also pushes us to take right action to get the life we want. Additionally, becoming familiar with the suits of the Tarot reminds us of the circular nature of things, how emotions rise up but fade away, how trouble comes but is replaced by luck, which is once again unseated by hardship. Ideally, such a study in the relative impermanence of it all helps us loosen our grip on whatever we're painfully trying to stave off or pull toward us.

We are living in a moment of renewed interest in the mystical. Call it New Age or "Woo," call it Witchcraft or the Intuitive Arts or Mind-Body-Spirit; name yourself Bruja or Conjure or Pagan or Priest/ess. The point is, I can't swing a magic wand without hitting someone who's got a crystal in their pocket, or just got their aura read, or is lighting a candle for the New Moon. Yes, I do live in the rarified land of California, but through the magic of

the Internet I observe a surge of people looking toward enduring mystical practices such as tarot, spell-casting, crystal meditating, earth worshipping, goddess imaging. It makes sense to me. Our future-focused, technology-obsessed world seems to be hurtling down a bad path. People are turning to ancestral practices for a sense of enduring longevity, and comfort. To help stay sane and grounded in the midst of so much cultural insanity. To source a different kind of power in hopes of making changes both personal and political. From learning meditation to fighting off a cold with some homemade fire cider; from indigo-dyeing your curtains to strengthening your intuition with the aid of the Tarot, such old-world practices are capturing our imaginations and providing us with meaningful ways to impact our world. Tarot offers moments of deep connection during a time when connection is ubiquitous but rarely delves beneath the surface. And in a time where most religions seem irrelevant—dated, boring, antagonistic to peace—the affirming and personal nature of the Tarot offers a spiritual experience that is gentle, individual, and aspirational.

The Tarot is divided into three sections: the Major Arcana, the Minor Arcana, and the Court Cards (which are technically part of the Minor Arcana, but which I treat here as their own section).

There are many, many different kinds of tarot cards available; for this book I've chosen to work with the Rider-Waite. It was my first deck, and for me it is the ur-tarot that most other decks start from. The cards in this deck will be numbered in accordance with that particular system. I also talk about the symbology unique to the Rider-Waite design, many of which details are not shown in

Amanda Verwey's illustrations. The underlying meanings of the symbols are present in Verwey's cards, as they are in whatever deck you choose to work with.

The Major Arcana are a procession of archetypes beginning with the inquisitive, risk-taking Fool and ending with the triumph of the World. In between are a lifetime's worth of ups and downs, from the positive power unleashed by The Magician to the wild inspiration of The Star to the nerve-racking Judgment, when you are called to answer for how you chose to spend your time. Often referred to as "The Fool's Journey," each of the Major Arcana cards lead into the next, a succession of life-lessons grandly illustrated. When a Major Arcana come up for you, usually something especially significant is at play in your life, for better or worse.

The Minor Arcana, which look more or less like very dramatic playing cards, track less grand movements. The minor Arcana is divided into four suits: Wands, Cups, Swords, and Pentacles. Each suit contains ten chronologically ordered cards, which tell their own story—a rise, a fall, a resolution. Though the energy fluctuates, the knowledge increases throughout the cycle. Each suit begins with Ace, which is the pure essence of the suit itself. Aces are all inspiration; they contain pure possibility. They hold the energy of every other card inside them, highs and lows, but they are ultimately positive as they indicate a hope, a dream, an intention, a pursuit of meaning and truth and pleasure. Twos are likewise fairly positive, though they can be unsettling. They represent the first real effort toward chasing down your dream. Threes provide a bit of welcome stability, a grounding, and fours more so, though with fours we see a bit of plateauing of energy, maybe some laziness

or confusion, a foreboding of problems to come. Fives just suck. In the Kabbalah five represents the sphere of war, and fives are full of conflict and strife. Sorry about that. Kindly, sixes represent the sphere of Beauty, and proclaim happy times and much success. Sevens bring some hardship, but on the heels of your awesome six you are more equipped to deal with it, and so the challenge is embraced and there can even be enjoyment in doing the work it represents. Eights pull back from the brute action of the journey and ask us to look critically at where we've come from, making changes as needed. It's a brainy, rational number. With the nine we are nearly at the end of the cycle, so some big pay-off (or disaster, if the cycle is a negative one) is at hand, but as it's not the end of the story there is still a sense of anticipation, even nervousness. Tens are the resolution, but they are not the big happy whiz-bang party card you might expect. Because the Tarot is a glyph of life itself, and life is about action always, the pride and happiness of a ten is tempered by a tinge of boredom, of "what now"–ishness. Because as one cycle ends, another is beginning, and the suit is ready to tip back into the Ace and start the whole thing all over again. This is sometimes a big relief—the Ten of Swords, for instance, looks like *the* worst card in the deck, but it holds the considerable silver lining of this lousy moment being finally *over.*

They also contain four Court Cards, a King, a Queen, a Knight, and Page. These individuals embody the energy of their suit, each focusing on a slightly different aspect. Pages are the students of the suit, suggestive of a person who has yet to master its special powers but who is earnestly engaged in figuring it all out. Knights are super action-oriented, ready to GO, on the double, like, yes-

terday! Queens are self-assured and generous, a bit interior, strong and meditative. Kings are likewise so but more extroverted and action-oriented. These gendered archetypes are more than a bit archaic, and many modern tarot decks mess with them in helpful and illuminating manners. Since this book is using the old-fashioned Rider-Waite deck as its model, let us just remember that any gender can be a King, and any a Queen, and likewise for Knights and Pages. Court Cards may also represent situations, not people.

Each suit has its own flavor and concerns a particular aspect of life. The Swords are brainy, mental, quick, tactless, painful, and are ruled by the element Air. They're like that brilliant professor you had in grad school, the very one you hoped to be critiqued by, who stepped into your studio wearing an impeccable, avant-garde outfit only they could carry off and proceeded to rip your work to shreds. The worst part—they were right.

Swords are the cool, harsh energy of rational thought. Lacking the merciful influence of emotion, Swords are like Spock. They have their own truth and value, but they're only one part of the whole. We also have the suit of Clubs, or Wands—ruled by Fire, they are fiery and impulsive, passionate and headstrong, playful and romantic. This suit is every Casanova of every gender who ever swept anyone off their feet. They're every start-up pitch that resulted in a shit-ton of capital being injected into a garage somewhere in Silicon Valley. They're pure, inspired *energy,* the kind you feel in your gut. Of course, such intensity can burn itself out (not to mention burn up those it touches). It can run from project to project or romance to romance with fickle swiftness.

The Wands are a rollicking good time, but nothing *but* Wands can leave you hungover. It's a good thing we've got the stabilizing, sensible energy of the Disks, or Pentacles, ruled by Earth. This suit has its feet *on the ground*! That's the whole point of it. No flights of fancy to be found here, unless it's a moderately fancy, *functional* abode, as this suit represents the home and does enjoy the accumulation of capital that makes the good life possible. Where the Swords might conjure up a fantastic idea and the Wands summon the charisma to sell it, it's the hardworking if sometimes dull Pentacles that understand the real-world effort that often must be put in to make anything happen—a book, a baby, a company, a relationship. Of course, though the Pentacles represent the posh heights of material success, they also depict what happens when *i*'s go undotted and *t*'s uncrossed. This suit contains the energy of failure and flat-out-brokenness as well as any and all future dream houses and signing bonuses.

If the energy of Pentacles has gotten a bit materialistic for your liking, let me introduce you to our final suit, the Cups, which represents the realm of emotions and is ruled by the element Water—here we see how you weep after your professor has hurt your feelings and how your heart swells when that player plants their first kiss on you, the joy you feel when you move in with your sweetie and the despair you feel when it ends. The Cups are all emotional energy—both uncontrolled emotion and emotion you have a grip on—crying jags and meltdown, glee and hope and unconditional love.

Taken together, the four suits encompass the variety of ener-

gies present in pretty much every human experience—anger and grief, wonder and innocence, disillusionment, excitement, everything.

The Court Cards, as mentioned above, can represent people, or situations, and sometimes they represent you yourself, the seeker.

Because the Rider-Waite deck is my first deck and, to me, the standard from which all other decks deviate, it's the one I chose to work with in this book. In recording my interpretation of the cards, I have tried to balance my respect and love for the tradition with my own need to deviate—for instance, bringing a card like Justice up to date with my own complicated, more contemporary take on the concept. My own biases are clear—I want to make some space within the Tarot for feminist concepts and for nonbinary bodies and personalities. This balance is perfectly captured by the artist Amanda Verwey, whose playful rendition of the Rider-Waite deck is intensely contemporary while staying true to the basic mood and symbolism behind each card.

The Tarot sees gender as a hard and fast binary, with the female and feminine standing in for one clichéd way of being and the heroic male taking the other. I do believe in masculine and feminine energies; I believe that most people have a swirl of each, with one perhaps more dominant than the other. But any individual at any time can call upon these energies to help them negotiate a moment, and throughout the book when I say "masculine" or "feminine" I am imagining those labels worn by any and all genders.

I'd also like to say something about my ubiquitous use of the word "energy." It's hard to talk about tarot without talking about energy, and sometimes the word seems like a handy little catchall to fling about when you're struggling to speak about the great unknown that the cards traffic in. So what does energy even mean, then? I like to think of it as an invisible force or vibration that emanates from animate objects and energizes the inanimate. Probably any of you can recall the sour sensation of being too close to someone who woke up on the wrong side of the futon, how even something so brief as ordering a coffee off a cranky barista can send your own mood plummeting, especially if you're sensitive. What is the mechanism through which such a thing happens? You caught a whiff of that person's energy—and it stank! Likewise, some people have energy that makes you feel like a whole bouquet of lilacs after an encounter with them. You've maybe even been able to feel your own bad mood leaving toxic drips across your landscape, or had the sweet experience of cheering someone up with a smile. We are all trading energy all the time.

It's not just people who traffic in energy—animals do it, trees do it, even this café chair my butt is currently planted on does it. Science has documented the draining positive ions our TVs and gadgets give off, as well as the oddly refreshing negative ions spread by ocean waves and thunderstorms. This sounds like good and bad energy to me! Science's tracking of the bounces and undulations of the atomic molecules that make up everything from our flesh-and-blood bodies to our paper-and-ink tarot cards furthers my belief in the vibrations—the energy—we can feel (or learn to feel) buzzing off the world around us. In this energy model of the world, everything is alive, and thus everything has the ability to help us practice magic.

I believe it is this unseen, stubbornly mysterious energy that makes tarot possible. The exchange of energies between the person reading the cards, the person being read, and the cards themselves creates a little energy vortex where synergy, synchronicity, and intent coalesce and make an intuitive communion possible. When everyone's energy is on point—open, healthy, aware, curious, accepting—the cards as they are flipped over seem to flow into a seamless story, the story of your life, right here, right now. When there is a glitch in the energy—anything from feeling physically compromised to under the influence of a negative belief system or a tenacious bad mood—the Tarot may seem uncooperative, confusing, broken.

Tarot and witchery in general operate on the belief that, like a cell-phone tower, we radiate energy 24/7. What pagan practices offer us is a way to engage with our own energy and, by using tools that stimulate our creativity, imagination, and intuition, consciously direct our energy for the good of ourselves and others. The Tarot is one of these tools. By using myth and color, story and symbol, glyphs and patterns, the parts of our minds that are receptive to art and play are engaged; all ritual, including Tarot, is just art and play for grown-ups (okay, for kids too). These subtler parts of ourselves are so easily overrun by rational thought and the very unmagical demands of daily life that it's like we need to trick that part of our mind into action, lure it out with beauty and intentions, just as Zen Buddhists trigger mindfulness in themselves by entering and exiting meditation spaces in deliberately fussy ways.

Don't ask me how it all works. Not even scientists can explain why an atom is sometimes a wave and sometimes a particle, or why

the energy of our observing it seems to have an effect. But through continued observations, scientists *know* things—like that galaxies are spinning so swiftly that there must be some sort of unseen, invisible matter out there giving the universe extra bulk and heft. Through my three decades of observing the Tarot, I can attest to *something* being at work. The combining of intangible energies results in a very tangible and generally uncanny tarot reading, one that illuminates the seeker's past, present, and future. It's a delirious mystery, like love and life and death. Even if it's not entirely comprehensible, it's enriching to contemplate, like a poem. Do you get it? Me neither, not entirely. Isn't it cool?

How to Use This Book

The concept behind this book—beyond adding my two cents about what these cards might mean for us today—is to create a new way to learn the Tarot and harness its energies through a magic practice. At the end of each entry I list one to three small (okay, some are sort of epic) spells that you can do to either bring the energy of that card into your life or get rid of it. I imagine picking perhaps a card a week to illuminate what is in your energetic sphere, and then following the instruction for one of the spells to further the vibes or banish them. Most of the ingredients for these spells are easily sourced; many can be found right in your spice cabinet. I made sure that more unusual things are accessible online, and I also avoided prescribing crystals that are too expensive. Regardless, you may want to enact a spell and find yourself falling short of the ingredi-

ents. I am a casual witch: I say, use what you have and don't sweat it. Magic, like the Tarot, is 100 percent intention. If you are working with less, send more energy. Of course, you can and will pick cards and use the book when you have a specific issue you need guidance on, and in a traditional reading you can always look at the spell prescribed for your outcome card and do that if you like.

I love doing spells—it's like spiritual crafting. I have no idea if any of it works or if it just makes me feel better, but I figure I'm no worse off than the rest of humanity with our shambling spiritual hopes and gestures. I believe your spiritual beliefs and customs should be joyful, fun, and inspiring, and the solo pagan mash-up you see here works for me.

The Major Arcana

✷

0. The Fool

Welcome to one of my favorite cards in the Tarot. Zero, the Fool, is our guide through the seventy-eight cards. As we advance chronologically through the Major Arcana, it is said to be the Fool's journey: we encounter, as he did, each archetype and its particular energy in deliberate order. In the Fool's own card, then, we are at the start of a terrific journey. Ahead lies all potential—the highest highs of love and money, career and intellect, and the lowest lows

of despair and destitution, loneliness and devastation. The Fool, like all of us in our lives, will experience it all, and all in due time. But right now, as we prepare to set off on our path, it is all joy and optimism, a feeling in our gut that we're doing the right thing, that we'll find the right way, find our people, our calling, our love, and our fortune. This sense of limitless possibility, of implicit permission to take a wild leap into the unknown, is what makes this card my favorite.

I was no doubt under the care of the Fool when I (foolishly) set off across the country with a shady girlfriend I desperately wanted to be in love with. It hardly mattered that our relationship was rocky; I was young, and everything was so new, and I was driving across the U.S.A. to live for a while in Arizona, which might as well have been Mars to me, a girl reared in urban East Coast blight. Nature was something seen on TV, but suddenly I was hiking down a canyon—a rather perilous canyon—in a pair of Tevas, a footwear choice my formerly punk-goth self would have barfed at, but this new me in this new environment demanded a sensible new sandal. I scampered down the canyon mostly on my butt, and enjoyed the secluded river washing over huge boulders it had polished and carved. Newly vegan, I ate an avocado straight from its skin; what else did vegans eat? I was having a hard time figuring it out, but I was enthusiastic about this new way of living. I splashed in the water and sunbathed on dangerous little perches, feeling invincible. It wasn't until we had to climb back out of the canyon that I was gripped by what I now understand was a whopper of an anxiety attack. Quite simply, the canyon was *steep,* and riddled with spiny cactus and probably scorpions too. There was no clear path. *I got down, so I'll get back up*, was a thought that seemed logical, but after a few minutes I was separated from my friends. Slowly I crawled up the canyon. Many times I stopped and had to breathe back despair, because it seemed there was no move I could make upward. I would carefully wedge myself against a rock, shimmy over a slight dirt patch, clutch at something that wasn't spiny, praying its shallow roots wouldn't pop out of the ground and send me careening backwards. Praying? Yes, totally praying. Through my silent, sweaty march upward I prayed to the earth itself, something I knew was very much alive, and somehow aware of my presence upon it. I trusted with my whole heart that the earth loved me and would not let me fall.

Thinking about this now I am astounded at my foolhardiness. A person completely ignorant about nature, with no hiking experience whatsoever, plunging into an advanced-level climb with the notion that the earth, which she imagined as a happy sort of goddess-planet, was keeping a Disney-esque eye on her well-being? I mean, what about the bazillions of people who perish at the hand of Mother Nature every day?

I finally reached the top, shaking and grateful. I humbly thanked the earth for her help and told her I loved her. And so I know that the Fool card was with me that day—and no doubt many other days throughout my life when I attempted something kind of dumb, or something kind of brilliant.

If the Fool card has come up for you, do not take this as an invitation to jump off a cliff, at least not literally. But off a metaphorical cliff? Well, yes, by all means, hurl yourself into that great unknown. The Fool wants you to be spontaneous. Book a vacation, quit your job, apply for a dream job seemingly out of your league. Leave your partner, take a lover, leave your lover, ask someone to marry you. Run away to another country for a while, or hop a train and write a book about it. Open a store, start a nonprofit, get pregnant. If it is bathed in optimism and takes you into unknown territory, the Fool wants you doing it. If you're an outdoorsy type and *do* want to conquer the next big physical adventure, climb Everest or whatever, okay, fine, do it. Do it knowing the earth itself has got your back. Whatever mythical deity watches over idiots, drunk people, and children is besties with the Fool; setting out on this new adventure with innocence and purity of heart ensures that you are being cosmically looked out for.

This isn't to say you won't have some downs with your ups; the Fool's journey is ultimately a long one, and though your initial experience will be affirmingly positive, you're in this for the long haul, and there may be some things to reckon with down the road. But that won't happen until you've experienced your first successes, and know that this crazy choice you've made, the one everyone told you not to do, is actually the right one for you.

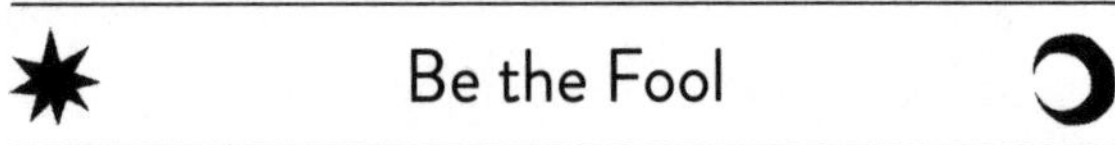

Be the Fool

- Make a Fool Pouch, to either wear around your neck or carry on your person during the day and to meditate with in the morning. Your pouch can be any of the following colors: spring

green, violet, yellow, sky blue, or white. It should contain as many of the following as possible: an anise pod, so that you move forward with passion; loose lavender, to see the beauty of your pursuit; a sprig of rosemary, for purity of intention; a bloodstone, to ensure your victory; and a piece of fluorite, to help you see clearly. Other things to energize your bag include butterfly and dragonfly wings (found in nature of course!) and the feathers of hawks, hummingbirds, and owls especially, but really the feathers of any bird will do.

Sit with your pouch in the mornings when you wake up (the closer to dawn the better). Ask it for bravery and glamour and innocence and triumph and focus. Ask it to help illuminate your path and to help you trust in yourself when the path is obscured. Touch it or sit with it throughout the day, as needed. It is certainly a foolish thing to believe that the Universe itself is looking out for you, that it's facilitating your plans, so such thoughts are protected and encouraged under this card and this spell. The Universe *is* looking out for you, and will lend you its energy as you set off into uncharted territory.

1. The Magician

This is an awesome card. The Magician asserts that you are in the right place at the right time in your very own life; that you have brought yourself here; and that you contain within yourself all the power, magic, and mastery needed to accomplish whatever you are dreaming of. Although this is a mystical card—I mean, he is a *magician*—it is a deeply pragmatic card too. It's about bringing all your dreamy feelings of inspiration and your out-of-this-world

longing and scheming and manifesting them in the here and now. What is possible under the Magician card may look like actual magic to the people who witness your abilities, but it is simply the result of you cultivating your interests and obsessions to the point that you are able to make them happen. The message here is that you *are* magic—that magic is just what comes about when you concentrate on something in so singular a way, with both purity of heart and an eye for what's possible.

Let's take a longer look at this person. In the traditional Rider-Waite deck, The Magician is depicted in white robes and a red cloak, in a garden of red and white flowers. The recurrence of the colors white and red, both in his garden and in his garb, speaks again to this magical balance of purity (white) and experience (red). *Purity,* with its connotations of sexual innocence or virtue, is sort of a gross word, especially when it's connected to the color white, so let's replace it with the word *singularity.* The Magician is here to manifest big goals, and in order to manifest you can't be all over the place. You need singular focus and concentration; you need to be able to synthesize all the elements of your desire into a single beam of light.

And speaking of elements, there they all are, laid out upon his altar. The pentacle represents the earthly parts of this manifesting and resonates with the color red, which represents experience. One reason why the Magician card is potent is that he's been around the block a few times. The Magician knows how the world works, and this is crucial, for he is a practical fellow at heart, despite his occult-y-ness. He's not going into this endeavor thinking he'll just bluff or charm or magic his way through it, and neither are you.

Magic of this caliber must be tempered with realism to give it legs in the material world.

The chalice on his altar, which represents his emotional link to that which he is manifesting, is very important, for there is much work to be done. If it is not feeding you emotionally, you're going to get bored or burned out and wonder what the F were you thinking. The chalice keeps you in touch with the emotional elements of this venture. The sword is your intellectual powers, as well as your communicative powers. It's how you conceptualized this effort, and how you continue to think about it, rearranging or even reversing your ideas as needed. And communication is key, because you'll have to explain your vision to others and inspire them to get them as excited about it as you are.

There are two wands in this picture: one laid on the table and a double-tipped one in the Magician's hand. Wands represent energy, the basic life force inside us that allows us to pursue our dreams, to persevere against obstacles, and to triumph when the haters are clucking their tongues and saying, *No way*. The wands say, *YES WAY*! The Magician lays one wand across his altar and then holds the other as high as possible above his head, to draw down the powerful chi of the Universe itself and bring that creative essence onto this plane. It's esoteric and also super-practical. In your own world, you should be looking around and seeing how these elements are present in your life, both esoterically and practically. What are the emotional stakes for you? Where is your emotional support coming from? Are you feeling energetically grounded in this effort? Do you have the nuts and bolts you'll need—the

money, resources, materials, investors, maps—to be successful? Have you not only thought it out in your mind but also put it on paper and run it by folks who might have more knowledge than you? Do you have a plan in place for when your energy is running low? Can you make a pact with yourself to get good sleep and eat healthy food and hydrate your body so it can go the distance?

When the Magician comes up, truly anything is possible; the infinity sign cycling around his head promises that. Spirit and effort, synchronicity and practicality, the mysterious timing of the Universe matches up perfectly with where you're at today.

When I was twenty-seven years old, flat broke with zero financial resources, I got it in my head to take some of the amazing, obscure, and similarly flat-broke female writers I loved on a cross-country tour so that we might expand our audiences and have a terrific adventure. With the help of my best friend at the time, Sini Anderson, a fellow dirt-poor artist, we fund-raised for a solid year and purchased a dumpy van. This being the era before the Internet, we sourced venues across America by word of mouth, punk touring publications, or gay travel guides. We called bar managers on the telephone, again and again. We sent our posters and press kits out in envelopes via the U.S. Postal Service. When the time came for our tour, Sister Spit, to hit the road, we navigated via the road atlas perched on the lap of whoever was in the passenger seat. There were no cell phones. We bought phone cards and called our promoters on pay phones, asking for directions, which we scrawled onto scraps of paper.

It was as if we conjured Sister Spit from the very air, and in

Magician style, we sort of did. We wanted this tour to work so very badly, and we focused all of our being on it, our bodies, minds, and spirits, for the entire year leading up to it. And in our way, we were practical. Personally poor, we looked to our wider community of writers and artists, queer people and feminists, who enjoyed the sort of work we did. We asked them for donations, or to come to our benefit shows, and slowly we amassed the funds we needed to make it happen. We were young, and living disastrous lives, but it was as if the Universe itself needed this to happen. Little did we know that the type of personal performance we were making was gaining popularity all across the country, from big cities like New York to small college towns like Athens, Georgia. Sister Spit was a success. Our inspiration, energy, emotions, and hard work merged with the magical moment and a movement was born. Nearly twenty years later, Sister Spit is still touring, now with different leadership, always with a different lineup, but forever with the same mixture of chutzpah, grit, love, and magic that got the first one off the ground so very long ago.

If the Magician has come into your life, get ready to dream big, and get ready to act. It is these two energies that you want to channel for maximum success. The time is right for you to manifest, so do not fear asking the Universe for the most that you can imagine; you're not going to be punished for being greedy. As my personal guru Yoko Ono sings in my favorite prayer, her song "Revelations," "Bless you for your greed / It's a sign of great capacity." But also make sure that your *t*'s are crossed. Magic will help you, but you will not coast into your dream life on a wave of lazy magical thinking. Balance all of your energies, keep your

feet on the ground, and raise your energy as high as the Magician's wand behind his altar, and all will come to you. Work, art, school, love, activism, family-making, scholarship, athletics—whatever realm you are trying to create within, the Magician card says, *yes, now, do it, go for it, make it happen.*

Bring the Magician into Your Life

- This is sort of a big ritual, but this is sort of a big deal! In this spell, you mirror the "as above so below" recipe for success that the Magician promises—that you yourself are a magical piece of the creative universe, with the ability to pull creative energy out of the cosmos. You will need a magical altar to inspire and stir the unseen energies that are available to help you. Find a surface someplace where you have some privacy. Maybe you keep a 365-days-a-year altar in your home; maybe you have to go out to the garage and brush off a carpentry desk for a while. Both are fine. What you will need is a cup of water to represent emotional power and a knife, pen, or feather to stand in for the powers of intellect and communication. A wand need only be a branch, a good, humble stick—ideally one with a little green or flowering growth on it, but no worries if that is not seasonally possible. Finally, for earth you can throw down some cold hard cash, or a hefty stone, or even a pile of lush, fertile dirt. If you can bring some flowers into the mix, I do think flowers are always lovely. If you can dress yourself in white and red, then I say, do it. In the best-case scenario, your second wand, the one mimicking what the Magician holds in his hand, would be a double-tipped quartz crystal. If that is not handy, another

branch or stick will do, but take time to whittle the ends into crude little points, okay?

Sit before your altar with some paper and a pen. You're going to do some writing. This is the practical part of the ritual. At the top of the page, write down what it is you are wanting to create, in all caps. Now let's run through the elements. Begin a segment titled WATER. Write down what this project means to you emotionally. Make a list of the people, places, or things that will emotionally support you as you take this idea to the next level. Next, write AIR. Recap why and how you know this is a good idea. Make a list of your knowledge-based resources that will support you—people, books, websites, communities that can answer questions or confirm you're on the right track. Under WANDS make a list of things that you can do to support your energy levels to prevent burnout. Think about what you need when you're feeling exhausted and make a plan to provide it for yourself preemptively. For EARTH, make a list of your hands-on resources, the material things that will help you build your dream.

When you're done with this writing, close your book and stand before your altar. Take your quartz crystal wand, or its stand-in, and clutch it in your right hand. Raise it up as high as you can, giving that shoulder a stretch. Imagine the magical, can-do energy of the Universe, the vibe that created the very planet that you are standing on. Imagine it coming through your wand and into the space around you. It is the air you are moving through, the very air you breathe. If this energy could create, say, Saturn, with its perfect rings and many moons, it can certainly offer you a hand up in getting your dream off the ground. Call upon the energy of the elements—emotional water, intellectual air, energetic wands, and practical earth—and ask them to bless you and be with you as you manifest your heart's desire. Name that desire. Say it out loud.

When you're all done, you can put the earth back where you found it, run the water down a drain (unless you are living such a magical life that you have a creek or ocean in your backyard, in which case dispose of the water there), and put your air stand-ins wherever they belong. Repeat this ritual as needed as your dreams become true and lead to bigger and bigger and even bigger dreams and that invisible infinity sign swirls above your very own head.

2. The High Priestess

Here we have the most mysterious, the most radical, the most feminist card in the Tarot, the High Priestess. A beautiful and enigmatic female figure sits upon a throne, a crescent moon at her feet. The High Priestess belongs to the moon, and all the moon represents in the occult—quiet power, secret magic, the unknown—is here in this card. The tapestry behind her, decorated with pomegranates, links her to her underworld sister, Persephone, but is also a

glyph for the Tree of Life, upon which the Tarot itself is based. The High Priestess is the keeper of the Tarot and the keeper of its mysteries; when you engage your subconscious to work with the cards, you are in her territory. She represents solitary magic, the witch without a coven, practicing alone. She represents all mystery schools and actions that seek to rupture the consciousness and reap the knowledge of the psyche. She rules your dreams, and if she has come to you, keeping a dream journal is mandatory.

There's something else about this card: the High Priestess represents the female individuals who in antiquity were crowned pope, or popess. She is the female or transgendered person who passed as male and was unwittingly crowned pope until their body betrayed them; she is the nun brazenly elevated to pope by her radical community and then burned at the stake as a witch for her wisdom and power. And so the High Priestess is all witches: those in our past who laid the foundation of magic and paganism we track today, who were burned and otherwise tortured and murdered for their wisdom and independence; those of today who gather alone or in groups to learn about the powers of crystals and heal themselves by the light of the moon; and those in the future, in whatever forms magic will take. The High Priestess is a powerful, radical card that disrupts gender dichotomies and oppressions and makes space for banished knowledge.

If the High Priestess has come for you, in the simplest reading it means stillness is called for. No matter what may be happening around you, you are to remain calm, prioritize serenity, make no sudden moves. You may have all sorts of people clamoring for you to make a decision, and you yourself may be chafing at the limbo you're in. No matter. When the High Priestess arrives, you do not yet have all the information. More will be revealed, perhaps even from your own heart or mind. You will *know* when it is time to make a move, and you will know exactly what that move should be, because this is the High Priestess's forte—the slow reveal of deep knowledge that changes or enriches a situation.

The High Priestess also rules the power of passivity. This is not the time for casting spells but for growing your own power so that future spells will be more potent and wise. It is a time for studying mysteries, especially the mystery of your own self, your self *behind* your self, your secret selves, the ones you dream about, the self who generates intuition. The High Priestess calls for a bit of hibernation, for time to allow thoughts and creativities to germinate without distraction and external influence. It is time for sitting quietly with crystals and doing lots of writing. Don't be afraid to say no to people, places, and things; everything will be waiting for you when you return. Some social activities, such as taking a class or starting therapy, are endorsed by the High Priestess, but if you drew this card to help you make a decision, her answer is: *No decision*.

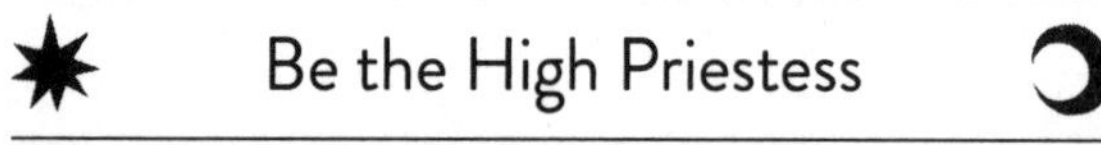

Be the High Priestess

- Bring all your water-safe crystals with you into the bathtub (some porous stones such as turquoise, pyrite, and selenite are water soluble and may become damaged by immersion). Hold

the stones and meditate with them in the bath. Feel free to make the bath as pleasant and perfumed as you like; the experience should be enjoyable. But the real point is to feel stillness and become purified for your next move, both spiritually and in the material world. Be very aware of what phase the moon is in and the current zodiac sign and acknowledge those energies, for they are at play around us and can be harnessed to strengthen inner wisdom. Light candles and if you are moved to make any offerings to the Priestess, do so.

3. The Empress

The core of the Empress, the archetypal earth mother, is connection. Not only is the Empress connected, but all of her connections run deep. She is connected in ways that we all long to be but that often seem somewhat out of our reach. She is heart-bonded to her partner and to her children. Her pets are her familiars—she understands them and communicates with them intuitively. Her

connections with her friends are profound and fulfilling, and she connects with strangers in ways that leave behind gladness and a sense of our shared humanity.

The Empress's primary connections are with the earth and its creatures and cycles, and with herself. This is illustrated by her placement outdoors, in the wild forest, seated on a throne there, the ultimate earth mother. Because she understands that she is *of* the earth, this primary connection allows her a deeper connection with herself, her own creatures and cycles. She wears a crown of stars, suggesting that her connection with nature does not stop at the earth but rises up to the heavens, and her scepter symbolizes her immense power. She is related to the Greek Goddess Demeter, the earth goddess whose joy causes the world to burst with life and whose grief brings winter. That is some serious power. Her robe of persimmons is said to represent fertility, and this mama is a real Fertile Myrtle, but to stick around in ancient Greece for a sec—pomegranates are the food of the dead, and I see in this life-affirming earth goddess a hint of her deep understanding of death as a part of life, as a part of nature. The heart-shaped shield leaning against her throne symbolizes self-protection born of love, and the glyph for Venus suggests she embodies many of the principles and traits classically ascribed to females—grace, compassion, patience, fecundity, maternal skills.

The Empress understands that the earth is her home, that it gives her every single thing she needs for her basic survival. The same is true of all of us, but as much as we long to feel connected to the earth and the natural world, such connections can be fleeting at best for most of us city-dwellers. Through a core spirituality that sustains her and colors her world, the Empress remains connected to the cosmos. Connected to her own creativity, she sees many of her activities, not just her more obviously art-making ones, as deeply creative. Most of all, she is connected to herself: loving herself effortlessly, she treats herself as she would treat any of her beloveds—kindly, sweetly, lavishly. There is no guilt or shame or toxic perfectionism in this person. Whatever her body may look like under her robes, she's into it, and it hasn't occurred to her that you wouldn't be too.

The Empress, the archetype of love, connection, and nurturance and the matriarch (regardless of gender) of our own little love tribe, comes to us when we are feeling super-loved. Maybe you are grooving on a special love or friendship connection, maybe there has been a birth, maybe your creative projects are blooming and bringing you joy, maybe it just feels super-good to be you today and you can't pinpoint why exactly but you're loving it. The Empress is reflecting this joy in life back at you.

Conversely, the Empress may have shown up for you because you're *not* feeling joyful and creative energies today. You're feeling disconnected, alone, as if life is a slog. The Empress has come to remind you that that is not the case—life is magic, and evidence of this is everywhere. If you're not able to snap out of your gloom, seek out the most Empress-y person you know and spend some time with them, soaking up their positive energies. You might even want to ask them what they're so happy about. Or what they like about you. If the Empress has come to you in a time of despondency, it means you are to look for her in your immediate surroundings and ask for her assistance. The Empress is always happy to oblige.

The Empress is a good time to say yes to anything that pops up—yes to a road trip, a romance, a collaboration, a party, a birth, a new job, a new friend. Yes yes yes. Whatever you say yes to now is bound to enrich your life and provide you with the soul-sustaining connections you need to thrive.

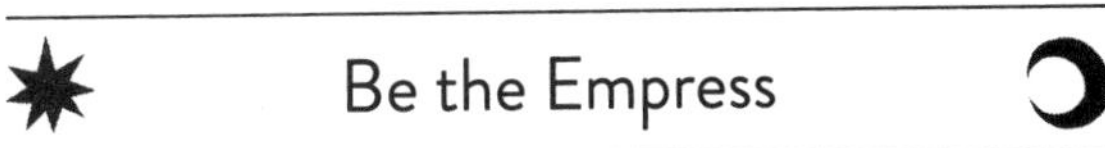

Be the Empress

- The Empress personifies connection. If you are looking for increased connection in your life, burn one of these incenses depending on your personal need and dedicate it to the Empress. Ask for her influence as you seek to emulate her openness and depth.

  Burning *amber* helps you connect to yourself, your primary essence, and the life experiences that shaped who you are. It also facilitates connections with your ancestors and lineage.

  - Burning *cinnamon* will help revive your connection with your beloved.
  - *Frankincense* will support your connections to your friends and deepen your relationships.
  - Burning *musk* will strengthen your connection to the earth and to nature.
  - Burning *Nag Champa* or *sandalwood* will grow your connec-

tion to your spirituality, your intuition, and your unconscious mind.

- ⋆ To connect with children, burn *patchouli.*
- ⋆ To open your heart to connecting with strangers, burn *jasmine.*

- Another way to bring the Empress into your life is to join a spiritual group or community. This might mean attending a ritual or a workshop, taking a class, or participating in a worship service. If truly nothing is available to you, invite into your home people with whom you have a connection you value and would like to deepen. Set up a simple group ritual that all of you will be comfortable participating in.
- A friend of mine began a monthly gathering called Femme Healing Arts Day: she gathered her female friends together and we all participated in magic, art, or self-care. We did tarot readings and passed crystals and incense; painted with watercolors and created magic oils; made baths salts and candleholders; dressed up for portraits; and ate foods selected for their magical attributes. Femme Healing Arts Day enhanced our lives tremendously and strengthened all of our bonds. The spirit of the Empress was clearly present at these gatherings and will be palpable at yours as well!

4. The Emperor

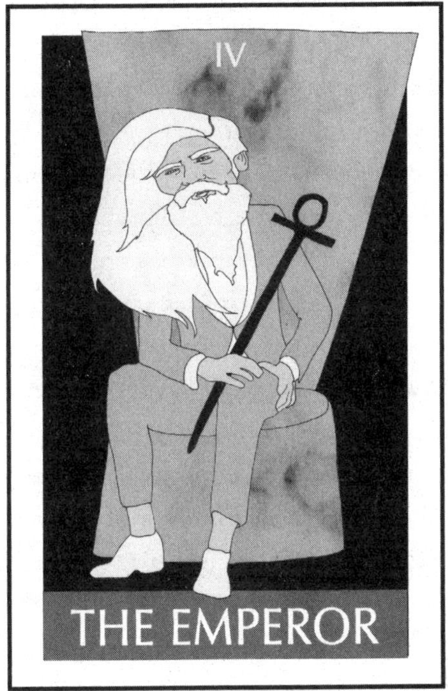

When the Emperor arrives, the left brain rules and organization, stability, foundation, and logic are the order of the day. If you are dealing with a challenge, the Emperor suggests that logic is your best tool. The Emperor doesn't have time for emotions, so keep yours tucked away lest you find yourself at a disadvantage. The Emperor is not afraid of conflict, so avoid passive-aggressive detours and get straight to the heart of the matter with strong, direct communication. This figure displays no softness; even the throne is made of hard, unyielding stone. The Emperor is a person or situation that is a my-way-or-the-highway type, come to cheer you on if you're finding it hard to stick to your boundaries. You're not here to take care of other people's feelings, the Emperor reminds you; now is the time to protect your own best interests, and perhaps those of the people closest to you.

If the Emperor is a person, I hope you're not on their bad side. The Emperor has no fucks to give and will not budge an inch. More likely, though, the Emperor has come into your sphere because you are being pushed to stick up for yourself, to stake a claim, to assert some leadership. His long white beard indicates a long and worldly life; like him, you have the experience necessary to take the reins.

In some instances, the Emperor means not that you are being oppressed by some hard-nosed bully but that you yourself are being a freaking despot. As one leader to another, the Emperor reminds you to be a merciful ruler. Are your charges miserable? Maybe you need to take a hard look at your management or communication style. If you're the victim of such an iron leader, the magic of the Emperor is just what you need to give them a taste of their own medicine and stand up to them with the same fierce energy they're projecting.

If the Emperor is a romance card, it suggests an unbalanced union. Maybe an age difference is keeping one partner invulnerable and the other a perpetual novice. Perhaps one partner is having a hard time opening up, suffering from depression, or becoming easily angered. If you're the one with Emperor issues, get some

help. If you're clinging to a block of stone, trying to eek some love out of it, call it a day and walk away.

Be the Emperor

The Emperor is a hardy, strong card that requires a hearty, strong spell to channel his energies. This dish, Emperor Tofu, is a spell dedicated to the powerful, fiery leadership qualities of the Emperor. Feast on it when you need to be fearless and to make a stand.

- As you prepare this meal, focus on channeling Emperor energy—intelligence, courage, masculine yang-vibes. Imagine yourself taking a stand, fighting to win, and succeeding. Continue the visualizations throughout your meal and into your cleanup process. This is best eaten the night before a big action, though leftovers can be snacked on at any point in the following days. If your need for raw, Mars energy is so powerful that you are craving some meat between your teeth, substitute the tofu for something bloodier.

  First, take a half-teaspoon of ground coriander (sacred to Aries, the Emperor's ruling sign), a half-teaspoon of black pepper (same), a teaspoon of salt (purification), a pinch of cloves (to keep people from talking shit about you), a quarter-teaspoon of cinnamon (protection), a quarter-teaspoon of cardamom (sacred to Mars, the Emperor's ruling planet), a quarter-teaspoon of cayenne (Aries), and a half-teaspoon of turmeric (good health). Mix it together and set it aside.

  Next, sauté an onion (Mars) and a jalapeño (protection

from negativity) in coconut oil over high, fiery heat for three minutes. Then add a tablespoon of fresh grated ginger (to move your plan along), three cloves of garlic (protection), and your pile of spices; cook for another minute. Throw in a can of coconut milk and a block of tofu that you've drained, pressed, and cut up into chunks.

Cover and simmer for twenty minutes. Before serving, add some fresh, shredded basil leaves (sacred to Aries) and a squirt of lime (to attract love and support). Voilà!

5. *The Hierophant*

The Hierophant represents a spiritual leader, someone who is learned in a particular tradition and acts to pass that knowledge on to others. The Hierophant is not just a wise practitioner but the public face of the tradition and a leader within a spiritual community. In the illustration, a triple scepter symbolizing domination over body, mind, and spirit is held in the Hierophant's left hand; through a lifetime of study, the Hierophant has learned to bring

spiritual discipline to these areas of living. The emotional right hand is held up in blessing; having become spiritually disciplined, the Hierophant can be of service to humanity. Two acolytes stand ready to be initiated into this tradition.

The Hierophant is a spiritual card, but it goes beyond religious traditions and in general rules traditions, groups, and situations that require adherence to certain rules, often for the greater good. This is not an innovative card, and it is not a radical card; the Hierophant does not welcome change. It stands for systems that have been in place for a very, very long time and is associated with a sense of reverence for the way things have traditionally been done. To seek the knowledge of the Hierophant, you have to follow particular orders, which may or may not be comfortable. This card rules organized religions, learning institutions, twelve-step groups, sports teams, and clubs of all kinds.

I have always been interested in Buddhism; its teachings seem true to me, and its traditions and myths capture my imagination the way a spiritual practice ought to. After reading about it for a couple of decades, I decided to begin studying Buddhism at a local temple in the Zen tradition. Initially I questioned the constraints placed on those who came to meditate in the zendo. Why did I have to step with *that* foot? Why did I have to place my hands in *that* position? Why did I have to turn my body *this* way? And why couldn't I wear brightly colored clothes? My own individualistic nature bucked against these strict and dour forms, but even though real frustration rose up in me, I tamped down that emotion. I wanted to learn the secrets and teachings of this particular school.

This *tradition*. As a queer, feminist person, I was accustomed to rewriting traditions to include me. Submitting to a set of rigorous rules felt oppressive, but I gave in and stuck it out. It was worth it. I learned to meditate, and I soaked in the eye-opening dharma talks given by seasoned Buddhists. I took a class and learned about Zen's history. I had revelations and adopted practices that I still keep. It was an experience I could not have had from the outside, through books. I had to join the group and conform to its expectations in order to take in the tradition.

Conforming rightfully has a bad reputation in contemporary culture; it's used to keep bright spirits down, we think, and to preserve a dying status quo. Likewise, the concept of "tradition" has been hijacked by people seeking to codify their dangerous opposition to a changing world. In the card of the Hierophant, we see conformity and tradition reexamined. There are millions of traditions, and much to be learned from the legacies of human culture and spirituality. Conforming to a set of standards can be enriching; moreover, fitting in with a group of like-minded people can be helpful—and sometimes even life-saving.

If the Hierophant has come up for you, you might be thinking about joining a group in spite of conflicted feelings about being a "joiner." The group offers something attractive to you, and drawing the Hierophant means that it is worth your while to seek it out. Swallow your ego and sign up. Perhaps you want to educate yourself by taking a particular traditional path; while it has its discomforts, this will pay off for you. Sometimes the well-trod path *is* the best path. If you are considering joining a spiritual collective,

or if you are being asked to accept a leadership role within a particular group, do it. At the end of the Hierophant's story is wisdom and an increased ability to help others.

 Be the Hierophant 

- Lapis lazuli is a beautiful stone that is sacred to the Hierophant. As you go forward and pursue knowledge and experience on a traditional path, bring this enchanted crystal with you as your truth-seeking, bullshit-sniffing detector. Hold it in your hand and meditate before a white, black, or purple candle. Ask it to sharpen your judgment and intuition as you leave your comfort zone and travel into an unknown landscape. Lapis lazuli will support your quest for truth, as it is a truth-seeking stone. Sit with it regularly to keep it charged with your intention, and if you find yourself confused about whether a choice is right for you, sit with the stone until clarity has returned.
- If you are seeking a spiritual teacher, this spell will call one to you. Find a paper image of an owl; you can tear one from a book or magazine, or you can draw it yourself. Over the image, write down your desire. Be specific—what are you looking to learn? What sort of a person are you seeking to learn from? Be as specific as you can. Next, light an orange candle. Say these words: *Owl magic I seek from thee, a Hierophant teacher to bring wisdom to me.* Fold the paper and place it under the candle; continue to burn the candle until your teacher appears. This might mean that you keep on burning your candle for a little while, especially if you are looking for a mysterious, cloak-clad mentor to swoop into your life. More practically, you might

burn it until you have clarity about the actions you can take to bring yourself closer to someone you might learn from. Maybe you have a revelation that someone close to you might be able to help, or you learn about a workshop or course of study, a trip that will bring you closer to practices you want to learn from. In any case, keep burning until you know your next move. Also, if you have any figurines or images of owls, place them around the candle.

6. *The Lovers*

Who doesn't squeal when the Lovers card arrives? Most everyone wants that glorious angel to come into their life, hands raised in blessing, a cosmic, holy *go for it*! The two figures on the card are certainly lucky: they've found one another, the grass beneath their feet grows in honor of the fecundity of their union, a mountain rises phallically in the background, one tree is burning up with

passion, and the other hosts the snake, the famous emblem of sex, knowledge, and temptation.

It is true that sometimes the Lovers card comes up to signify a nonromantic union—maybe a new acquaintance you've got a friend-crush on, or a blessed collaboration. It often signifies a sexual connection, something that feels magical and destined, something that has triggered all the infatuation chemicals in your brain; suddenly you're a romance poet, feeling compulsive and obsessed, sensitive to music, to flowers. You're in love.

Or you're not. The Lovers card also comes up for people in long-term relationships, often when the choice to leave or not to leave has arisen. More than just a ticket to ride the hot sex highway, the Lovers is about making choices. An important aspect of this card speaks not of love but of building up your personal value system and figuring out who you are and what you believe in. It's interesting that such a theme would be paired with the Tarot's major love card, but it makes sense. If anything has the power to challenge our personal ethics, it's the lure of attraction. In recovery circles, the biggest threat to a newly sober individual is said to be "romance and finance."

If the Lovers card has come up for you, you may be trying to make a romantic decision using the barometer of your morality. Is the person you are intrigued with already committed? Are you? Is it an office or academic situation, with a host of potential problems, that has piqued your interest? Is the object of your affections somehow off-limits—perhaps the ex of a close friend? Maybe you know the person you're drawn to isn't good for you, or maybe isn't a good person at all, and you're trying to figure out how you can indulge your powerful attraction without really letting this person in. Romantic complications present endless possibilities. What the Lovers card always wants you to do is take the high road—which is challenging. In fact, science has shown that obstacles placed before lovers only increase the brain chemicals that make them want each other so badly.

If the Lovers card comes up and you are in a relationship that feels happy and healthy and exciting, consider yourself blessed by that angel. If it comes up while you are struggling with the ethics of a relationship, know that the snake of temptation is hissing in your direction—what will you do? Perhaps you're like me after one round of dating that left me aching and confused: I was forced to draw up a set of standards to protect myself from my tendency to jump in too quickly with any cutie who winked in my direction. Entering my forties, finally willing to get serious about the romantic choices I was making, I started parsing out which cuties were perhaps fun for a roll in the hay *only*, and which had the gravitas required for a more substantial something. Age was newly considered, as was employment (as in, they should be employed), proximity (no more long-distance time wasters) and overall mental health. No more sex on the first date, to ensure I didn't let pheromones blind me to red flags. The Lovers card wants us to have standards, as well as a noble love of the highest level. It does not want us to settle. If you are settling, recognize it and do what you must do. If you have found a high-caliber, high-quality love, bask in the Tarot's blessing.

 Working with the Lovers 

- To bring high-quality, Lovers-approved connection into your life, make this fragrant potion: to two ounces of almond oil, add a tablespoon of orange oil and a tablespoon of citrus. Add the zest or peel of an orange and a grapefruit. Drop two apple seeds into the oil, and sink a single amethyst in it. Mix it all up. State your intention: you want this potion to bring you a royal love. Anoint yourself with this oil behind your ears, on your throat and wrists, between your legs, and behind your knees before you leave the house.

  Before it brings you love, or in addition to bringing you love, this spell may bring you information *about* love that will heighten your understanding of it, and of who you are and what you want. Be patient and allow the fullness of the spell to take. Be alert for individuals outside your normal taste, and ask the potion to help you be open to them.

- If you are unsure whether the person you are with, or trying to be with, is truly a good person for you, ask the Universe to do what you're not able to do yourself. Take two of the same type of coin (i.e., two pennies or two dimes), hold them in your hand, and say: *If we are true, please bind our heart, if we are false, tear us apart.* Toss the two coins as high in the air as you can, and then walk away from them. Do not look back. More information should come to you now, in the form of communication or circumstance. If something arises that comes between you and your beloved, allow it. It means you're not good for one another, and the spell is sparing you both pain and guiding you toward others whose hearts are more in synch with your own.

- Here is a simple ritual to help you come to a clear and healthy decision regarding your love life. Make a strong tea by placing an entire bundle of fresh mint in a deep bowl and filling it with boiling water, then letting it steep for thirty minutes. Take a ritual shower. As you cleanse yourself, know that you are washing away indecision, denial, excuses, and clouded thinking. You are cleaning not only your body but your aura, your protective shield. When you are done, make sure the mint tisane has cooled to skin temperature, and pour it slowly over your head. Mint is powerful for breaking spells; ask it to help you come out from under the spell of attraction, so that you may make good decisions for yourself. Mint supports mental toughness; ask it to keep your mind sharp and help you stay focused on what is best for *you*. Don't rinse or dry yourself off. Allow yourself to air-dry. This spell works best before sleep. Climb into bed with mint leaves in your hair and allow it to work its magic on your psyche as you slumber.

7. The Chariot

If the Chariot card has come into your world, it's looking like you're the boss. Even if you're chewing your cheeks, you're biting your nails, and butterflies are swarming in your stomach, the Chariot will not take no for an answer, and it demands that you refuse to take no for an answer too. The Chariot—called the Chariot of War in some circles—heralds that it's time for you to fight to get what's yours.

Taking a peek at this card, we see some royal-type person clad in a chic yet practical outfit of armor, with some witchy, art-deco moons on the shoulder and a shining image of the sun on the crown. Since this is the Tarot, fashion is never just fashion—it's symbols. Since you probably are not going to be jousting or dueling, the armor is a symbol of the invulnerability achieved when you gain control of your emotions. Although a lot may be riding on this situation and the stakes feel high, it's imperative that you keep your emotions in check while in "battle," whether that's a professional or romantic negotiation. I generally advise a life philosophy that encourages tenderness, emotional honesty, and noncompetitiveness; what the Chariot represents are those moments when such an approach will fail you. There is a time and a place for all things, and the Chariot is about fighting, competing with, and besting your opponent. If you've pulled this card from the pile, that's what the scenario is calling you to do. Pull on your suit of mental/emotional armor and hit the battlefield.

Much of the imagery on the Chariot points to duality: the moons on the shoulder versus the sun on the brow, and the Sphinxes, each the negative twin of the other. These images speak to the essential duality within all of us. Each of us is both confident and nervous, capable of both love and hate, and proficient in both emotional and rational wisdoms. Although the Chariot does require us to take an aggressive stance to get what we want, it does not require us to become total beasts in the process. It acknowledges that the supreme confidence you must channel to succeed lives alongside profound doubt. What is required to triumph under the Chariot's direction is not banishing your softer side but balancing it with the part of yourself that wants to win at any cost. Generally, this sort of single-minded drive must be relegated to the background if you're going to make nice with others, but in the Chariot your bloodthirsty prowess is called to the court. Bring it!

I'm not going to lie: the Chariot is a challenging one for me personally. As a codependent, people-pleasing dreamer, I want to smile and charm my way into the things I want; I want my special ideas and uniqueness to be what gets me what I'm after. Most of the time, being easy to work with and an ace brainstormer works out. But all of us have moments when we have to roll into a room like a baller and make demands. Such situations have surfaced for me when I've edited collections of other people's writing or edited a collaborative film. I had to trust my vision and stay true to it by requesting, then demanding, that people make changes to their work that they didn't necessarily want to make. I could have been more of a people-pleasing team player, but I felt certain that my vision was the best one, and so I went to bat for it. I think I bummed some people out; I still don't like thinking of that part. But the projects turned out exactly the way I wanted them to, and I'm proud of them *and* of my decisions to fight for what I wanted and not take no for an answer.

If the Chariot comes up for you, know that it's time for you to put on your thick skin and go to battle. It's okay if this goes against your nature, if you're trembling, if you feel like a total faker. *Fake it till you make it* is a great mantra when dealing with the Chariot. You're not required to be a 24/7 warrior to work with this card and get what you want. You only need to *pretend*, for a moment, that you're a tough-ass bitch who spanks the competition. After you've successfully scored, you can lock yourself in a little room and cry your nerves out. But really, you might not want to. You might find that accessing and flexing that particular muscle actually feels *good*. Rather than cry, you might want to take yourself out for a celebratory drink, after tucking your brand-new bossy pants into your dresser to be worn again, as needed.

Be the Chariot

- Get yourself some pyrite. It's a great crystal for balance and control, two qualities you need if you're going to pull yourself together and go to metaphorical war. You want to find your inner control freak for this one, and pyrite is your ally. Meditate with it, ask it for help, tell it what you want, and keep it on your person while engaged in your battle. Once you've won (the Chariot always wins), bury the pyrite in salt for twenty-four hours to cleanse it. It will be ready for you the next time you need it.
- Red and orange candles will stimulate the fiery energies required for any battle, and white and black candles are helpful for silencing and controlling the less confident, more emotional parts of yourself during this time. Or do your one-stop spelling with a single purple candle, for dominance—over yourself and over the situation.
- Here's a serious domination spell to help you beat your competitor. Take a piece of paper and write out the name of your

nemesis clearly. On top of it, write your own name—darker, bolder—three times. Roll the paper up and tie it to a mandrake root. Wrap it up in dark cloth and bury the bundle in dirt some place where it's unlikely to be disturbed. Go home, hold some pyrite, or sit before a candle and imagine yourself winning.

8. *Strength*

Look at the person on this card, draped in flowers and handling a wild lion as if it were just another kitty. You've gotten the Strength card, one of the most beautiful and complicated cards in the tarot deck. It is easy for the delicate meaning of the card to be distorted by our feeling-phobic, male-centric culture of today and yesteryear. I don't know about you, dear reader, but for me, being told

that I'm being too emotional or sensitive smacks of patriarchy and betrays an unwillingness to bear witness to legitimate gripes because of discomfort and denial. And yet, in this image of a, yes, female subduing a wild beast happy to submit, we have a glyph for bringing our often raging feelings and passions under control in a validating and loving way, and for the express purpose of enabling ourselves to get what we want in the world.

The lion represents our inner wild thing, the sensitive beast of our heart. Ruled by the zodiac sign Leo, this proud and touchy person is as quick to tear up at being left out as to dominate a party with charm and charisma. In many ways, Leos are ruled by love, which leads to a sign full of ups and downs, wild roaring passions and tragic heartbreak, crazed lust and dramatic proclamation, and a tendency to scurry away to lick wounds in isolation when the pendulum swings the other way. All this makes for a character we'd prefer to observe on a television, from the safety of our couches. And no doubt many of us have fallen under the captivating spell of such a person. But what if you *are* that person? When the Strength card comes to you, it suggests that your native passions, though sacred to your person and the source of so much of your precious individuality, have spun a little out of control. And though you may have spun up quite a tornado, in the end the person sustaining the most damage is likely to be you.

As a rather wild thing myself, I've been greeted by the Strength card *many* times. It came to me when my drinking, once a source and symbol of my liberated spirit, had degraded my spirit to the point of terrible depression and stunted creative growth.

It came when my lust for life—and many people, all at once—created a string of hurt feelings, people I cared for turned sour and betrayed, and I lost my sense of myself as a just and fair person.

So what did I do? I got sober, and I reevaluated my dating philosophies. These were tough projects, and if the Strength card has come for you, you're probably struggling in a similar way over some aspect of your life, or your approach to it. The golden trick of this card and the way to make the work easier—even rewarding—is love. Compassion. Empathy. The maiden on the card—a slight, Mona Lisa smile on her face—uses a gentle hand. She has boundless affection for the lion and all his lion-y ways. Her efforts here are not aimed at changing him, but at simply bringing him under control so that he might stop devouring small children and destroying the villagers' thatched huts. And the lion, in his submissive pose, is ready to be tamed. He gets that the delicious taste of small children isn't worth the mad drama of a hundred villagers on his tail, torches lit.

And so what we see in this card is a collaboration. It is up to you to collaborate with your own wild side, for your mutual benefit. To continue using the examples from my own life, it would not have worked to say to myself, *You drunken loser, you've ruined your life. Why are you such a weakling? Quit acting like such a low-life scumbag!* Instead, a reckoning with what drinking meant to me was in order, including a salute to the aspect of myself that craved wildness, had an endless capacity for *more,* was brave and daring, and longed for arenas in which to explore my daredevil nature. This was all good, holy stuff. It just needed to find a different, safer avenue for expression. Same for my super-sluttiness. How wonderful it is to be so genuinely liberated in a culture that stops at nothing to shame women for being sexual. But when my lust for lust tipped into the compulsive, when I felt at its mercy and unable, or unwilling, to consider the consequences of my indulgences, the pleasures of sexuality became deeply marred.

As you go about correcting the proportions of whatever energy is giving you grief, never ever blame yourself, beat yourself up, or demonize your demons. These aspects of yourself are gifts—they make you both universally human and individually *you*. It is only a matter of bringing these energies under your conscious control so that you will have maximum agency and autonomy in your life and be able to seize the career, the relationship, the creative project, or the basic happiness you desire. You are both the maiden and the lion, each in rapturous love with the other, engaged in a dance of mutual benefit and understanding.

Be Strength

- Make some crystal chakra magic. Your ally in this work is carnelian, a handsome, reddish-rusty-orange stone that is great for courage and stamina. *Courage* is synonymous with *fortitude,* the original name for the Strength card, and so this is as close to a namesake crystal as it comes, tarot-wise. Carnelian rules the second, sacral chakra, an orange whorl situated between your belly button and your pubic bone. Your basic life force nests in

this chakra, and it is a crucial conduit for body-mind communication. Like carnelian, your sacral chakra is a big helper in all efforts to bring rampant energies under control.

Sit or lie with the carnelian held or lying on your sacral chakra. Imagine its raw, red courage seeping into your guts. Imagine the spinning crimson light of your sacral chakra melding with the crystal, both harnessing its strength and infusing the stone with its own. Continue the meditation by thinking about what it is you are wishing to transform. Acknowledge the energy's wisdom and value, and look honestly at the havoc wreaked in your sphere by its current unformed state. Envision what your life would look like with this energy under your control. Imagine how you would feel. Sense how close this reality is to you, and ask the carnelian to keep you brave and motivated, to impart its psychic wisdom to you. Carry the stone with you always, holding or touching it whenever you feel your old patterns rise up. Continue to sit quietly with it for a moment each day, and check in with your sacral chakra too. Feel that energy and know that it is yours, sitting there to help you however you need it.

9. The Hermit

It's the Hermit—an older person of advanced style who has been around the block, who has lived a long, full life. Traditionally this person is male with a long white beard, but there's no reason why the Hermit couldn't be an elder female with a head of wild, gray curls poking out from under the hood of her monastic robes. When the Hermit card comes up, one thing is super-duper clear: you are alone. Maybe you hate this. Maybe you're trying like hell to get

laid, or to turn some sort of affair into a lasting relationship. Maybe you're trying to get an ex back, or trying to reconcile with a good friend, maybe even a group of them. It's not going to happen. The Hermit comes up when life itself, the Universe, needs you to be alone.

We live in a culture where being alone feels like a punishment, especially for women, who are supposed to be both immensely popular queen bees with a buzzing social circle *and* the deeply desired loved one of your Mx. Right. The Tarot, however, holds aloneness in a different esteem. The Hermit card represents the deep and deeply important things we gain from our time alone. By being with ourselves, we can gain insight into the nature of our personality and the nature of personality in general. We can see our weaknesses as well as our strengths. Indeed, our inability to be alone is often the first helpful thing we learn about ourselves when we do it. Being alone can be heartbreaking and scary, but it is also simply a part of life—an important aspect of the human experience that not even a dozen social media accounts could ever banish.

Possibly this card is a welcome sight. The Hermit rules the sort of serious scholarship that can only be accomplished by shutting yourself away from the world for a while. Maybe you are writing a novel or trying to create a different kind of masterpiece. The Hermit will help you eject all distractions. It rules retreats—artistic retreats, silent retreats, health retreats. The Hermit understands that sometimes you've got to get away if you're going to accomplish something meaningful. The Hermit does not get FOMO. Maybe it's because the Hermit is old and has sort of done everything, chased the same ultimately meaningless things we all find ourselves chasing. Worn out by the rat race, The Hermit climbs a mountaintop, which provides a metaphorical look at the big picture. The Hermit is literally above it all, with a staff to help along the way.

What is your staff—your one trusty tool, coping skill, or talent you will bring on your own retreat? Think about it. Because when the Hermit card comes up, you are retreating. Perhaps only to your bedroom to listen to music and stare at the ceiling, to play with the candles on your altar or hunker down with a book. Perhaps you're doing something truly awesome, like an endurance walk—hiking the Appalachian Trail or Spain's El Camino. When Cheryl Strayed embarked on her hike along the Pacific Coast Trail, which she'd later document in her best-selling book *Wild,* you can be sure the Hermit was along for the ride. You may be imagining a hermit all bunkered down in a cave somewhere, but the Hermit of the Tarot can also be found on the move. Perhaps your retreat is an epic walk along the ocean, or through your city with a pair of noise-canceling headphones jammed over your ears.

Let's talk about the Hermit's lantern, which is super-important, especially for those social animals who, like myself, cringe whenever this card comes into their lives. The lantern is what allows the Hermit to walk this nighttime landscape alone. Night in the Tarot always represents the unknown, the uncertain, the problem that must be solved. When the Hermit arrives, some type of soul-searching is in order, and the lantern represents your inner compass, your inner light, that thing that will guide you through this night and help you solve your current puzzle. You have everything you need to achieve the breakthrough you need.

Occasionally the Hermit's lantern represents an actual person

whose knowledge can benefit you—a mentor, a helper, a teacher, a therapist, an especially wise friend. You're still going to have to do the solitary heavy lifting, though; this is *your* soul you're searching for. Other times the lantern augurs the arrival of an individual who will point you toward the mountains you need to get lost in.

Inside the Hermit's lantern is a six-pointed star, a shape that has been used by dozens of cultures since ancient times to represent the perfect arrangement of the cosmos and humanity's place within it all. You are seeking no less than this: your own place in the world, the space you are to take up within your own life. Any quest you're currently on can be viewed this way, and perhaps seeing your path in such a mythological way will help it feel less annoying. In the Tarot, six is the number of beauty, perfection, and harmony, and the Hermit promises that this inner gorgeousness awaits you on the other side of your solitary journey.

Also, a word about the snow. I *love* snow symbolism. If water is the emotions and air is the intellect, then snow is the emotions made tangible, and understandable, by the cold air of logic. Getting a handle on our emotions, gaining an understanding of why we feel the way we do, learning to master our emotions and not be victims of them—this is a crucial step in growing up and establishing a baseline of happiness so that we can enjoy our lives. And it is by and large an inside job.

The Hermit came into my life—quite unwelcome, I might add—while I was in the stark, stoic city of Warsaw, Poland. I had been traveling with a boyfriend, and it did not go well. I arrived in Warsaw alone, to teach a series of workshops, and I brought with me the knowledge that this relationship was over. Having sunk a lot of hope and love into it, I was devastated. And what a place to mourn a lost love! Gray skies, brutalist Soviet architecture, unsmiling people, a history of war that felt palpable. Not versed in Polish, I spoke so rarely that it was as if I had taken a vow of silence. On top of it all, I was sick. My vague hope of distracting myself from my heartache by smoking cigarettes and having affairs with some cute Poles went out the window. It was just me and my heartache, alone in the little room provided by my host, with a mattress on the floor and a cat that came only to pee on it, never to snuggle.

In this bare-bones, Hermit-y environment, my heart's truth erupted in my chest with a force that brought tears to my eyes: *I want to be loved so bad*. The raw reality of it embarrassed me, but I found a way to wrap my arms around it. It was true: I wanted to be loved *so bad*. This desire was everything: an expression of my highest self, but also a distraction from an untreated anxiety disorder, which I could feel jittering me throughout my Polish retreat. During these two lonely weeks I did a lot of thinking, free from the distraction of people, of cell phones, of even a good book to lose myself in. I made a lot of connections between my anxiety, the hypomanic state it left me in, and my knack for falling in love way too quickly with individuals sporting lots of flashy red flags. When I returned to the U.S., I promptly got myself on some medication that smoothed out my crazed interior, and then I gave my aching heart a firm talking-to: *It's perfectly fine to yearn for love, but there will be no more desperate grasping at inappropriate love-objects*. With the Hermit's help, I got comfy with being on my own and acted on the insights that would only have come to me in that stoic, solitary situation.

Be the Hermit

First of all, don't resist. All the downer cards in the Tarot are rougher rides when you fight them. If the Hermit card is coming up for you, or if you have the wherewithal to know that you could use its solitary energy in your life, here are some spells to make friends with this wise, unwavering icon.

- The Hermit rules all night-blooming flowers, one of which is evening primrose. Ingested as a powder, tincture, or tea, this medicinal plant is full of fatty acids and has long been used by people struggling with PMS and pregnancy symptoms; in fact, it's a main ingredient in a lot of medicinal teas for women. In this spell, we will use evening primrose tea, which you can find on the Internet (of course) or at your local Chinese medicine provider. Check the ingredients list: if evening primrose is listed first, you're holding a tea that will work for our magical purposes. A note: if you happen to be pregnant, congratulations and *don't drink this tea without first consulting your midwife or whomever.* This powerful plant has been known to bring on labor, and you may not want that to happen.

  Wait till the sun has fully set and the moon has risen (though this spell, like most others, works best during the darkened new moon), then brew your tea and go for a walk. I imagine you winding through quiet streets, sipping your tea and connecting with your essential aloneness, though I don't know why; for the majority of my life I have in lived in wild urban areas, and perhaps you do too. If possible, get yourself to a more natural location—a hilltop would be especially nice, or even a park—but if you can't, never fear; we city witches practice our medicine

in the belly of the beast. It might feel a tad strange to stroll along teeming nighttime boulevards while sipping a cup of tea, but embrace the possibility that being solo in a crowd will make you feel most alone. Wherever you wind up, drink your tea with the intention of embracing your aloneness, and call upon the universe to help you be open to whatever lesson is yours to learn right now. It would be nice to sit quietly with your eyes open when you're done with your tea, achieving an alert, meditative state. I also recommend using a portion of your tea, or a tea bag, as a magical sachet bundled in cloth and kept in your pillowcase while you sleep. Make a nighttime wish for Hermit wisdom to come to you in your dreams, and keep a notebook and pen close enough to write down your dream upon waking, before you get out of bed or say hello to your bedmate or do anything else.

- The Hermit rules licorice root, which is turned into a popular candy these days but has long been used in magic. Take a bundle of nine licorice roots, the Hermit's number, and throw the bundle into a hot bath. Baths are great because we typically take a bath alone, and a bath can't help but encourage introspection. Ask the Universe to bring Hermit energy into your life. If the Hermit is already present, ask for the strength and the wisdom to work with its important, challenging energy. If you feel like super-charging your Hermit bath, throw some dried evening primrose flowers or tea into your bath and the crystals howlite or kyanite, both sacred to the Hermit.
- On small pieces of paper, write down the emotional situations you would like to gain clarity on. Place these scraps of paper in a small bowl or jar and cover them with water. Place the container in the freezer and let it stay there for nine hours. During this time, reflect often on whatever your issues are. At the end

of the nine hours, take the bowl or jar from the freezer. Carve or scratch a six-pointed star into the ice and place the bowl of ice before a candle. A white candle would be good, as would a black candle. Sit before it and meditate, pray, and wish. Ask the Universe for clarity. Ask the Hermit to grant you mastery over your emotions. Let the candle burn until the ice has melted, then extinguish the candle and dispose of the water and paper in running water (in other words flush it all down the toilet).

10. Wheel of Fortune

When the classic rockers sing, "wheel in the sky, keep on turning," this is probably the wheel they're talking about. When this card pops up, you can be sure that you are really *living* and that whatever gnarly, sad, or embarrassing pickle you may have recently gotten yourself into is on the outs. The Wheel of Fortune promises that change is the only thing you can rely on, and while that can sometimes suck (who wants their lovely relationship to end or their flush bank account to drain?), this card promises that the changes heading your way are happy ones that will tug you out of whatever rut you're in and thrust you deeper into the bigger, richer themes of your life.

The Wheel of Fortune card is deeply connected to destiny. It makes me flash back to being twenty-two and brand-new to San Francisco, knowing only one single person, and having just scored a cheap room in a clean house but with really no plan beyond wanting to write poetry and fall in love and start having some sex. Standing in my tiny room—four short walls with one window that looked out onto a freaky, Seuss–ian bottlebrush tree—I recall leaning against the humble desk that came with the place and having the strangest sensation come over me, a revelation so powerful that, though it started in my mind it swiftly bled into my body: everything, *everything*, in my life had led up to this moment. While this possibly mundane thought is surely true for everyone at any moment, the intensity with which it struck me marked *that* moment as a profound one for me. I *had* been through a lot recently: My heart had gotten busted up after I codependently flung myself into a love affair with a straight lady on a girl-cation. A stint in the sex industry had left me frazzled and bewildered. And my family of origin had fallen apart, unable to function in the wake of sexual abuse revelations. Some dark stuff, but standing there in my cozy room, I felt the exhilarating rush of the precipice I was on. Far from my family, free from that disappointing relationship, and with a wad of sex industry cash hid-

den in a hiking boot in my closet, I knew that my life was *finally* about to happen. I would write, and fall in love, and begin great friendships, and bond with this city, my new home. What was this breathtaking full-body *whoooooosh*? Well, clearly it was the Wheel of Fortune. That pleasantly dizzying sensation was vertigo as I took my place at the top of the wheel, my whole life spread out before me.

Let's take a peek at the Wheel of Fortune. If you enjoy esoteric symbolism, there is hardly a more densely packed card in the deck. There's the wheel itself, etched with the alchemical tags for sulfur, salt, mercury, and water, the chemical elements that correspond to the four suits of the Tarot (wands, pentacles, swords, and cups). The corners of the card are occupied by emissaries of the elements in the form of zodiac signs—that's the Aquarian water-bearer up top, next to a Scorpionic eagle (having evolved out of both a reactionary scorpion and a manipulative snake); Leo the glorious lion and lovely bovine Taurus rest at the bottom. Each sign is the *fixed* sign of its element, meaning the most stable. All of them read the Torah, which is maybe declared as TORA on the wheel itself, or maybe it's to be read as TARO—who knows? A bazillion esoteric scholars have weighed in, but all we need to take away from this glyph is that stability is change, and this knowledge can keep you rooted no matter what storms life throws your way. You hunker down in the cellar of your heart, and when the debris stops falling from the sky, you crawl back out and behold the new day and the rest of your golden life.

Let's keep puzzling out the mystical creatures plastered all over

this card, shall we? On the wheel's left we spy poor Typhon, a murderous, monster-begetting monster in the midst of his downward spiral. Typhon has had his time on top, but that time has come (temporarily) to an end. On the opposite curve of the wheel we spot the Egyptian god Anubis, half-jackal, half-human, protector of the dead and guider of souls, exhibiting elegant form as he allows the wheel to spin him back on top. But not so fast—currently enjoying fifteen minutes of positive karma is a pretty blue Sphinx *literally* at the top of her game, wielding a sword, symbol of a sharp mind. This, my friend, is you.

At a glance, most of us can relate to all three beasts surfing the great wheel. We've been on top, riding high like the (slightly smug?) Sphinx; we know what it's like to work our ass off to clamber back on top like crafty Anubis (who doesn't seem to be breaking a sweat about it actually), and we've squiggled down the backside, undone by our own fecklessness or the whims of circumstance. The takeaway here is the inevitability of these ups and downs and the relief in remembering that everything, everything, *everything*, changes. Sure, you might currently be belly-flopping, but the wheel promises that you will once again have your moment on the diving board, where the view is gorgeous and everything seems possible. The ultimate optimism of this card comes courtesy of its ruling planet, Jupiter, a jolly god who doesn't spend too much time licking his wounds, not when there is so much *fun* to be had. Though the card is a predictor of change, that change tends to be positive. In its representation of the entire success-failure-success cycle, it aims to be nothing less than a glyph of human life, karma, and destiny.

Bring the Wheel of Fortune into Your Life

- Create a Square of Fortune, those grade-school origami games known as fortune-tellers, cootie-catchers, or salt cellars. In the place where eight silly fortunes once went, write out eight different actions you can take to guide your destiny. These should all be things you actually *want* to do! Don't write down "go back to school" if the thought fills you with dread. Don't put "break up with so-and-so" if you're in a happy relationship. *Do* list educational paths if you want to learn things, and relationship-enders if you need to bail on a connection that's holding you back. Other good ideas include—write a book, make a movie, move to a new town, move to a new country, volunteer somewhere far away, volunteer somewhere nearby, have a baby, have someone else's baby, ask someone out, get a driver's license, learn to sail a boat, invest some money, quit your job, go train hopping, start a band, adopt a puppy, take a solo vacation, shave your head, get a tattoo, make a new friend, quit drinking, drop acid—the list goes on, the options being as endless as destiny itself.

  Write your eight destinies in shorthand on small pieces of paper, then fold them and shuffle them so you don't know which is which. Paste them into your Square of Fortune and play the game, picking a number and counting it out, picking a color and spelling it out, until you land on your destiny. That shiver you feel as you read the chance you've committed yourself to take is the sensation of *being alive*!

- If you already know what big move you want to make to propel yourself harder into your destiny, make an altar to the four

SQUARE PAPER

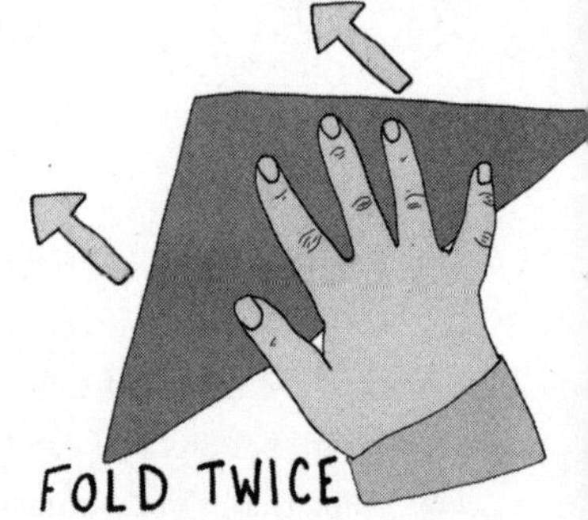
FOLD TWICE

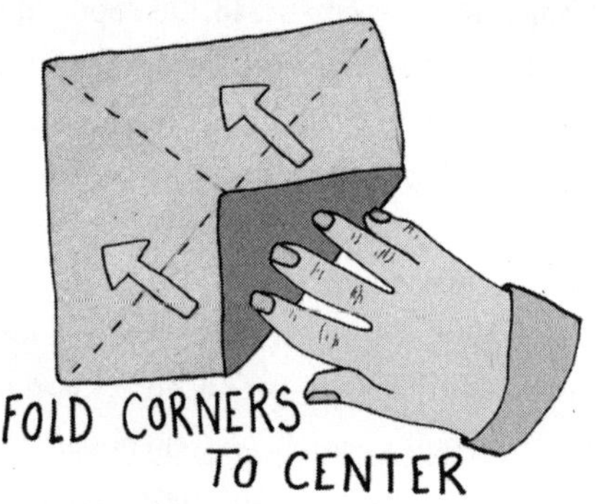
FOLD CORNERS
TO CENTER

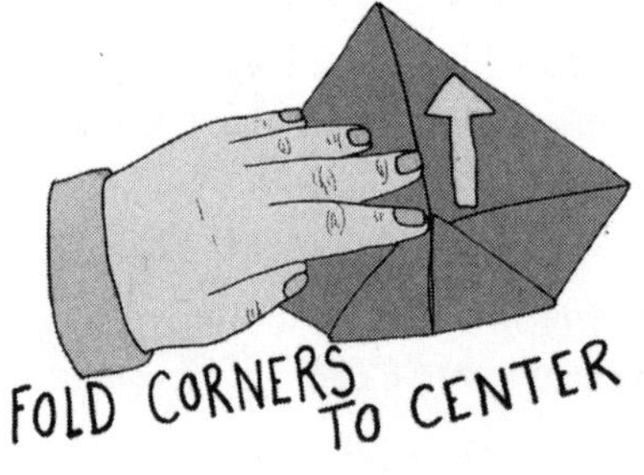
FOLD CORNERS
TO CENTER

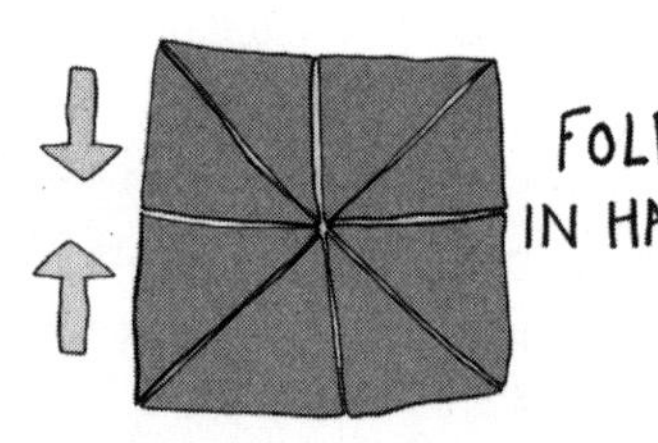
FOLD
IN HALF

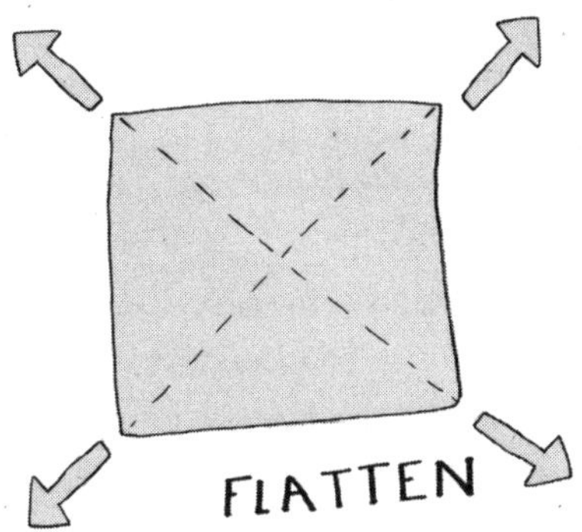
FLATTEN

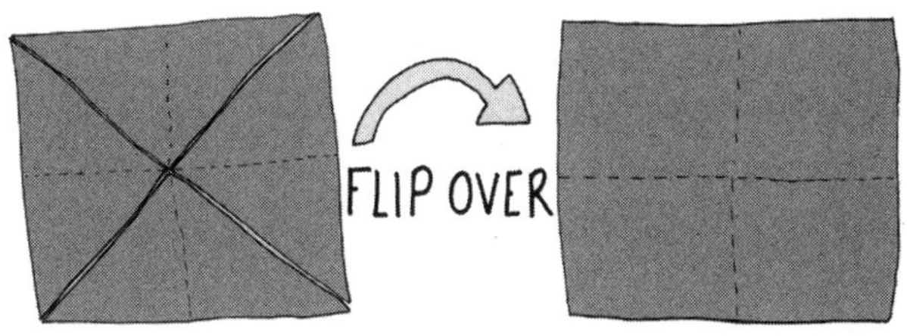
FLIP OVER

PINCH CORNERS
UNDER THE FLAPS

VOILÀ!

directions. Place upon it a book that has been meaningful to you or has some relevance to what you are trying to accomplish. Also a glass or bowl of water (make it pretty) and a candle (blue would be good, for the vastness and clarity of a brilliant blue sky). And something from the earth—a flower or plant, a branch or twig or rock or crystal.

Sitting before your altar, take a moment to meditate on what it is you wish to do. Visualize yourself successfully doing it. Go wild with this best-case scenario! Finally, write out ten things you can do to help make this happen. Do you need to purchase things? Save money? Talk to people? Reach out to strangers? Train your body? Change your attitude? Get focused? Be creative in thinking of the ten things that can support this decision. Some things may not seem immediately related but will promote your overall well-being in ways that help bring about success, like eating healthy, getting enough sleep, and spending time in nature. Keep this list at your altar, and keep your candles lit for ten days in a row minimum (No maximum! There's never any maximum where Jupiter is concerned!). Generally with candle spells you're encouraged to *literally* keep those candles going, even when you're out at work or walking the dog or what-have-you. One way to do this is leave them in the sink while you're gone. You might even fill the sink with an inch or two of water to be doubly safe. However, if this gives you an anxiety attack, feel free to blow out your candles and re-light them when you return. Remember, magic is 98% intention, and I don't think the benevolent energies of the universe are going to punish you for being concerned about your house burning down.

- Create a Wheel of Fortune charm for luck and focus. Find a round object from nature—a stone or crystal, a sand dollar, anything that resembles a wheel. Hold it while meditating on

everything, good and bad, that has brought you to where you are in this moment, and feel gratitude. Clean the object and place it in a glass with water and mint. Set it outside during a full moon or on a sunny day. Say this incantation above it: *Lead me / To my destiny / Happily / So mote it be.* After the day or night passes, remove the object and boil the water and mint into a tea for drinking. Your object is charmed! Keep it with you as a reminder that you are being led into your future. Use it in rituals to help bring what you want toward you. Meditate with it for gratitude and clarity.

11. Justice

When the Justice card comes into your realm, issues of fairness—quite possibly the concept of justice itself—is up for you.

The Tarot traditionally treats Justice as a real, true solid *thing*. Optimistically it believes that justice prevails, but most of us know that such a belief is naive, often dangerously so. We live in a world where legal systems are corrupt, and laws are unfair and unequally enforced. Huge social movements have come into existence for the sole purpose of combating unjust justice. The justice system that the Tarot represents—judges, lawyers, police, courtrooms, and jails—does not uphold the values of fairness, justice, and the victory of right over wrong. What does value the optimistic tone of the card are social justice movements—people driven by fairness and seeking justice by taking to the streets, working to change policy, to free wrongly incarcerated individuals, to banish unfair laws and create new ones that actually help people.

The figure of Justice holds a sword in one hand, blade up, to demonstrate victory, and the scales of justice in the other hand, reminding us all that our analyses always need to be tempered by mercy, compassion, heart. The symbolism embedded in the clasp that fastens the cloak of Justice is to me even more appropriate when applied to social justice struggles—it's a protective square that protects the circular unity of community. In this understanding of Justice, that square protects the people from the abuses of those in power, especially those in charge of our judicial systems, from the police in the streets to the judges who sit on the highest courts.

Now that I've brought a little *justice* to the Tarot, let me tell you how getting the Justice card could shake down for you. Generally, it means that an ethical or moral issue has come into your sphere and you are having to deal with it. Maybe you are directly involved—you've been done wrong, or someone feels you've done them wrong. Maybe you've witnessed an injustice, and it's giving you feelings. Whatever side of the conflict you are on, the Justice card beseeches you to act fairly. Now isn't the time for vengeance or martyrdom; it's not time for gossip or defensiveness. The Justice card asks us to sit with ourselves and meditate on the issue at hand, how we did or did not play into it, how we might have handled it differently, how we will conduct ourselves in the future. We see in the larger world how conflict begets conflict; it doesn't occur to us that our own smaller spheres are subject to the same chain reactions, but they are. Justice asks you to work for peace, for Justice.

If you have been the victim of a crime, you are probably feeling tons of righteous anger. The Justice card recommends funneling it into activities that are healing for you and for others—becoming an advocate or activist, creating art around the larger issue, connecting with others who have had similar experiences.

If you are being justly accused of something, it may be time for you to face up to not just your actions but the underlying belief system that enabled them. Maybe you got caught talking shit and now have to eat some humble pie. Maybe you got caught stealing and need to take a hard look at your scarcity issues. Maybe you're like me: after decades of heavy drinking, I had to look at the consequences of that behavior in other people's lives and make amends. Facing issues like these doesn't feel good, but it's crucial to the health and caretaking of your soul. When the Justice card comes up, you are being called to do the right thing, pure and simple.

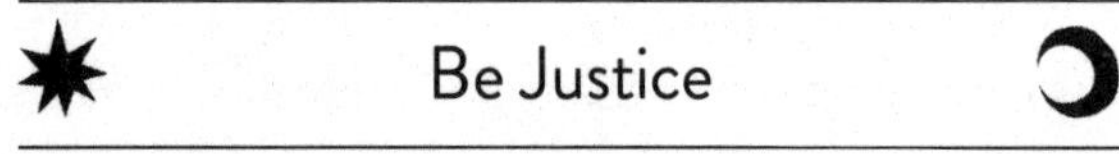

Be Justice

- When the Justice card shows up, chances are there are a lot of hot feelings flaring about. Some cooling water magic is called

for. Get yourself to the nearest body of water you can find—the ocean, a bay, or a river, creek, stream, lake, or pond. Walk along it for as long as you can, taking slow, meditative steps. As you walk, repeat in your mind, *Water, cool my heated thoughts, please bring me the justice sought.* Water Justice is cool, tempered by mercy, the kind of Justice our best selves desire. As you walk, pick up any rocks or shells or blossoms that call to you from the banks (only where it's legal to take such things of course). Bring them home with you and set up an altar to water justice. Let the universe take care of the outcome; you take care of yourself.

If you have no body of water nearby, take a lovely bath. Add some Epsom salts to detox. Bring into the water with you any objects from the natural world that can withstand it—crystals, stones, shells, etc., and use the same chant, spoken aloud or in your mind. Return these objects to an altar when you're through with your bath.

- For those actively involved in seeking justice through the activism or work they do, here is a recipe for a pouch spell to support both you and your work. The pouch should be colored black or white. If your work focuses on justice for people of color, in particular black people, make High John the Conqueror root the central point of your pouch. Sacred to African American magic, this root is the physical manifestation of the power of a magical African man who left his magic behind when he outsmarted the Devil itself, stealing the demon's horse and returning to Africa with his daughter, whom John loved. The root is incredibly powerful for supporting work that seeks to undo the damages of slavery in particular and to banish racism in general.

  Other herbs to add to this pouch, or for use in other social justice work, are chamomile, to help relieve the stress of the

fight; coriander and fennel, to help destroy the systems of oppression; sage, to keep you alert; and dry barley, black pepper, chia seeds, and/or eucalyptus to protect your body, mind, and spirit. Use as many or as few of these ingredients as you like. Keep the pouch on you, especially when you are actively engaging in social justice work, and under your pillow at night to help restore your psyche.

12. The Hanged Man

A person in a tunic hangs by the ankle from a leafy tree—and looks pretty chill about it. Is this some sort of ancient yoga move, or perhaps a sadomasochistic ritual of yore? Um, in a way, sort of. The Hanged Man represents all situations in which you've put yourself somewhere on the spectrum between slight discomfort and deep pain, and you've done it consciously because you know at the end of your bondage a new and improved reality awaits you. The card

can represent undertaking a yoga regimen or any new physical endeavor that puts your body through the ringer but does something for your spirit in the process. Exploring fantasies of submission and pain can leave a person high on endorphins and brimming with new insights about power, sexuality, and the self, so these activities are also watched over by the Hanged Man. Other scenarios that come to mind include scholarship (the Hanged Man is all about sacrifice and what's a bigger sacrifice than grad school?) and pregnancy (your body is in an immense purgatory while creating a kid, not to mention the sacrifices parenting requires). Retreats both silent and artistic resonate with the Hanged Man and his resolve to withdraw from the world for a greater personal good. And yes, the greater good of this card *is* personal. Look at the sunny yellow halo beaming out around his head! It's as if he's reached a meditative state, and the Hanged Man does rule meditation. Those who have practice sitting with monkey-mind understand the hell of it as well as the clarity it engenders.

When the Hanged Man shows up, retreat is recommended. Perhaps you have come to a point where the only way for you to get what you truly want is to give up something else. You've weighed the choices, you've made your choice and decided it's worth the effort, and you're settling into your self-imposed purgatory. Aspire to do your time like the Hanged Man does his: relaxing into the discomfort of it (look at the lax bend of that leg!), not dwelling on what you've lost but anticipating what lies ahead (a peek at his facial expression shows a radiant acceptance). Sometimes what you need to give up are assumptions, or ways of thinking. Sometimes more concrete action is required; like taking a dream

job that requires a faraway move, or adopting a new way of eating to deal with a health problem. Whatever it may be, the discomfort you feel will be proportional to your inability to let go of it. The heart of the Hanged Man is surrender, letting go. If you've accepted that there is no way around letting go of what you need to let go of, you'll be ready to endure the deprivations and discomfort of your sacrifice with his egoless charm.

The Hanged Man came up for me lots when I stopped drinking. I was at a terrible crossroads, and crossroads are sacred to this card (just look at the intersection his legs make). I neither wanted to drink nor cared to *stop* drinking. No, wait, it was actually much more extreme than that: I knew I couldn't drink anymore, that it was killing me. I also knew that I couldn't live without alcohol. I lived in this state for quite a miserable while, trying to achieve some sort of balance by making ridiculous rules for my drinking (rules I couldn't help but break) or taking tiny alcohol breaks (breaks I rewarded myself for by drinking copiously). It wasn't until I admitted I was actually powerless over my alcoholism and let go of my attempts to control it that my misery began to abate. I began to accept that I was in fact an alcoholic and couldn't drink like a normal person. *Powerless, control, accept*—these are all Hanged Man buzzwords. So is *letting go*—quitting drinking required me to let go of the way I saw myself, the way I saw the world. I had to reconfigure my priorities and learn new coping skills, not to mention new ways to socialize and pass the time. It took a while to get the hang of. For a while I felt like I was in a strange cocoon, shut off from most of my boozy former social groups, with no new social circle to relax with. Not knowing how to handle my feelings but

knowing that diving into a bottle of wine wasn't an option. I experienced cravings, I *wanted* a drink with my whole body, mind, and spirit. But I didn't have one. I existed in a painful state of thwarted desire, until slowly, slowly, it got better.

When I stopped being so self-obsessed and began paying more attention to what folks in my recovery groups shared, I was reminded of why I had taken this rocky road. Their lives sounded like miracles. Their lives *were* miracles. I understood that all I had to do was stick hard to this path, to dangle here on this tree—the tree of *life* no less!—and eventually it would all make more and more sense. *I* would make more and more sense. The life I wanted, one with healthy relationships and less regret, a healthy body and less sickness, a stronger career and less floundering, would only ever be mine if I passed through this time of darkness. By cultivating qualities that the Hanged Man represents—flexibility, serenity, patience—and by practicing meditation (another of his jams), I got through it. On the other side was a drastically different life, one that was worth the sacrifice.

If the Hanged Man has come up for you, know that everything is in motion, even if it feels like nothing is moving. That's the nature of the Hanged Man. It's a waiting game, and the waiting can be interminable. It's not a time for activity. If you're considering making a move to help a situation along, *don't.* You'll probably just mess it up. If you've been insulted or threatened, the best recourse under the Hanged Man is to lay low and wait it out. Passivity is rewarded. Don't send that email, don't make that complaint, don't hit back. Just scramble up that tree, get yourself in the most comfortable position you can, and count your breaths until the situation remedies itself. And it will. Movement is always occurring within the Hanged Man; it's just happening away from you, or so deep inside you that you can't see it clearly. If you're considering whether a sacrifice you're tempted to make will be worth it, the Hanged Man says yes. And always, the way through this card's trials is the dropping of the ego. Get out of your head and get going.

Be the Hanged Man

- If you're ready to take the plunge into a significant life change, one that you know will require serious sacrifice on your end, then it's time to get into training. In the absence of a way to safely hang upside down for as long as it takes, meditation comes very close to embodying the energy of the Hanged Man. Meditation is many things—people practice it for its health benefits, or to bring about a spiritual experience; the entire discipline of yoga grew out of it. Meditation can also be a spell.

  First of all, you're going to be physically uncomfortable, especially if you don't do this kind of thing very often. I want you sitting up, preferably on the floor, with a pillow jammed under your butt. Settle into the most comfortable posture you can. Then, with your eyes half-open and sort of spaced-out gazing at some fixed point on the floor a foot or so in front of you, start counting your breaths. Here comes the mental

discomfort. Watch as your mind annoys the shit out of you by bouncing from one stupid, meaningless obsession to the next. Sometimes physical and mental discomfort will coalesce as your meddlesome mind begins harping on how sore your ankle is, or your knee, or whatever. Of course, if you are in *real pain,* you should stop what you're doing, but meditation is a physical drag for most people. Part of the point is to endure it. Enduring those bouncy thoughts is significant; as your ideas and observations make themselves known, it's your job to bat them away gently without getting riled up about it and insisting that you're like *the worst meditator ever*!

This is the way we begin to know our mind. You're not going to have a fab out-of-body experience, and it's unlikely you're going to get knocked out by a euphoric, one-with-the-Universe sensation, but that's not what we're doing here. Through meditation, you get to understand the mind in general and your mind in particular. By enduring discomfort and trusting that there is a greater good for you at the end of it, you are physically and mentally embodying the Hanged Man card.

At the start of your meditation, state your intention to the Universe. Something like, *Hi, Universe, it's me. I'm ready to move into the crossroads, into the liminal space between where I am now and where I want to be. I understand this is a big change, but I am ready and getting readier. With this meditation, see that I want my life to change. Help me to intuit what I must do. Help make me strong and wise enough to endure what must be sacrificed. I offer this meditation to the future I am ready for.* Then meditate. Do it for as long as you're able. Your intention will bring about the change you desire, and the skill and discipline you'll gain will help you through the Hanged Man energies with maximum grace.

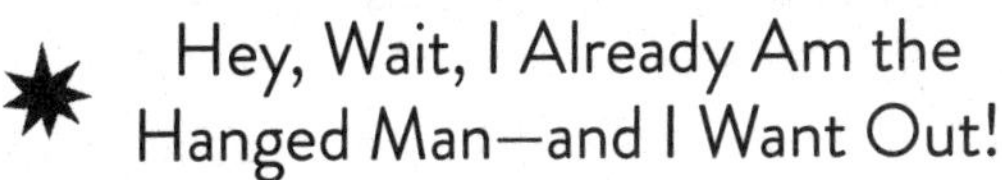

Hey, Wait, I Already Am the Hanged Man—and I Want Out!

Okay, if the Hanged Man popped up in your life and you like have *no idea what the hell it's doing here*, then we got a problem. The Hanged Man is always a *voluntary* sacrifice, so if you feel like things are being ripped away from you, it's possible you are deeply out of touch with your own wants and intentions. You could be setting things in motion subconsciously, which then leaves you feeling powerless and resentful. To get on top of your life you need to own whatever the Hanged Man has brought your way. I'm going to prescribe a fire ritual for you, so get yourself in a place where you can safely play with some fire.

- Before a candle (black or white ones are best), take the time to write down adjectives that describe all the ways the situation at hand has you feeling. If there is something you feel ashamed to admit, make sure to get that down; describing what brings you shame has the most potency and will bring about the greatest transformation. Tear off each word from the paper and one by one feed them to the fire.

  When the words you wrote are nothing but ash, sit with a new sheet of paper and consider all the good that could come out of what's happening. This can be really hard—it's possible that you really can't see how the situation could benefit you. Nonetheless, go out on a limb. If something has been taken away from you, imagine and write down the many things that could eventually fill that space. If something unpleasant has been thrust upon you, think hard about and write down how

the experience might enrich you, tangibly and intangibly. At the end of your list, in all caps, write I ACCEPT IT ALL. Draw a triangle around that sentence. You will not burn this list—you will hold on to it and refer to it whenever you feel yourself resisting your reality. "I accept it all" will become your mantra.

For an extra boost, do this spell when the moon is in Pisces. The Hanged Man is ruled by Neptune, the ruler of Pisces, and the watery sign is an expert at letting go. If you (like me) would like to involve a crystal in your ceremony, aquamarine is the Pisces sacred stone, but it's a bit pricy. If your rich aunt didn't pass one down to you, amethyst works just as well.

13. Death

Okay, you got the Death card. Don't freak out. It doesn't mean you're going to die.

Actually—wait a minute. You *are* going to die. So am I. So are all the people you spoke to today, everyone you passed on the street, everyone whose status you liked or hated or ignored. We're all going to die. And while a tarot reading doesn't have the ability to predict the time or manner of your death, and while

99.9 percent of the time drawing that card has *nothing* to do with physical death whatsoever, I hesitate to relieve you of your mortality anxiety so quickly. Though the Death card, a difficult, almost uniformly painful card to draw, deals primarily with change, transitions, and transformations, it is largely the primal fear of death at our core that makes these and so many other endings excruciating for humans. When the Death card comes up, something is being taken from us—our marriage, our livelihood, our most rewarding friendship. A treasured talent is no longer available to us. We're being evicted from our home.

These changes occur against our will, often in spite of our clinging and keening, but Death governs other losses besides these, such as quitting drugs, changing an identity-defining point of view, gender transition, or becoming a parent. People generally choose these changes—which often bring them much joy—but if Death pops up for you, it means there is a shadow side to the happy new era you're ringing in and you ignore it at your peril.

Sometimes I think the Death card would benefit from being renamed Grief, or Mourning, for that is the real heart of the card. There has been a profound loss, and whether you are grateful for the loss or devastated, a time of processing is upon you, of consciously letting go. It's a time of feeling your feelings, your anxiety, of raging and making peace. You are becoming a new person, and whether you worked for this change or had a crisis rudely thrust upon you, the only way through it is to embrace it and find your agency within the situation.

Let's look at the card. I guess if we did rename it Grief or Mourning, we'd lose the iconic Goth imagery—the Grim Reaper

Herself, clad in armor, as she is unconquerable. No one outwits death, and no one outwits change. A king lies on the ground, as trampled and prone as a *Walking Dead* extra. A pope, a kid, and a pretty lady—*no! not a pretty lady!* jeez—all await their fates, communicating that neither piety, innocence, nor adherence to the current cultural beauty standard will save us. Let's unpack these little archetypes, shall we?

Are you the king? Your stature can't help you in this situation. You can't buy yourself out of this loss. I mean, I guess if you're a billionaire with dubious ethics you could, for instance, buy yourself a mail-order bride if Death has come for you in the form of a divorce. But unless you dig into your stony heart, locate a smidgen of humanity, and weep for what once was, whatever is left of your soul will continue to degrade inside your body, like Dorian Gray's secret picture.

Are you the pope? You're not going to be able to pray-meditate-chant-yoga-cleanse-crossfit your way out of this one. While all of those pursuits are killer support systems, tools to help you through this moment, sitting down to meditate in the hope that you'll be lifted away from your pain is (always) incorrect. Meditate in order to bring yourself closer to the razor's edge of your fear. Look it in the face. Accept it and make peace with it. If the fear of death underlies all fear, and fear is what stops us from acceptance and letting go, then getting into a practice of accepting that you're going to die will have the ripple effect of assisting you with all loss. Personally, I especially like to think about how we're all going to die when I'm feeling choked by economic anxiety. *Can I really spend $150 on a ticket to that super-fun celebrity gala that supports a totally* *worthy feminist nonprofit?* Well, we're all going to die. How much time do I want to spend stressing about this? How much *yes* do I want to say in whatever time I have left?

Are you the child? Innocence can't save you. Perhaps you did everything right in this situation, and you're *still* getting screwed. Oh, well. C'est la vie. I'm not being cavalier with your feelings—it's just that "c'est la vie" is the order of the day when Death comes trotting up. Also, don't think you can trick Death by playing your innocence off as ignorance. Pretending you don't know what's going on, or falsely embracing the situation as positive, will both backfire. Yes, the Death card has a totally gorgeous light at the end of the tunnel, but you are required to walk through the dark night of your soul to get there. There are no shortcuts.

Are you the pretty lady? I hate to make a conventionally attractive female a feminist metaphor for being a tool of the patriarchy—*I honestly and truly do*—but the Tarot deals in arche(stereo) types, so go with my flow. To me, the pretty lady speaks to how supporting the status quo, not rocking the boat, cuddling up to conformity—none of these are going to stave off this loss. You might as well be your messiest, most authentic self. The Death card ain't pretty, and neither are you while you're in its thrall.

I remember sharing at a support group about the recent ending of an eight-year relationship. I was shell-shocked and still couldn't speak about it without crying. When we all stood to hold hands, I clutched the palm of an elderly lady. She turned to me and said, simply, "It's like a death." Nothing anybody said to me in those long months of wrestling with this card resonated so clearly. I thought it was generous of her to say what she did; I surmised that in her long life she'd experienced her share of actual deaths, not to mention figurative deaths through heartbreak. It was kind of her to lend me the power of this word, *death*. It helped me when I struggled to come to grips with my new situation, my new life, my new me. What I was experiencing was a death.

We can't leave this card without speaking about the flag Mx. Reaper carries. A chic black flag embossed with an enormous, elaborate rose. What could be more beautiful? And truly, as sure as that sun setting in the background will rise again, there is beauty at the end of this struggle. You *will* love again. You will create art again, or make money again. You will know friendship again, find shelter again, feel whole again. The death of my relationship helped show me what I needed most from my relationships; it gave me the motivation to look for it and brought me to my soul mate, whom I'm married to today. There is a bounty of beauty waiting for you. You just have to cry your way to it.

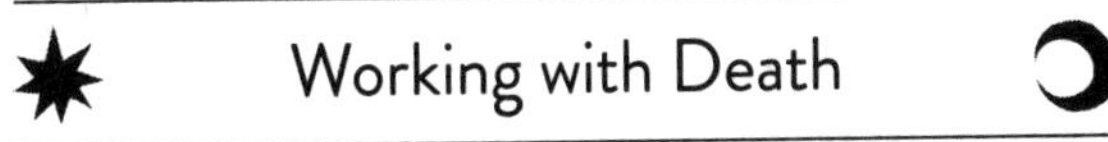

Working with Death

- Make a Goddess Box. Make it a God Box, if that's your jam, or a Buddha Box, a Unicorn Box, a St. Joan of Arc Box or a Chango Box, a Kali Box or a Kwan-Yin Box. Create a box in honor of whatever deity you like to imagine watching over you. (You *do* imagine a benevolent force watching over you, don't you? Try it! It feels nice!) Inside this box will go every single thing that you have no control over, the terrible things you're having a hard time letting go of, everything you're fighting against ac-

cepting. These things can be big-concept, like injustice; that's super-hard to accept. They can be downright trivial, like your bestie's annoyingly shitty taste in dates. Write down each one, fold up the paper, and slip it into your Goddess Box. It's out of your hands now—you've handed it over.

Keep doing this and the strangest thing will happen—when that stressful feeling rises up inside you and you start mentally rehashing the painful thing that's beyond your control, something in your mind clicks and says, *Oh hey, wait, you put that in your Stevie Nicks Box. Stevie Nicks is taking care of that for you now, so you can let go.* Letting go is the swiftest and easiest way through the Death card. Sometimes what you're letting go of is your inability to let go. It can get meta up in here when the Death card shows up.

Oh, and make sure you decorate your Goddess Box. My own is just a cardboard pencil box I bought for a dollar at a drugstore; I think it has puppies on it. But I grabbed my trusty glue gun and covered it with every piece of broken jewelry I ever hoarded, plus stray rhinestones and feathers and sequins. It delights me to look at it, and delight is one way to access magic.

- In a culture that discourages crying and views it as weak and sloppy and all things traditionally and hatefully female, it is a radical act to embrace your tears. When you're working with the Death card, it is your tears that will save you, so let's honor their salty power and have a sacred cry bath for them.

  Gather around you as many of these magical tools as you can: bath salts, like Epsom salts or a big chunk of Himalayan pink salt or even some table salt if that's all you've got to work with. Salt draws out impurities—it detoxes. It has a lot in common with crying, another detoxing activity that's very salty.

Make yourself a cup of elderberry tea. Elderberry is sacred to Scorpio, the ruler of the Death card. As such, the Death card is also ruled by the dwarf planet Pluto, known as the ruthless surgeon who goes in and cuts away whatever is poisoning the system. It's painful and you need to recover from it, but it's for your health.

As you lie in your tub, sipping your elderberry tea, think about how whatever is being taken away from you was actually a poison. It didn't work for you anymore. The you emerging from this loss will be a healthier, happier, more unified person. What else? Grab a rose quartz. This crystal of love, particularly self-love, is nice to have around when times are tough. Similarly, grab some rose petals. An homage to the bloom on the Reaper's flag, it will remind you of life's sweetness and the sweetness that awaits you. Roses are flowers of love, so the petals will support the work your quartz is doing. Grab some jet too, if you have it, and pour all your teary bad feelings into it. Jet can take it. It absorbs negative energy. Let it help you. If you want some candles around your bath, I recommend black, white, and pink.

Now, sit in your bathtub and cry. If you want to bring some real style into it, invest in a gorgeous, vintage handkerchief. A frequent crier, I learned some time ago that sobbing feels much more elegant when you are blowing your snot into an embroidered flower. But what do you do if you've set the stage, and you're still deeply miserable, and the tears won't come? The bath created too much pressure! You're cry-shy! No worries. Enjoy your bath. The salt will still detox you, the crystals and candles will do their magic. A little bit of healing will happen. Repeat as necessary.

14. Temperance

Behold Temperance, sweet, peaceful, balanced Temperance, a glyph of serenity, sobriety, and the esteemed Middle Path. Have no idea what a Middle Path might mean? Then it's probably good that you drew this card—you probably need it. But before we get into the meat of this card, let's take a look at its heavy and inspiring symbolism.

First, notice that we're dealing with an *angel*! A supernatural

winged being. According to some lore, this is the dragon-slaying archangel Michael, but frankly that's both a little too violent for such a temperate card and a little too Christian for me. Others name her the rainbow goddess Iris, and the card does give this deity a shout-out with the yellow irises growing by the riverbank. But my favorite identity for this spiritual creature is Hermaphroditus, the intersex child of the love goddess Aphrodite and the flickering communication god Mercury, from Western mythology. As problematic as it is to employ any body as a metaphor, I can't turn away from one of the few representations of intersex beings in Western culture and would hate to ignore the patron deity of effeminate men and androgynous everyones. In a culture that remains heavily gendered and punishing to those whose genders defy expectations, Hermaphroditus's healing and benevolent energies are crucial. On the Temperance angel's robe is a triangle held within a square, a symbol of feminine energies held and protected, making this angel a feminist spiritual hero. The glyph can also be interpreted as the merging of feminine (triangle) and masculine (square) vibes, making the Temperance angel an icon of androgyny, a touchstone for anyone working with genderqueer magic or energies.

There is a lot of sunshine in this card, from the literal sun rising in the background to the encircled dot on the angel's third eye, the glyph for the sun. A new day has dawned, and so long as you pledge yourself to the positivity this card embodies, it is a day that can last forever. With one foot grounded on rational terra firma and the other dipped in the waters of the subconscious, symbolic and intuitive, Temperance walks in perfect balance, pouring the waters of life back and forth between two golden chalices, effortlessly mixing the lower and higher energies of life into a perfect stream. Some interpret the angel as pouring the waters *up*, as a metaphor for consciousness ascending. I like that idea, but I also believe that true enlightenment on this material plane comes when we can accept the ups and the downs without getting too attached to either. The Temperance card is a total, pure representation of this acceptance.

Okay, okay, enough with the woo-woo dip into Temperance's symbolism. What the frick does this card mean? Well, when you pluck this card, it means it's time to slow down. While the Tarot honors all of life's extremes, when she hands you this card it's time to chill the fuck out. Maybe you're drinking too much. Maybe you've been insanely social, at the expense of spending some much-needed time with yourself. Maybe your job or even your beloved creative work has been taking too much energy from you and it's time to withdraw from that world of doing and seek some stillness. If you're afflicted by a conflict, this card advises you to be a peacemaker, to see the other side regardless of how abhorrent it might be to you. As the angel joins the waters, it could be a great time for you to synch your energies with another's; collaborations and marriages thrive in this card. If you have been involved in serious activism, this card gives you permission to withdraw for a spell. It even relieves you of the often painful experience of having an opinion. The Middle Path, the road the Buddha strode to enlightenment, is a path of neutrality. In a culture that tells us to define ourselves by the passion of our beliefs, neutrality may seem sacrilegious, but in fact traveling the Middle Path gives you the space, for at least a moment, to transcend the righteous battles for justice that define this plane and access something higher.

I have experienced the Temperance card in many life-changing ways. It came to me during a time when my allegiance to my political beliefs had veered into serious fanaticism. My interpretation of feminism had made it almost impossible to live on this earth; it certainly had removed all the joy from life. I had forbidden myself the pleasures of food, fashion, sex, romance, art, friendship, and community. I denied myself the basic pleasure of kindness, of allowing kindness to pass through me, of giving other people the benefit of the doubt. I'd forgone the complicated pleasure of trying to see the world through another's eyes. I fetishized mythologies of female warriors—amazons, harpies, gorgons, girl gangs, Valerie Solanas. Our culture needs women to embody these extreme energies to somewhat offset the overwhelming force of misogyny. But for the individual running these energies it can be excruciating. To me it is no surprise that ardent feminists are disproportionately afflicted with immune disorders; when every cell in the body is attuned to the energy of fighting, the body eventually will give out.

At the apex of my own fight, I was considering blowing up the frat houses that lined the university district of my town, certain that they harbored rapists. Probably they did, but they also probably harbored men who cared about women, men who were as lost and confused by the way our culture distorts female and male as I was. At some point, a type of grace entered me. I allowed myself to be burned out. I allowed myself to be drawn back to things that my anguished feminism had outlawed—the poetry of Charles Bukowski, handcuffs in the boudoir, artisanal cheese, male vocalists

(welcome back, Prince, how I missed you!), dildos, candy bars, drag queens. Slowly I recommitted myself to being alive on *this* planet, not some other planet I thought I could create if I could only get the entire world to fall in line with *my vision*! My feminism, and all my politics, became right-sized—something I believed in and engaged with daily, but that did not dominate my psyche.

 Be Temperance 

Though devoted to gentleness, Temperance is a powerful card. Its Middle Path is deceptively tranquil; the transformation you can access by conjuring its energies is life-altering and has staying power. In stepping away from extremes, you are able to access a truly radical existence.

- Meditate. This is the essence of Temperance energy, and a relatively easy spell to cast on yourself. To bring the serene energy of this card into your life, simply sit quietly with yourself for a set period of time. Start with five minutes, amp it up to ten, and strive for twenty. Count your breaths, one to ten, then begin again. When your chattering mind kidnaps your counting, begin again. And yes, your chattering mind *will* kidnap your counting. This does not mean you are "bad" at meditating, or that your Temperance spell isn't working. It means you have a human body and a human mind, made for thinking. You are casting a long, slow spell over it, like a lifestyle spell. It will get easier as your sessions slowly reveal to you the nature of your own mind and how it sabotages your serenity. Play with this

spell by meditating in chaotic, busy places; I like to meditate on a city bus. Like the Temperance angel, you are mixing the waters of chaos with the waters of peace when you meditate.

- Create a Temperance stone. I recommend amethyst; it's not too expensive, it's beautiful, and it's known to be helpful in achieving sobriety. Obviously, if you are trying to stop drinking or imbibing any inebriant, this stone is especially powerful for you. But we can work with the idea of sobriety as becoming clear about and getting rid of *anything* that is enslaving you, bringing out your worst self, or causing you to act against your best interests. A job that needs quitting, a relationship that needs to be severed, any habit that is hurting you.

  Hold your amethyst in your hands while meditating. Imagine a column of pure water coming down the center of your head and moving through your body; imagine it changing course and flowing upward out the top of your head. Once you get into the rhythm of this, moving the water with the motion of your breath, place the crystal on top of your head for a moment. Breathe, and move the water. Place the stone at your third eye (the space between your eyebrows). Place it at the center of your throat. We're moving through the chakras here, both charging the crystal with your life energy and offering the healing vibes of your magic rock to your spiritual power centers. Place the crystal on your solar plexus, on your belly button, on your junk. Finally, let it chill for a moment on the sole of each foot. Now reverse this movement. You may feel like a total goon while doing this. Who cares? You're alone in your bedroom or bathroom and taking the time to goon out with your magical astral body.

  When you're done, you will have a supercharged serenity stone. Wear it in a pouch around your neck, pop it into your

pocket, or carry it in your change purse. Just keep it somewhere on your person so that you can access it in moments of tension, when you feel the pull of that old way of being entering your sphere. You have everything you need to resist it. The power in that crystal is your own sweet, gentle power.

15. The Devil

When the Devil arrives in your sphere, it is time to get serious. The broadest explanation of what this card is signaling is that you are under the spell of a lie, and its consequences for you will be real. The hardest part of the Devil is how likely it is that you have no idea that what you are believing in so fervently and spending so much of your energy on is a dangerous falsehood. When the Devil card comes, it is asking you to do the heavy-duty soul-searching

required for the difficult work of cracking the belief system or denial that is protecting the problem. What are you doing or believing that is causing harm to yourself and others?

Addictions of all kinds are ruled by the Devil, and it is truly possible to be addicted to almost anything. When something that once offered pleasure has grown into a compulsion you have no control over, the Devil has stepped in. Chemicals, shopping, sex, love—whatever it is you're putting between your lower self and your higher self. Belief systems that demonize others or encourage you to be self-loathing are the work of the Devil. Like the two devilettes chained to the big beast's throne, one with the wino's tail of grapes, the other with the flaming tail of a sex addict, you too are chained to a negative force that is bigger than you are. To remain there is to settle for no freedom, for no movement, for a life that becomes ever smaller and devoid of joy. The pentacle on the Devil's head points down, encouraging us to let our basest energies run amok, leaving spiritual and often physical destruction in their wake.

If you have drawn the Devil, it is time to get clear about what your master is right now. This could be a lighter issue—maybe you're spending too much time on your phone and its grip on you has been nagging at you. You must come up with a plan to correct your relationship with your device; the consequence won't be destitution, of course, but weakened social bonds and comfort with not being present in your own life are still pretty chilling destinies. On the other hand, the Devil in your life might in fact be a grisly life-or-death situation. Are you on a roller coaster of soaring highs and crushing lows? What is taking you on these trips? Maybe it's chemicals you're taking in, or maybe it's the chemicals that are naturally present in your body—being slaves to our own painful brain chemistry is the Devil's work too. So are low self-esteem, self-hate, all philosophies that see humanity as cold and hopeless, and all punishment-based religious beliefs. Any spiritual tradition that does not prize individual autonomy and unconditional love is the Devil's work.

Whatever scenario the Devil is pointing to in your own life, try to be willing to look at it honestly. There is no doubt that a lot of denial and justification and a lot of fear have chained you to his throne. But in life everything is possible—including liberating yourself from whatever has you in its stifling, unhealthy grip.

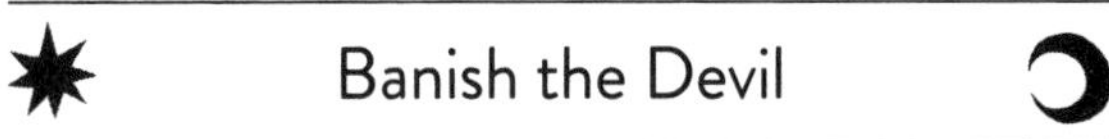

Banish the Devil

- Thyme is a powerful herb for working with the Devil card. It can stop nightmares, and as your life becomes, or threatens to become, a waking nightmare, thyme can help you halt this progression and wake up to reality. Since our own bondage can be hard to see clearly, what wakes us up to reality is a gift. Thyme is also cleansing, and those in the grip of the Devil have accumulated a lot of spiritual toxins (and probably some physical ones too). And finally, this is an herb that protects. You will need a lot of protection as you work to break yourself of whatever habit is bringing you down. Fresh thyme is more powerful than dried thyme, but work with what you have access to.

  Place the herb in a bowl and cover it with boiling water, making a very strong tea. Take a ritual shower, and as you clean

your hair and body, imagine that layers of soot and grime are being removed from your very aura, allowing light and clarity and acceptance to enter. When you are done, pray over your tea. Ask it to help you wake up to reality. Ask it for the courage to look at life as it is. Ask for the strength to change your life and the dedication to keep on your new path, no matter what. Make sure the tea has cooled to skin temperature and pour it over your head. Do not rinse or dry off; allow yourself to air-dry. I recommend doing this spell every night for thirty nights. During the day, carry a sprig of thyme or a pouch filled with the herb on your person.

16. The Tower

The Tower is one of the most feared cards in the Tarot, and for good reason. Few people love change, and the Tower is nothing but change. Even fewer people like sudden change, and it is true that the type of upheaval this card brings is the kind that strikes out of nowhere. You didn't see it coming. You *should* have seen it coming, but you didn't.

When you stay cocooned in denial, when you refuse to face re-

ality, when you shy away from making the life changes you need to make in order to grow, the Tower will show up for you. How painful this card is will depend on how tightly you cling to the walls that are falling down. This card demands complete letting go—a tough order for anyone, but especially for one taken by surprise, or one who has been consciously or unconsciously resisting change for quite a while.

At the heart of the Tower lies a revelation. Either you or someone who impacts you has experienced a sudden clarity—a truly paradigm-shifting understanding has arrived. There is nothing to do but change in accordance with this new information, no matter how devastating it might be. As an ex of mine came closer to realizing our relationship was no longer good for him, the Tower card came up repeatedly. Once he saw with his heart that he had to go, then he had to go, regardless of how much this change destroyed us both for a little while. His Tower became my Tower; I should have listened to my own gut many times and perhaps ended the relationship, but I didn't. Now my resistance snapped back on me, and I was in a lot of pain.

When all the debris and rubble are cleared and the smoke fades from the sky, the Tower offers you a way of living that is much more in accordance with your heart and mind. The structures that the Tower brings down are always things that need to go—unhealthy connections, bad living situations, dead-end jobs, lousy lifestyles. But the Tower does not always bring devastation; once I picked it for a friend who wanted information about a new date. He drew the Lovers, the Sun, and the Tower. Stunned at this combo, I could only surmise that it meant they were crazy soul mates who were going to force each other to change in profound ways. The two just celebrated the birth of their first child!

When the Tower comes, allow it to humble you. You don't always know the right way, and the Universe has intervened, dramatically, to push you in the proper direction. There is a saying in recovery for when hard but beneficial things happen: God is doing for you what you couldn't do for yourself. I was way too codependent to ever break up with my ex-boyfriend, but the Tower intervened and all parties are happier for it. Trust its knowledge and follow the path it is pointing you down. The pain won't last forever, but the benefits of this period will.

Working with the Tower

- Lots of people might think you're crazy to willingly call the Tower into your life, but if you need extreme and drastic change and cannot figure out how to get started, summon this energy into your sphere. Beware, though: it's quite wild! Do not do this spell unless you are ready to deal with the consequences (though the consequences of this spell are better, in the long run, than the consequences of sticking in your rut). But the Tower will come for you eventually, so there is a little boost to not being taken by surprise.

  Take a piece of tissue paper and carefully draw on it the image of the Tower—a building struck by lightning, with people jumping from it. Bring lit candles into the bathroom, white, black, red, or yellow. Pour Epsom salts into your bath and get in. Bring your sigil—the image of the Tower—into the water with

you. As it dissolves, call out to the powers of the Tower and ask it to knock away everything that is keeping you from living your best life. Then relax into your bath. Draw upon the element of water to help you be accepting and flexible in the time to come. Water is a great element to use with Tower magic, because it is impossible to hold on to it, and when the Tower comes you must let go.

Your bath is done when the sigil has fully disintegrated. You may bottle a bit of your bathwater and keep it as a talisman. As you enter this new period of your life, it will remind you that you called this destruction, and you possess the power to let go.

- If you are going through a Tower period, allow a magic pouch to emotionally support you through this tough time. Into a black or white bag put hawthorn (an herb with deep powers that can stand up to Tower energy, helps with hard situations, relieves pain, and brings sweetness); rosemary (supports your heart chakra and heals the pain of disillusionment); and cacao and schisandra berries (both great for letting go). Add an amethyst crystal, which will help attune your intuition and psychic vision and allow you to be in touch with the big picture of why the Tower is ultimately positive for you. Carry or wear this pouch with you and sleep with it close by. You will know when you no longer need it.

17. The Star

The Star, the beautiful Star, has come twinkling into your world with her immense generosity of spirit and hope, creativity and inspiration. I must admit that I am deeply biased in favor of this card, as she is ruled by my sign, Aquarius, and when I am under her influence—feeling inspired, hopeful, like I can make my dreams come true—I feel at my best and in my essence. Like the symbol for Aquarius, the card features a woman bearing water; in the

zodiac, she is in space, pouring water down onto the earth; here in the Tarot she is still pouring water onto the earth, while also pouring some into a pool. Water represents many things, all lovely—creativity, tenderness, inspiration, love. The water also represents the unconscious mind, the place where love and inspiration are first sparked. This is very much an image of making wishes come true, taking the raw material of the creative subconscious and bringing it onto the material plane. We also see the Star replenishing the dream state by pouring water back into it, communicating that our creative coffers need time for rest and recuperation via sleep, nurturance, daydreaming, and art.

If the Star has come into your life, it is time to dare to dream, and to dream big. What would you like to create right now? A community center or a small business? A novel or an epic play? A day care center, a magazine, a bakery, or a nonprofit? It can be as small as a poem and as grand as a festival. All such things begin with a moment of inspiration, the flicker of a great idea taking hold and becoming a wish, a desire. This is that moment. Let the glorious mantra *Why not?* echo through your heart and mind, because with the Star card anything is possible, including and especially those projects that haters and naysayers like to say just aren't possible. The Star is here to tell us they *are* possible, if we dare to believe in ourselves.

Of course, there will be lots of hard work down the road. The Star is super-magic, but that doesn't mean you get to simply click your heels and watch your dream spring to life. The Star is here to pour her rejuvenating waters of inspiration onto you, to bless your goals and keep you motivated and dreamy enough to get your project off the ground.

Be the Star

- The Star may correspond to air, way up there in outer space, but what is a star if not a burning hunk of fire? Honor the Star's burning core by doing a candle spell to summon inspiration. At night, light eight candles—white, black, blue, yellow, and purple work best. Summon the energy of the Star, dedicate the candles to her, and ask that she lend you her fires of excitement and belief. Isn't that all inspiration is? Excitement about an idea and a belief that you can do it? Keep the candles burning, when you can, for eight days. Each night go outside and wish upon a star.
- Place in a bowl the herbs blue violet leaf (to bring inspiration and a lust for life), horehound (creativity and inspiration), lavender (emotional connectivity), sage (inspiration and smarts), bay leaves (inspiration and psychic attunement), and frankincense (inspiration and transformation). If you can't source all of these herbs, use what you can, but be sure you are pairing something with the lavender—that flower alone won't be enough. Pour boiling water onto the herbs and let them steep until cool. Take a shower. Standing beneath the spray, imagine the Star pouring her healing waters of inspiration and transformation on you. When you are ready, pour the bowl of herbs over your head, and do not rinse them off. Air-dry, allowing the potion and the herbs to settle on you and fall away on their own. Yes, this is a little messy, but so is creativity!

18. The Moon

Behold the Moon. A reflective ball of stone orbiting our planet, tugging all the water on the planet, including the water inside our bodies, as it moves. We all know everyone goes a little crazy when the moon is full. Everyone knows the moon is female, its wide, pale body open to everything we can project onto it. The Moon card in the Tarot is a repository of fear, from anxiety and jangled nerves

to outright insanity. It represents nightmares and confusion, the experience of the vanishing sun made individual, personal—who turned out the lights? It represents both confusion and confusion's opposite, intuition. Even with electricity, nighttime is still the bed of sex and violence in our world, the time when crime strikes and magic is made, when people are most likely to alter their consciousness, to become a bit more like the moon perhaps. Possibly more fears arise, more tears are shed, at night under the moon than during the day under the sun. Perhaps the card deserves its status as representative of madness, but feminist histories of madness and lunacy make it a little hard to cosign.

As someone who works with moon magic regularly, dutifully making new moon intentions, charging my crystals under the full moon, tracking what's left of my menstrual cycle through its phases, I think the Moon card could use a tune-up. If there is a fear it represents it is fear of the unknown, in all its terrible permutations. When the Moon card comes for you, there is likely to be some element in your life that you can't get a grip on. More needs to be revealed, and you are antsy or scared. The Moon always does reveal more and more of itself, but takes its own sweet time. The Moon requires you to be patient, and to trust.

The Moon dares us to make friends with what scares us, to get familiar with our bogeymen, shake paws with the monster under the bed, look ourselves in the mirror at our most emotional, and love ourselves. When working with the phases of the Moon, following it as it moves through the zodiac, something calming occurs. In our world, being in synch with even a single natural cycle can feel profound and full of magic. With moon magic, more is always revealed.

If the Moon has come for you, it is not the time to make any sudden moves. Do not commit yourself to anything or anyone until you have more information. And trust me, more information *is* coming. The Sun always follows the Moon, which always follows the Sun. The Moon might be drawing your attention to your own cycles of emotion and energy. Is there anything there worth noting? If this card represents a person or situation, it is one best avoided for now. If you find yourself battling fear, dare to look it straight in the face. What is your monster? Is it possible to befriend it? Could you, at the very least, make friends with the ebb and flow of life itself, so elegantly illustrated by the phases of the Moon?

This is a great time to trust your intuition, to cast spells and keep dream journals. The card is ruled by Pisces, who is, in a sense, afraid of nothing, being one with the Universe and the Universe contains all. Remember that when pondering your fears by moonlight: this thing that so frightens you—is it inside you as well?

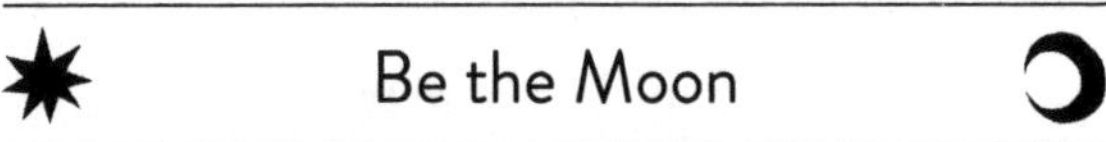

Be the Moon

- The most powerful thing you can do to bring moon magic into your sphere is to start following its course and track its effects on your mood. Begin on a new moon, with the intention to channel the magic of the moon, familiarize yourself with its energy, and become sensitive to its effect on you. Note what sign the moon is in—it is always new in the same sign the sun

is in—and continue to note the sign as you keep your evening journal, noting any moods and sensations or revelations. By the full moon, your connection to the moon will have you inspired, you will understand what exactly you are doing, and you will feel a bond with the moon you previously did not.

- Leave an offering for the moon outside, whatever feels appropriate. Let your crystals bathe beneath it, becoming recharged and purified. You may also set a cup of pure spring water outside to be charged; use it later for magical work. I find it exhausting to pay *too* close attention to the passages of the moon, but you might find that this experiment becomes a practice. At the very least, try to keep a tradition of observing the new and full moons. They are very powerful nights for wishing, magic, and reverence.
- Arrange a simple, DIY crystal grid to honor the new or full moon. Though some grids are meticulously arranged, with this one you don't need to use a template. Simply bring your stones to a place that feels right, inside or outside, and take a moment to meditate with the stones and connect with the moon's energy. Keeping in mind the moon's phase and zodiac placement, as well as what you are hoping to get out of your crystal magic, allow your intuition to guide you as you place your crystals in a pleasing pattern. Allow the grid to stay in place until the moon has moved into its next phase. Doing this outside during a full moon has the added benefit of supercharging your stones!
- Mix sandalwood, which is sacred to the moon, with frankincense to honor the full moon; burn it on charcoal and ask for its assistance as you work to face your fears. Because it helps banish negativity, sandalwood is very supporting when you're confronting fears or dealing with unknowns.

19. The Sun

What a super-beautiful card. A naked baby cavorts on a pony beneath a brilliant, radiant sun, its rays shooting out in linear beams of activity and undulating beams that represent vibrations. The secret of the Sun's utter joyfulness is this balance of the active and visible, on the one hand, and the hidden and the felt, on the other. The Sun card represents the dichotomy of the conscious and the unconscious minds, and when it arrives, it

means those two aspects of your psyche are in a skillful, harmonious balance.

Think, for a moment, what it means for our two forms of consciousness to *not* be in harmony. When we are all conscious mind with no unconscious, materialism reigns and spirituality is ignored. We can't hear our intuition, and we're cut off from sources of knowledge about ourselves and the world. Likewise, when we are all subconscious, we are out of touch with reality, plagued by nightmares, and prone to debilitating fantasy and paranoia. In the Sun we are whole, the embodiment of psychic health, able not only to enjoy a material world suffused with magic but to bring our magic into the world to manifest our dreams.

In our culture we follow mostly sun-sign astrology. We celebrate our birthdays when the sun returns to its position at the moment of our birth. We identify with the zodiac sign that the sun was in when we were born. We believe that our sun signs represent us in our element. And so when the Sun card pops up, you are likely in your element. You are feeling on top of your game, on top of the world. You are being rewarded for being you, often in little ways you may take for granted. The people who love you for being you want to spend time with you because they enjoy you. Or maybe you've scored some kind of award, probably for doing something you are innately good at.

The Sun's mandate is to enjoy the day. Get out under the sky, do something pleasurable, something luxurious, something wonderfully simple. Get an ice cream, sit on some grass, get a massage. Enjoy being who you are, enjoy this life that you have. Know that your good vibes in large part made it all happen.

Be the Sun

- If you are looking to call Sun energy into your life, there is a very simple way to do it. Go outside and lie beneath it! Yes, do put on your sunblock, but depending on where you are in the world right now, get as naked as you can and spread yourself under its wonderful rays in gratitude for the life it gives to our planet. Allow yourself to become drowsy like a sun-worshipping cat as you relax in its magic glow. You will actually feel yourself taking in the powerful energy of our star and will be able to see its effect on your body. We know the science of this, but think of its magic too. Say a prayer to the sun and ask it to bestow upon you the positive radiance it is famous for. Repeat as necessary.
- In ancient Greek magic, roosters were sacred to the sun deity. Collect chicken feathers, ideally naturally shed ones. Bind them together with red, yellow, or orange fabric. Go to the place in your home where you feel the most powerful—perhaps where you work your magic. Dedicate the feathers to the sun, asking that they be charged with its positive energy. Take a smudge stick, light it, and use the feathers to fan the smoke around the room. Fan the smoke onto yourself as well, bathing in it. Allow it to purify you, and ask the Universe to help you channel the golden, positive energy of the sun. Leave your feathers in place where you can see them often.

20. *Judgment*

A slightly foreboding card, with its angel calling the dead from their coffins, Judgment has a Christian flavor that makes me personally, as a heathen, step back. If this is about "Judgment Day," I know where I, as a feminist, socialist, witchcraft-practicing, capitalism-destroying lesbian, am headed, at least according to the god of Pat Robertson, a sadly popular deity right now. Plus, judgment has a bad rap. Nobody likes judgy people; in fact, the phrase "nonjudg-

mental" has a soothing, spa-like holiness around it in my corner of the world. What are we to do with its "avenging angel calling out spooky zombies" vibe?

If you banish the judgmental god association from the Judgment card—and I suggest that you do—what we have is a card about karma and your ability to look yourself in the eye and honestly call yourself on your bullshit. When this card pops up, it is absolutely time for you to do it.

Karma is so misunderstood in America, don't you think? The word has been hijacked by business owners who want to brand their commercial endeavors with a "chill," vaguely spiritual vibe. It's also been abused by people damaged by Western religion, those who think it means if you do something bad over *here* (you're rude to a waitress), then something bad will happen to you over *there* (you stub your toe or step in dog shit). This notion of karma is inherently Judeo-Christian, because it presumes a petty-ass deity is up in the clouds monitoring depressingly common human foibles and meting out equally depressing punishment. That's not karma.

Karma, as I understand it, is cause and effect. Basically, if you sow seeds of misery, you will reap misery. If you sow seeds of kindness, you will reap kindness. Sometimes karma strikes big enough to satisfy our schadenfreude, such as when a public figure known for wreaking havoc on humanity gets a comeuppance. Sometimes karma's impact is big enough to give us a fleeting hope in some sort of cosmic justice, like when something marvelous happens to a downtrodden person. But mostly karma operates internally. When we spew hate, hate grows in our heart, hurting our bodies and creating an internal environmental wasteland. When we work toward peace and serenity, it's like we plant a garden inside ourselves that benefits our bodies, our minds, our social lives, our capacity for abundance—everything. Karma is not about big prizes and plagues of destruction. It's mostly about how well we are living up to our own best selves, and when Judgment comes up, it is asking us to take some inventory. What needs to be tweaked? Where can we do better? Do we need to forgive anyone, let go of anything, offer an overdue apology? Do we need to change our habits, mental or physical? Major shifts in life philosophy, revelations, and "callings" are not unknown when this card comes up.

We don't have many rituals that encourage us to take stock of our lives and give us the tools to do it. We have New Year's resolutions, but whatever the lofty origins of that tradition may be, by now it's fodder for glossy magazines, with a clichéd focus on "fitness" that has turned the celebration of the New Year into our top body-shaming holiday.

My best experience of how periodic introspection can change your life happened when, as a spiritual seeker who rarely turns down a religious invitation, I accompanied a Jewish friend to temple for Yom Kippur. Yom Kippur, for all you unchosen people, *literally* means "Day of Judgment." In fact, the Jewish New Year celebrations seem to have a significant affinity with the Judgment card, what with its biblical name that can also be translated as "Day of Blasting" and "Feast of Trumpets." Having been brought up Catholic before creating a hodgepodge, paganesque, occultish spirituality of my own, I wasn't familiar with Yom Kippur's tradition of looking back to consider whether you harmed anyone in the past year. Imagine if the secular American New Year's celebration, with its emphasis on inebriation followed by smoothies and a treadmill, encouraged such annual soul-searching! What would our culture be like?

I felt enchanted by the trappings of tradition I encountered that Yom Kippur, and took up the dare to look back. I didn't have to look far: the resentment I had nurtured all year was still thumping its nasty thump in my heart, which had been broken nearly a year earlier by a girl I had dated for a scant nine months. Whatever—I was twenty-three and had been *in love*! But Yom Kippur's somber demand struck a chord. This lousy negativity I was carrying around was way past its prime. For the past year I'd let this bummer define me: I was the girl who got dumped, the dumped girl, the heartbroken. I couldn't have imagined letting that go—forgiving my ex for finding another girl to love and actually *apologizing* for my unsportsmanlike behavior—without the framework of tradition and spirituality to hold and inspire me. I ran into my ex that very night at the gay disco, which is where I forgave her and apologized. Being a gracious and mellow sort, she accepted. Many years later she married a good friend of mine, and now I get to visit them on their farm in the country. Taking a look at the stories I was perpetuating about my own life and the negativity I was blasting, and then summoning the courage and humility to stop—these were life-altering experiences.

If you've gotten the Judgment card, the Tarot is asking you to take a hard look at your stance right now. Can you lighten it up? Is there something you can let go of, or an apology you need to give or accept? Perhaps your conscious mind is urging you to change something about the way you live and you've been ignoring it because the ramifications are too big, too scary, too inconvenient. Part of the Major Arcana, Judgment is a big card. It dares you to allow your life to change, to take the one step that can make the future be different. It is, despite the image of the gray undead crawling from their coffins, an auspicious and highly positive card. Take up the challenge it is presenting to you. With a little introspection, you probably know what it is.

Work with Judgment

- It's hard to do a strong self-assessment without some structure; as I said earlier, without the occasion of Yom Kippur showing me the way, I might still be writing shitty poetry about my faithless ex. Another tradition that leans heavily on personal inventory is the twelve-step program. Utilized by alcoholics, loved ones of alcoholics, various and sundry drug users, folks who earn too little money and spend too much, outright gamblers, and the sex-crazed (the love-crazed really), a twelve-step tradition is out there for anyone afflicted with the human condition who needs to hunker down and deal with it. And why not? The twelve steps proscribe a path out of whatever compulsion you've indulged in to push the abyss away, but that inevitably brought the abyss right up to your doorstep. However, if you'd like to work with the energies of the Judgment card, you don't have to be in need of recovery to benefit from the type of inventories found in the twelve steps.

  Get a notebook, a pen, and some representatives of the elements for support: a candle for fire, a glass of water (which you

will drink—self-assessment is dehydrating!), a feather or blade to represent air, and a rose quartz crystal to keep you grounded and self-loving. Make a list of your resentments. Get 'em all out, especially if you've never done anything like this before. Okay, now write down *why* you're so pissed at the people you resent. What did they do?

Next, we're going to unpack it a little deeper. How did what they did affect you? Usually we get a beef with someone if they affect our pride, our self-esteem, our romantic relationship, our standing at work, or our standing in the community.

Once you really get into what the core problem is, it's time to take the tough look at how you fed into it. Maybe your expectations were unrealistic. Maybe you were being controlling. Maybe you just couldn't accept a particular reality. Possibly you were truly wronged, but you took that wrong and ran all over town with it, trying to get people on your side, really nurturing your grievance. You couldn't let it go. Being a victim can bring a little bit of a high with it, as can gossip, fighting, and conflict in general. Be as fearlessly truthful as you can right here. What's at stake is your psyche and your spirit. Being able to look honestly at yourself, no matter how unpleasant or embarrassing it is, helps create new patterns and increase your happiness. It's worth it! Looking at each situation, ask yourself how you could have handled it differently.

Finally, think about what you can do now. Do you owe someone an apology? Do you need to change your point of view, your way of being? Ask your elemental support for the courage, clarity, and self-love to do what your inventory has shown must be done. Self-love is a real important bit here; if you end your inventory engulfed in shame and self-hate, you've done it wrong. There is a joy in seeing things—including yourself—for what they are. What you, like all of us, are struggling with is nothing less than the human condition, complicated by those impulses to protect our tender selves at all costs. Honor your coping skills, however warped or misguided they were. They meant well! But now a new day is dawning, as it does in the Judgment card, and your angel of truth, a vision of color, is waking you up and inviting you to join him.

21. The World

And so the Major Arcana come to a truly glorious end. In the World, a joyful, ethereal, gender-fluid or transgender individual dances in the sky, one with the cosmos, batons of pure energy in her hands. In each corner of the card we see the same figures from the Wheel of Fortune card—the Aquarian human, the Scorpio eagle, the Leonine lion, and the Taurean bull. Representing the Suits of the Tarot, they suggest that the enormous accomplishment this card heralds has come about through the wise and intuitive manipulation of the elements. The intellect and the emotions, passion and hard work, were all employed, and the result is a magnificent celebration. The dancer is surrounded by a giant laurel wreath, the symbol of victory, and the wreath is decorated with symbols of infinity. All is as it should be, and all is beautiful, forever.

When the World comes into your life, you have, quite simply, won. Your hard work, perseverance, and intuition have paid off grandly, and you now find yourself in the giddy situation of having made your dream come true. You may be receiving accolades right now; if so, accept them humbly but absolutely enjoy them. You're receiving no less than a congratulations from the Universe! Your World may be a bit less worldly: perhaps you successfully arranged a reunion of all your far-flung best friends, or made sure that family got together for a holiday, or just celebrated a meaningful birthday. Whatever your achievement, be it a prestigious award or a hard-earned night to yourself, the World is acknowledging that there's something special about what you achieved and it wants you to recognize that too. Do not sabotage your achievement with story lines about your unworthiness or by dwelling on what you have to do *next;* the World insists that you are worthy, and to question this is to insult the very Universe. As for your next move, you are not allowed to think of that until the last bit of confetti has been swept from the floor.

 Be the World 

- Make yourself a magic wreath. It might sound like advanced magical crafting, but if I can do it, I promise you can as well. All you need is a wire wreath frame and some florist's tape, both available at your local craft depot. If you can get your hands on actual laurel branches, making a laurel wreath would be so perfectly synched up with the World's energy. If you can't access laurel, however, other herbs that are usually available also hold the insanely positive energy that the World card represents: eucalyptus, rosemary, and lavender are all wonderful (and fragrant!) for magic wreath-making. Or feel free to use whatever is available to you; almost all plants have magical properties, and a quick trip to the Internet can affirm the vibing goodness of the one you choose. Simply affix the herbs or branches to the wire frame and secure with the tape. Voilà! Feel free to accent with additional herbs whose energy you'd like to bring into the mix. In fact, those bay leaves you have in the kitchen are actual laurel leaves, so tuck some into the wreath and dedicate it to the magic and grandeur of the World. Ask the World to come into your home and to stay with you.
- After making so much magic happen, you must be exhausted. Or maybe you haven't made your magic yet and are working to bring the victorious energy of the World into your sphere. Either way, this healing, invigorating magical bath rules. Draw a bath and add to it Epsom salts, roses, and bay leaves. Toss in some cinnamon sticks and, if you're lucky enough to have any around, some vervain. Get into your tub. If you are currently luxuriating in the type of success the World brings about, relax

and enjoy yourself. If you're hoping to pull such energy into your life, meditate with more focus, asking the Universe to assist you in your efforts to make your dreams come true and to bring you big-time success.

- Make an altar to the World. This can be done as a celebration, as an expression of gratitude, or as a way to bring World energy into your life. Use candles of many colors, and lots of them. Also your entire crystal collection. Put feathers, seashells, and water in your finest crystal. Burn some frankincense. If you have representations of what victory looks like to you, bring them to the altar. A mirror and something blooming or alive would be nice. Stand or sit before your altar and cast your spell of celebration, gratitude, or coming victory. Say it aloud in your own words. Then spend some time before the altar enjoying its beauty.

The Minor Arcana

Wands

The Ace of Wands

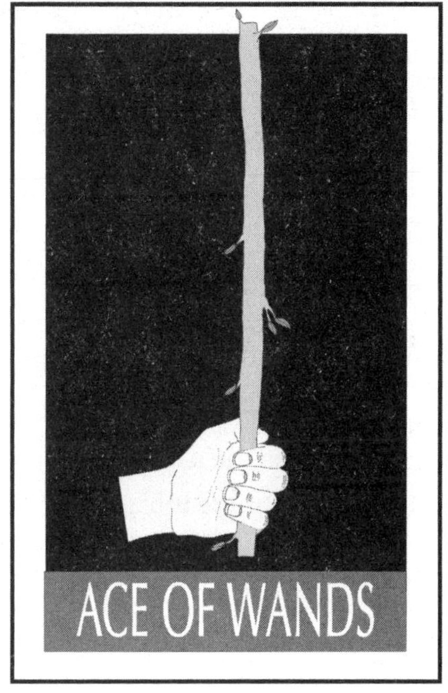

Get ready, you're about to get thumped on the head with the boldness stick. Or is it the creativity stick? Or the inspiration stick? Or the pure passion stick? All of these things and more, the Ace of Wands is a tremendous *YES!* from the Universe, pushing you to run not walk in the direction of your nearest inspiration.

What is it you've been thinking of doing? Starting a school? Going on tour? Trying out for something you're barely qualified for but have a deep gut feeling about nonetheless? Do you feel creativity surging through you like you'll go *mad* if you don't have some place to put it? This is the all-fired-up blessing of the Ace of Wands, the card that packs every bit of crazed, visionary, energy-to-burn fierceness from the suit of Wands into one simple little card featuring a hand holding a branch. From this humble illustration, pretty much everything happens. If you've been feeling stuck, you can happily expect everything to start moving. If you've been wondering whether to make a particular (bold, daring, potentially foolish) move, the answer could not be more affirmative.

Of course, the Ace is simply the start of this journey; along the way you will get stuck, burn out, and feel overwhelmed. But you will also experience achievement, you will also celebrate, and you will also learn. When the Ace of Wands comes for you, an exciting new chapter of your life is beginning. Say yes to it as loudly as you can.

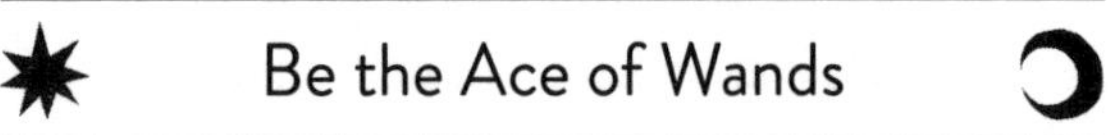

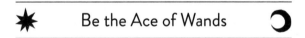

Be the Ace of Wands

- Wands, as you probably know, are frequently used in magic. If another spell in this book hasn't made you go out and make yourself one yet, this card would be a great occasion to do just that. Wands are sold in most magic shops, but honestly, you could find a child's wand at a toy shop (you know, with a shiny

star on top, ribbons, etc.) and use that if you like. Or it can be super-fun to pull out your craft box and make a wand. You don't have a craft box? Errr, well, get yourself some or all of the following—colored thread, yarn, ribbon, small crystals, faux flowers or greenery, tinsel, sequins, feathers—whatever strikes your fancy as you cruise the aisles of your local craft shop. Find yourself a nice sturdy branch in some natural space and get to work decking it out with magical intention and flashy decor. Make your wand as serious or whimsical as your temperament requires.

When you are done, stand before your altar, outside in some natural space, in your bedroom, wherever, and raise it up in your hand like that ethereal hand in the card. Then proclaim it to be *your* wand, to do *your* magic, and to help you bring about the changes you desire. So mote it be, man!

- Fire agate is a great stone to channel Ace of Wands magic. It revs up your physical energy and your libido and helps you run high energy without burning out. It also helps the Universe guide your action, hooks you up with courage aplenty, and guards against the sort of boring, lackluster, ho-hum existence that is your nightmare. This crystal wants to go on an adventure with you! Pledge it to the Ace of Wands, then pledge yourself to it, and see where it takes you.
- For a potion to conjure potent power à la the Ace of Wands, gather cinnamon, ginger, and lemongrass essential oils. Add a couple tiny drops by the dropper to a one-ounce base of almond oil. Play with it until you get it to a scent you find appealing, but be aware that cinnamon can irritate sensitive skin. When you go out to command your day and seek your destiny, daub it behind your ears, on your throat, on your wrists, and between your legs. Dedicate it to the Ace of Wands.

The Two of Wands

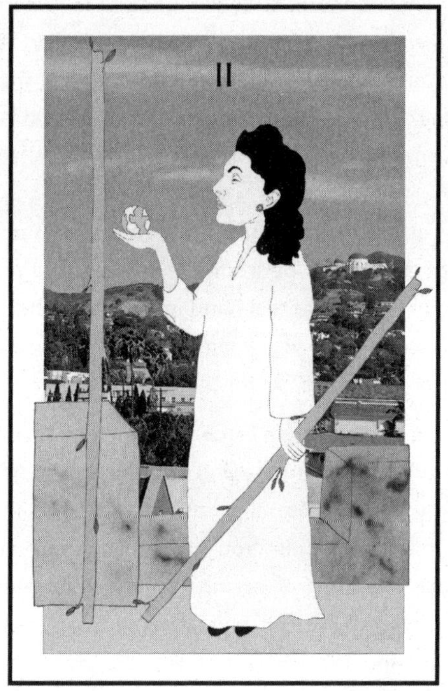

The Two of Wands depicts a pretty well-to-do person standing on the turret of their personal castle. They look out on their primo landscaping, holding a little globe in their hand as if wondering, *Where in the whole wonderful world will I explore next? Where shall I expand my reach? Should I book a European tour? Or should I stay put where my business is wildly flourishing and enjoy the fruits of my labor, all while kicking my creativity up to the next level? Whatever shall I do?*

If the Two of Wands has come up for you, chances are you are contending with luxury problems such as these. The card suggests that you are experiencing some pretty uplifting success, and the best part is that you did it on your terms, while being your totally weird self. Not an everyday occurrence in this world! You have a lot to be proud of—and a couple of decisions to make. Every possible move seems like a good one, which makes your process more challenging, not less. The only thing the Two of Wands requires is that you keep working. If you're itching for a vacation, make it a business trip. Just because everything is coming up roses doesn't mean it's time for you to take a breath. This is but a Two, early in the suit, a wonderful follow-up to the explosive energy of the Ace. But you still have work to do. The good news is that you almost certainly enjoy the work. The even better news is this: the outcome it will lead to is awesome. Get to it.

If the Two of Wands has come up in regards to a new relationship or an intrigue, it doesn't look too good. Starting a new relationship is likely to be a distraction from looking at yourself and making the big move you're meant to make. There is a restlessness and even a boredom at play in this card, and new crushes fizzle fairly quickly. Better to walk away now, though chances are a friendship can come from it that might be mutually beneficial in the future. If this is a longer-term relationship that's hit a snag, perhaps the card is calling you to make a big move *together.* Start a shared project, move, travel, go to couple's counseling, anything that brings you together in a way that is new, creative, and honest.

 Be the Two of Wands 

- Want to recharge before you take your project to the next level? Simply draw a bath and toss a bundle of fresh rosemary into the water. It provides the relaxation you're craving while also energizing you for the coming activity. For extra magic, dedicate the rosemary to the success of your project before you add it to the bath.
- A magically fortifying tea to drink as you begin your Two of Wands course of action is honeysuckle. It will amp up your confidence (not that you need it!) and attract people predisposed to help you achieve your goals.

The Three of Wands

Sometimes I think of the Three of Wands as a pat on the back from the Universe itself. When it arrives, you can be sure that the plans you have laid and executed are solid. Your energy is right on, you're operating with vibrant dynamism, you do not risk burnout, and you can keep going, full steam ahead, in pursuit of your dreams. You are on the track to making it happen.

The card shows a figure taking a meditative moment to sur-

vey the landscape, while leaning a bit on the wands they've firmly planted in the ground. This is totally you! Those wands may be work or a project, a relationship or a significant leisure plan such as travel. Whatever it is, it required a bit of a strategy and you nailed it. As you get ready to take the next step, take a moment to make sure you're taking advantage of all that is available to you. Push the boundaries of your awareness to see if there is anything you're not seeing, any potential allies you may have, or any challenges you can anticipate. If you are thinking about expansion, this card bodes well for taking things to the next level. If you are considering travel, this card looks favorably on that as well. When the Three of Wands comes around, you can pretty much go after anything you want, as you've already laid the necessary groundwork and your passion will continue to carry you forward.

Be the Three of Wands

- If you are looking to call into your life the type of success the person in the Three of Wands card is experiencing, try this potent candle spell. With a pin, carve into the wax of a red, gold, or orange candle a word that symbolizes what it is you want to see success in. Dress the candle with almond oil, which attracts abundance. If your candle is in glass (I prefer these), drip some oil on top; if it is not, apply the oil to the whole candle. The three herbs to use in this spell are kava kava (the bark, not the tincture), allspice, and patchouli (again, the herb, not the oil). Mixing them together in a small bowl, ask these herbs to bring success to you and to your endeavor. Either sprinkle the mix-

ture onto the top of a glass candle, or spread it on paper and roll your (nonglass) candle in it. If you can handle it, toss a little gold, red, or orange glitter into the mix! Now you have infused your candle with serious success-summoning magic. Light the candle and sit before it, meditating on what your next move should be.

- If you are looking for success in a particular physical location, bring a galangal root to that place. Chew up a mouthful of it while envisioning how hard you are going to rule. Then spit the galangal out. You're done!
- A super-strong crystal for success is citrine. Get yourself a stone and dedicate it to the success of your project. Meditate with it and have it on you always as you go about your work. Check in with your citrine each night and always sleep with it nearby.

The Four of Wands

When the Four of Wands pops up, true celebration is upon you. It could simply be your birthday, or maybe there's been a special achievement or occasion in your life—a promotion, an art show, a film premiere, a graduation. Those in a committed relationship might find themselves being proposed to, those who are engaged might be welcoming their wedding celebration, and other couples may be approaching an anniversary. Whatever it is—a birth, some good news, a visiting friend—the Four of Wands wants you to take the celebration to the max. Really get into how much you love your partner, how happy you are to have been born, how psyched you are to visit with a friend. Spare no expense to make the event a special one.

I feel the Four of Wands in my life whenever I have a book party planned. It feels so good, after trudging through my own brain for months, to bring my creation out into the world and have a party for it. I'm celebrating myself, I'm celebrating the book—which, oddly, is of me and yet not of me—and I'm celebrating my friends who support me and my community of readers. It's just super-fun. The Four of Wands especially likes celebrations that come at the completion of some hard work, but don't worry—the completion of the earth's trip around the sun was full of hard work too. Birthdays and new years are important occasions too!

Often the Four of Wands is foreshadowing a surprise. If this card has come up and you've got nothing—like, really, *nothing*—going on, perhaps a surprise is coming your way, or a reason to throw a party. It also could be that you're being called to throw a party for someone else. If this is the case, get lavish—it's a special moment to really show someone else that they matter. You shouldn't be satisfied unless your efforts bring tears of joy to the person of honor!

Life is too short, and the Tarot is too full of pointy swords and tearful cups. When the Four of Wands comes your way, the Universe wants you to take advantage of this moment and really, really celebrate it. Make up an excuse, invent a new holiday, but do what you must to conjure some joy for you and yours.

 Be the Four of Wands 

• Though the Four of Wands is absolutely a fire card—it's some fiery activity, resulting in success, that's the cause of celebration in the card—what came to me is a water spell to bring this lovely energy into your life. In a large bowl, I want you to float as many flower blossoms as you can without them getting too cramped. Sink your crystals to the bottom and shake some chunky salt (preferably pink Himalayan) into the bowl. On an altar, light as many candles in as many colors as you can without creating a fire hazard. Now get dressed up—like you're going to the fanciest event you've got the wardrobe to attend. If you wear makeup, pile it on. Have fun, be creative. Bring in a dish of honey and add that to the altar. Spritz yourself with your favorite scent and spritz it about your magic space too.

Now meditate. Talk to your altar, ask for what you need. Do you have a hard time celebrating yourself? Do you need help opening your heart to positivity and attention? Do you need some glamour and adventure? Is life feeling a little too dull for you right now? Ask for it. Perhaps you can see how to make your life more joyful, or more exciting, but you feel scared to make the move. Ask for bravery. Do you want to celebrate someone close to you but the thought makes you feel like a nerd? Again, ask for courage. Keep this altar up until you have made definite plans for an actual party, an occasion to wear that incredible outfit out into the world, a celebration with actual fellow human beings.

The Five of Wands

The Five of Wands is a total pain in the ass card. Generally petty in nature, it signifies anything from a stupid day that can't end soon enough to being surrounded by people who have become so consumed by ridiculous bullshit that it's affecting everything around them, yourself included. This card also rules competition, but not in a heroic way—more like the soul-deadening, annoying competition we experience in work and social circles.

First, let me share with you the practically iconic Five of Wands day I experienced recently. The diner where we'd hoped to eat breakfast was closed—because a driver had rammed their vehicle through the front door in the wee hours of the night. Poor me, right? Because it was raining, we chose to run errands in a horrible mall, but immediately felt spiritually poisoned by the environment. The things we had hoped to get weren't available. We allowed a fast-talking steam-cleaner salesman to hijack us for fifteen minutes. I attempted an intervention with a total stranger whose drug problem appeared to be compromising his parenting ability. Depressed, we decided to cheer ourselves up by visiting our favorite ramen house. It wasn't open. Later, when we were starving, my wife drove back to get food to go. It took forty minutes, and as you can guess, they gave us the wrong order.

None of this hurt my life at all; even the serious problems I encountered (the diner, the parent) weren't actually my problems. But still. When the Five of Wands pops up, you can expect pretty much nothing to go right for you. You will be *certain* that Mercury is in retrograde, but it's not. You may think the Universe itself is out to get you, but it's not so personal. To everyone such shitty days must fall. At least they come to an end.

The Five of Wands also represents groups of people who are incompatible, who cannot work together and allow themselves to be separated by the pettiest conflict. Make sure you are not participating in this dynamic. If you pull yourself out of it and work to become a peacemaker, you might be the big hero; at the very least, you won't gain a reputation as an idiot.

If this card arrives, it may also mean that competition is getting

you down. It isn't fun competition, and it's annoying and possibly soul-crushing, but you have to engage because something that matters is at stake.

The key to getting through these Five of Wands problems is right there in the imagery of the card itself. Look at the fight depicted; it's *play*! Those are children, clad in the play clothes of their time. Get a sense of humor about your situation. Regarding your situation as a game might make its competitive aspect a bit more enjoyable. None of these conflicts are at all important, so try not to take them seriously. Even your crappy day might be the goddess playing a trick on you for no good reason. Maybe she's bored, and you're cheering her up. Show up with a smile on your face and lean heavily on your sense of humor. This card will pass before you know it.

Working with the Five of Wands

- This is a great moment to weigh yourself down with stones, because you need some earth to ground the crazy, unfocused Wands energy running amok in your world. As I traversed the mall from hell I desperately clutched the one little crystal I had in my pocket, wishing I had ten more. Load every pocket you can with grounding stones. I have a friend who carries hers in her bra; if you wear such things, fill 'er up. If you can walk comfortably with a thin crystal in your shoes, give it a try. As for the rest, dump them in your purse or man-purse or duffel bag or whatever. If you don't have a ton of crystals, even

some everyday rocks from your garden will work. They might not sparkle, but they are still sacred to earth energies and carry their own magic. Say a prayer to the Universe before you head out the door: *Keep my energy on the ground, let laughter be my only sound.*

The Six of Wands

Oh fun, a victory parade! The big winner trots through town, a laurel wreath on their head and another held high on their staff, while all around them townsfolk clamor like paparazzi. When this card gallops into your life, it means you've won! Maybe you've scored a job or promotion, or a project you've been working on has been green-lit. It could be a creative breakthrough profound enough to share; it could be that the seemingly thankless chari-

table work you've been doing has earned you some serious accolades. Often there is more work to do—this card is a six, after all, not a ten—but when the Six pops up, it means the work you *have* completed has hit a sort of critical mass and the time has come for some props and recognition—just the boost you need to keep your energy up and directed toward your larger goal.

The Six of Wands doesn't always refer to winning a competition—sometimes you've bested yourself, or won against the odds—but for me this card does bring up winning the Lambda Book Award at the tender age of twenty-eight. I never, ever thought that dirtbaggy old me would get a *literary* award, and certainly not for a book that featured the snorting of drugs and the having of threesomes. Having my work recognized and celebrated by a literary community I didn't even know I was part of was heady and humbling and affirmed that I was on the right track with this writing thing. It wasn't the end of my story, but it was a critical moment of accomplishment that would influence the rest of my career.

If the Six of Wands is up for you, enjoy it! You've worked hard to bring about the triumph of the moment, and you should feel free to bask in the glow of admiration. I don't have to tell you not to let it go *too* much to your head, do I? I mean, of course you *do* want it to go to your head in that you want to allow this experience to inform your sense of yourself and your abilities, what you are able to accomplish. Let it build your confidence, and go to work on any imposter syndromes you have lurking in your shadows. What the Six of Wands *doesn't* mean is that you're through, you're done, you can rest on the card's numerous laurels. And though you may be experiencing a personal best that involved literally besting some others, it doesn't mean you're literally better than anyone else, right? Duh.

If your efforts are still too close to their starting point to have earned any real praise but this card came up anyway, know that the universe sees and applauds your work. Keep going! Whether your achievement is worthy of a victory parade, replete with horses, or it's more like a yay-for-me-I-went-twenty-four-hours-without-drinking, the Six of Wands is here to crown your accomplishments and give you a hip, hip, hooray! Keep doing what you're doing, with joy and confidence.

Be the Six of Wands

- If you are looking for a charm to help you straight-up triumph, source the herb woodruff and keep some in your shoes. Wear the shoes whenever you're looking to be victorious.
- To call the victorious energy of the Six of Wands into your life, light gold, red, and orange candles while burning frankincense. Lie back and visualize yourself totally ruling. If you happen to have any turquoise or turquoise jewelry, bring it into the mix, as Six of Wands is ruled by the planet Jupiter and turquoise is sacred to the planet. Consecrate it to your future success, and carry or wear it whenever you are looking to win!

The Seven of Wands

When the Seven of Wands comes up, you're probably having to defend your position, whether it's a role that someone is trying to knock you out of or a belief that you need to stand up for regardless of how contested it might be. The card shows a person who literally has scored the high ground; this can mean either that you've clawed your way to the top of your field or that your beliefs have inflamed the townspeople and they're coming after you with pitchforks. Both the defensive posture and the aggressive stance of the individual are fully warranted. It is also noteworthy that, while fully engaged, the figure doesn't seem particularly scared. The Seven of Wands all but guarantees that you will remain on top—whoever is competing with you will fail, whoever is spreading gossip will get their comeuppance, whoever is debating you will be seen as feeble. Your strength and perseverance combined with your hard-won skill in the area under attack have imbued you with confidence, and this unstoppable combo will keep you king of the hill.

It is worth mentioning that, if you are part of a group attacking or intervening with a particular individual, it's probably not going to go the way you hope. If that person has an enviable position, they've earned it. If they've behaved badly, matching them with rumormongering will backfire. If their beliefs are terrible, it is their right, sadly, to have them. One day during the 2016 presidential election, I saw a Donald Trump sign on the front lawn of a very fancy home in my neighborhood. It took all the maturity in my body to not rip it from the grass. Leaving the sign alone felt bad, but it was the right thing to do. The Seven of Wands wants you to do the right thing. Also, for some reason, the figure under attack is wearing two different shoes. Truly don't know what to make of that one.

Be the Seven of Wands

- If you're looking to be the Seven of Wands, you want two things: to be undefeatable, and to have unshakeable energy.

A glittering, glowing sunstone is here to help. A sunstone supports being independent, fighting for your beliefs, and going against the grain. It assists people involved in competitive arenas and promotes vitality and strength—not just inner strength but physical strength as well. *And* it protects against enemies. Sunstone is basically your all-purpose Seven of Wands crystal. Acquire one, dedicate it to the card's energies, and bring it along with you as you fight for what's yours.

The Eight of Wands

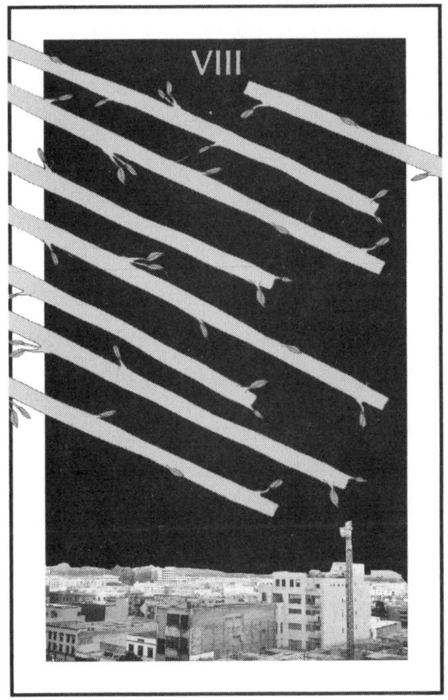

The Eight of Wands is traditionally illustrated as a bunch of sticks flying across the sky. It's meant to convey swiftness, the card's primary attribute. Imagine the sticks as arrows being flung toward a bull's-eye by an expert archer. Imagine them as currents of pure fire or electricity pulsing outward, energizing everything in their path with passion.

The Eight of Wands is associated with the fearless and fun-loving Sagittarius zodiac sign, depicted as a randy centaur aiming its bow and arrow out into the universe. Sags get their fearlessness from their ruling planet, Jupiter, the planet of luck, so no matter how many planes they sky-dive from or drugs they jack into their body or romances they tumble into, they're sure to emerge unscathed, sober, and heart fully intact. That wild, headlong, *Fuck it, let's GOOOOOOOO!* Sagittarian energy propels those wands upward and onward, and Sugar Daddy Jupiter is there to make sure they hit their target with room to spare. Another planet associated with this card is quick-witted Mercury; the fastest planet in our solar system, Mercury is believed to govern everything communication-related—not just communication technology, like social media, computers, and cell phones, but actual communication, like when you speak directly to another person.

I was having an Eight of Wands moment when, in the midst of fertility treatments and sick of hating every single mommy blog on the Internet, I created *Mutha* magazine, a space for all sorts of nontraditional "moms" (plus the occasional dad, baba, and grandparent) to tell personal stories from their experience raising children. I conjured the name in a flash, Googled the domain name, whipped out my ATM card, and *whammo, Mutha* was born. My totally supportive wife was a little confused, as would be anyone upon learning that their person just up and started a website with no real plan. But taking a page from the intuitive archer Sagittarius, I just *felt* that the time was right—and it was. *Mutha* has run for over two years now, with new content nearly every day, the majority of it unsolicited. I wasn't the only weirdo mom or mom-to-be jonesing for a dose of refreshing reality on the Internet. This virtual community kept me focused and inspired as I trudged along the often heartbreaking path of technology-assisted reproduction.

The Eight of Wands wants *you* to start *your* website—like, right now. It might feel a little rash, but the thing is, it's an eight. Cards higher in the 1–10 cycle suggest that work and preparation has been happening, even if they were happening in your subconscious mind. Your burst of inspiration isn't coming from nowhere, even if it feels like it is. It's just a plan that has gained enough underground momentum to burst into your brain with a fevered *now!* You are more prepared than you know.

So buy that domain name. Or take a trip, preferably out of the country, and with as little planning—and baggage—as possible. Do that thing—you know, that *thing* you always say you're going to do but you just haven't got around to, because you're lazy or scared, because your parents poo-poo'd it or your friends sort of laughed at it. The big thing, the crazy thing—that's the thing you want to do right now. The quit-your-job thing, the break-up-with-your-g'friend/b'friend thing. The start-your-own-business thing, the fling-yourself-at-the-feet-of-that-person-you've-been-salivating-over thing. There doesn't need to be a lot of thought here, just muscle. Sign up for that class, register for that silent retreat, move across the country or, better yet, *out* of the country. Sagittarius governs travel to lands not your own, so now is the time to go teach English in Tokyo or walk the Spanish El Camino or finagle your way onto a ship bound for the North Pole. The Eight of Wands says, *Yes! Go now! Quick!*

Be the Eight of Wands

- To bring Eight of Wands energy into your life, buy a fat red candle. With a pin, score eight strong lines into the wax. Light it and ask the Universe to help you make your move. Burn it for eight days (eight days straight in your sink or re-light as you come and go).
- Go outdoors someplace where you can light a fire without setting a national park ablaze or otherwise endangering anyone. Gather eight little twigs or sticks. Make a little structure with them, and light them on fire. As you watch them burn, imagine all your inhibitions, your restrictive fear, the negativity that immobilizes you, going up in smoke. Imagine the powerful heat of those eight burning wands infusing your blood, making it roil and shimmer. This is your life, and you can do anything you want to do.
- Create an Eight of Wands talisman (or talis*woman*) to carry with you and keep your fires raging. Many of the properties of fire are attributed to fire agate; procure either a single crystal or eight of them. (If you go with eight, get yourself a little bag, red or orange, to hold them in.) If you can't come up with a fire agate, grab something that suggests fire to you. A wooden kitchen match. A lighter (but only if it is a handsome silver Zippo). Whatever you use should have some sort of aesthetic charm to it, so don't use a pack of paper matches (unless they hail from a faraway land you're looking to explore), and don't make magic with some crappy plastic Bic. Honestly, you can even take some orange and red crayons and color yourself a little flame. (Feel free to be as abstract as your artistic talents require.)

Whatever you wind up with, hold it firmly in your hands and ask it to help you keep your fire high as you embark on whatever new project or adventure the Eight of Wands has inspired for you. Lie back and place your talisman right below your belly button. This is the site of the chakra that holds all your energy and vitality, your will and strength and purpose—your fire. Imagine this space right below your belly button as a veritable cauldron of hot, fiery energy! Imagine it infusing your talisman with your very own life force! Next, imagine the metaphorical flaming qualities of your talisman sinking into your body, your guts.

You know how we say something takes guts when it's daring? Or how wild, go-for-it types are called gutsy? This is what we're doing. Fueling up your guts with intention and imagination and loading your talisman with gutsy energy so that whenever you feel yourself falter you can whip it out of your purse or pocket or wallet and remind yourself of the well of badass life energy you have access to.

The Nine of Wands

Who is this sketchy-looking, stressed-out person with the bandaged head, defensively clutching a stick behind his self-created fortress? Well, if you picked the Nine of Wands, it's probably you, and chances are you're feeling more than a little put-upon by the world. When the Nine of Wands comes up, so do your dukes; this is a fighting card. Look at the weary, glowering expression on our guy. He's hurt, and he's exhausted. He's been up all night building

his protective encampment to make sure he's not taken by surprise. In spite of all this, he's ready to go. If a problem shows up, he's going to have at it like a one-man ninja army.

When the Nine of Wands comes up, it's time for you to stand your ground. Someone or something is going to try to talk you out of your best interest, out of your personal truth, out of your heart's desire. The stakes here are high—wands symbolize our creative energy, our life force. It reminds me of the time I turned in a book I loved—*loved!*—to a publisher, only to be told it was more or less a piece of crap, the first hundred pages needed to be deleted, and the entire manuscript could use rewriting. I'd thought this publisher was a done deal; the book cover was done, and I'd excitedly bragged about it on Facebook already. And the publisher was highly respected, a press I'd been honored to be working with. What to do? For a moment I flirted with the idea of following my editor's harsh instructions. She was a super-wise woman, both warm and intimidating. I knew she only wanted the best for both my book and her press. But when I sat down to make her changes, my heart broke. As a person who has written a lot of stuff, I knew how rare it was to actually *like* something this much. Usually I feel a combination of embarrassment, relief, fear, and pride when I finish writing a book. But for this one I only felt excitement and joy. And all the parts that made me feel so illuminated were the parts my editor wanted me to get rid of.

My ego was as bruised as the Nine of Wands warrior's forehead. I concentrated on making sure my response wasn't defensive so much as protective. I loved my weird little book! If the esteemed press didn't feel that they could put it out, I accepted their decision.

But I had to remain true to my vision and trust that my book would find a home in the publishing world. And did it ever! After licking my wounds for a bit, I gathered the courage to share it with another editor, at an equally esteemed publisher. My stubborn faith paid off—she loved it! My beloved book was going to be released to the world by a publisher that understood and believed in it.

The Nine of Wands assures you that the fight is yours to be won, so long as you don't give up. It promises that you've got more energy than you think, and commands you to not succumb to the easy way or the stronger voice. Take care that your fortress isn't defensive so much as protective—of yourself, your project, your people, whatever you're sticking up for—and do what you must to guard yourself against the forces challenging you. At the end of this experience you will probably be a little less innocent and a little more cynical, but you will also be a lot stronger and more in touch with your inner strength. Trusting yourself is a powerful thing, as is fighting for what you know is true. On the other side of the Nine of Wands is a newfound confidence, a bit of swagger, and that big blue sky you see in the card.

Bring Nine of Wands Energy into Your Life

- Go into nature and find yourself nine wands—sticks, branches, twigs, driftwood. Arrange them on the ground in the shape of a circle and sit down inside it. Consecrate this temporary pro-

tective space by asking the forces of wands, cups, coins, and swords (that would be emotion, spirit, the body, and the mind) to join you and make your circle sacred.

Take out a notebook, a piece of paper, or the note app on your phone and do some writing. What do you want to protect? How come? What does it mean to you? On the other side of this battle, what would you like to see happen? Dream big! Ask the Universe to give you the clarity and strength to stand up for your truth. If your sticks aren't buggy or gross, bundle them up and tie them with a ribbon (red would be nice). Keep them someplace where you will see them often, maybe on your altar or your front steps. Let them be the visual manifestation of all the inner power you cannot see. When your battle has ended, untie them and scatter them where you found them.

The Ten of Wands

My shoulders hurt just *thinking* about this card. The figure clutches a cumbersome bunch of wands in the most awkward way possible, limping painfully into their future. How can this person even see where they're going with their oppressed head tucked into their burden? The ten poles are taller than the figure and probably weigh more. Surely there was a cart handy, or someone they could call in a favor to, but our friend decided that this was the way to go.

Why would this person do this? Well, maybe they're an eccentric thinker, and this seemed like a good idea, and when they realized they were wrong they were in too deep, the town is *right there,* they can make it! Was the person too proud to admit the plan was a bad one? Does this happen a lot? Is our eccentric thinker actually a person who does things the hard way all the time? Are you that person? Is it super-hard to ask for help? Do you believe no one will do as good a job as you, so you take on all the responsibility and then resent everyone for not being as capable as you? Maybe it's not as psychological as all that (though I bet it is). Maybe you just enjoyed the challenge of physical endurance was the struggle for a bit and found it engaging, and now here you are at the end of your journey feeling burned out and alone.

When the Ten of Wands comes into your life, it's time to take a hard look at how you handle responsibility. Our responsibilities are often work-related, but not always. Sometimes we have caretaking responsibilities: maybe you are responsible for another person's health and well-being right now. Or maybe you've *assumed* caretaking responsibility—like, no one really wants your help but you are hell-bent on giving it anyway. Whatever might be sapping the life force from you—a creative project, a collaboration, a relationship, a commitment—one thing is for sure: it is no longer sustainable. On some level it doesn't matter if you are truly responsible for someone else or just assuming that responsibility. Either way, you are at your breaking point, and you need to drastically change your relationship to your commitment.

A rigorously honest investigation of your motives will reveal whether becoming burdened is a recurring problem of yours that calls for a larger solution, or whether it's just that one thing has gotten out of control and you need to rethink your method. If you frequently find yourself doing more than the people around you, helping people who seem totally ungrateful for your assistance, or burning up with resentment that other people are so lazy and incompetent, then the problem this card is calling you to address is yourself. You need to go on a *NO* bender—that is, start saying *no* to all the people, places, and things that are sucking your energy.

I know this is harder than I'm making it sound. This propensity of yours to take on a disproportionate amount of responsibility probably began a looooooong time ago. Maybe it started as a coping mechanism, but now it's morphed into something that is seriously hurting your quality of life. Perhaps you are surrounded by manipulative people (your family, your frenemies, your toxic coworkers) who know exactly how to guilt *you* into doing all the things *they* don't want to do. Regardless, you are the only one who can make it better. The number ten here signifies the end of a cycle. It's a perfect time to break this pattern and begin a new chapter featuring better boundaries and increased self-care.

Or okay, maybe it isn't all that deep for you. Maybe you just innocently took on more than you could handle and you've hit your breaking point. It happens. I once accidentally created a legitimate literary nonprofit and almost lost my mind. I'd been doing the work of a nonprofit—programming readings, events, even tours—but hustling it DIY-style, making next to no money for my efforts. A nonprofit mentor swooped in, and within months I was getting thousands of dollars in grant money, which allowed me to support myself doing what I loved *and* share the dough with my community. It was absolutely life-changing.

But I was actually unprepared for the success of my nonprofit. Like Notorious B.I.G. said, *Mo' money, mo' problems*. With the grants came piles of paperwork, new financial rules, different tax issues. My Ten of Wands looked like this: me hunched over sobbing, understanding that this nonprofit was the best thing to ever happen to me but simultaneously knowing that it was killing me. I phoned my mentor to tell him I was done—sorry about all the time and work and money you sank into building this with me, but I'm *out*. It didn't occur to me to ask for help (a hallmark of this card). Thankfully, my mentor was accustomed to helping artists who collapse into a heap of despair when faced with a pile of paperwork. He told me to use my grant money to hire someone to do the work I couldn't do. And I did. And the nonprofit continues to thrive today.

In this context, the cycle signified by the number ten is a positive one. You've hit a goal, maybe more than one, and achieved beyond what you'd imagined. This problem is the result of good fortune, hard work, and bright ideas. Nonetheless, if you think you can go it alone from this point, you're mistaken. You risk ruining everything you worked for, not to mention your health and sanity, if you don't find a way to make your workload more manageable. And it doesn't matter if you think the end is in sight; the end *is* in sight for the person on the card—look at that little village awaiting the arrival of his bundle of sticks! But he won't make it in this hunched, pained, slow, blind way he's going. He's going to have to stop, lay down his burden, and reconsider. So are you.

 Stop Being the Ten of Wands 

- Get your hands on some wormwood, the herb used to create absinthe. It's a bitter, powerful, mysterious herb, good for repelling and creating boundaries. Take the roots or leaves of the plant, boil them in some water, let it cool, strain it, and mix it with three tablespoons of apple cider vinegar. Or if you're working with wormwood tincture, mix ten drops of the stuff with two cups of water and three tablespoons of the apple cider vinegar.

  Go take a shower. Not a bath—I don't want you soaking, stewing, marinating in this problem! We need movement! Give your body a thorough scrub. Any old soap is fine, but if you've got something special, even something really gritty and scrubby, use that. Think about this Ten of Wands problem you're having. Imagine you are scrubbing away this burden. You're washing away your guilt-fueled feelings of toxic responsibility. You're cleansing yourself of beliefs that you must suffer for your work in order to deserve its fruits. Whatever your issue is (do take time to figure it out before hopping in the shower), wash it down the drain. Give your head a vigorous shampoo, then shut off your shower. Pour the wormwood potion over your head, really soaking whatever hair you've got. Sit there and let it saturate your crowning glory. In so many cultures hair represents power, and certainly most of us get a modicum of personal power out of our hair; that's why bad hair days bum us out so bad. Let this concoction *empower* your hair. You're soaking in a very strong *no*. Ask the wormwood to help you create and keep boundaries, to say no, to cut off people, places, and things that are toxic and draining to you. Ask the wormwood to give you the courage to ask for help. Then rinse. Add therapy as needed.

- Make rhodonite your best friend. Rhodonite is a pink-red stone shot through with veins of black, and it's the perfect crystal to keep in your pocket when life gets traumatic. It is a confidence-boosting stone, so it will help you stick to your guns and make changes you believe in. It's a self-esteem booster too, so if any of your Ten of Wands issues involve feeling "less than," it can assist in your efforts to believe in yourself. It is a good one to meditate with during moments of extreme lousy feelings—anxiety, fear, rage. Ultimately rhodonite is a stone of love and will remind you that saying no, asking for help, breaking toxic ties, are acts of love.

  Before using the stone, share your intentions with it, asking for its assistance in the way you need. Then sit with it quietly for five minutes. Keep it on your person at all times; sleep with it nearby too. When you feel that your Ten of Wands problems have been resolved, thank it and put it on your altar, dresser, desk, or what-have-you until the Ten of Wands pops up again.

- Here's a simple candle spell to help you move this energy along. Use either a black or a white candle. Carve either NO or HELP into the wax, depending on whether you need to hand out a whole lot of *no* or need to ask for some assistance to make your life more balanced. Light the candle and sit before it, imagining what it will feel like on the other side of NO and HELP. Imagine feeling more relaxed, more at peace, less manic, harried, depressed. Think about what you will do with the extra time your NOs and your HELP will bring you. Find a little bit of time every day to sit with the candle for ten consecutive days, and let this spell support you while you go about making these challenging changes.

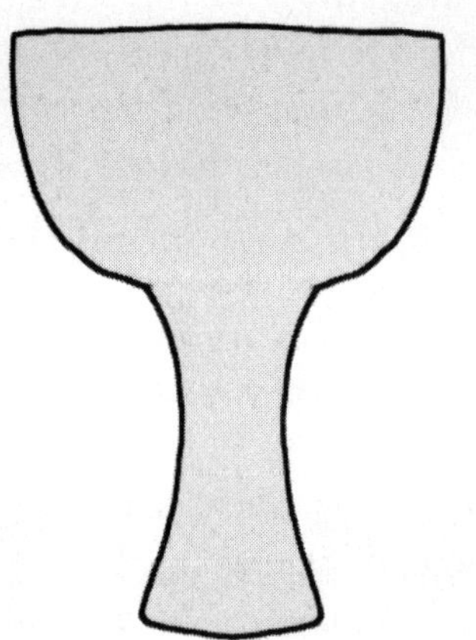

Cups

The Ace of Cups

The Ace of Cups is a beautiful card of feelings and emotions, love and newness. It is the idyllic springtime of the Tarot, a time for wonderful beginnings, the sort of beginnings that swell your spirit with inspiration and anticipation for all the additional magic soon to come from them. If the Ace of Cups has come to you, you're

probably dazzled by the sheer potential of a new person, place, or thing in your life. Obviously, the Ace of Cups is a great card for romance; it denotes finding a person who will be very, very important to you and relationships that have a bit of staying power. Especially inspiring friendships and collaborative or business partnerships can also begin under the blessings of this card; if that happens, you can know it was meant to be. Not all soul mates are romantic ones!

The Ace of Cups can also rule travel to realms that feel deeply magical and inspiring to you, places that unlock heady, positive new ways of thinking about or seeing the world. The Ace of Cups can also come your way when you get an opportunity to begin or join something that connects with all your beauty receptors or touches a place very, very close to your heart. The radiance coming out of the hand bearing the chalice suggests that what you touch right now has a magic or holiness to it. Enjoy this moment. All Aces are simply the beginning of a new cycle, and all the cycles contain both ups and downs, heartache as well as bliss. But right now, at the apex of something new, you're probably feeling pretty euphoric. Get into it.

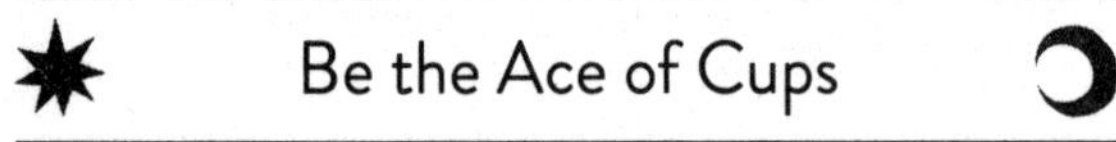

Be the Ace of Cups

- I'm sort of obsessed with celestite right now. Its raw, pale blue sparkles and sweet periwinkle polish call out for angelic assistance, tap into big, universal love vibes, encourage trust

throughout the ups and downs of life, and help us remember our dreams. Its blue abundance makes me think of the overflowing waters of the Ace of Cups. Dedicate your celestite to calling toward you a new emotional beginning or helping you navigate a blissful new chapter in your emotional life.

The Two of Cups

The Two of Cups is always a welcome card. In this image of lovers coming together, there is no mistaking that romantic adventure is the order of the day. One tenderly reaches for the other, and both are already so dizzy with limerence that they appear to be totally checked out about the winged lion head popping out of their cups. Oh to be so drunk on love that one misses even the supernatural

affirmation of such love! If it sounds like a good time, that's because it is.

If the Two of Cups has come into your sphere, you are very likely in love. The card, pleasant-looking in all ways, does suggest that this is a happy thing, and most of the time it is, but here's a shout-out to those of you feeling like your love-cups are empty. If you are on the make, it's entirely possible some lust-luck is heading your way. If you are in unrequited love—oy. I'm so sorry. You can *feel* how good everything could be if the object of your affection would just *get it together*! You're probably right. And he might actually get it together—the optimism of this card is occasionally shocking. But a word to lovers everywhere on the happiness spectrum—this card, though it does offer up true, life-changing love, does not guarantee the lifetime love of committed soul mates. I mean, sure, that might be your story, but it is just as likely that the person who comes along now will eventually become the one who got away, the one who haunts your dreams and pops into your mind when you're spacing out. You will learn something from this love affair (or one-sided, desperate crush), and it will change you. Even if you end up among the one percent who feel keen pain from this card, ultimately you won't regret it. You are learning something valuable: that you can love. You can hit emotional highs (and lows, yes). You finally understand what all those songs and movies and books are about. Welcome to the club, and when I say, enjoy it while it lasts, I'm not trying to be a killjoy. It's just that you never know with these things. So stay in the moment, take it all in, love your heart out.

Of course, it is worth mentioning that other committed relationships may come your way when this card comes up—best friends, collaborators, business partners. These relationships are destined to last a long time, so only sign on with people who fill your heart with joy or certainty.

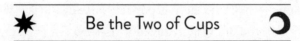

Be the Two of Cups

- To draw love your way, create this magic oil: Take two ounces of almond oil, for luck. (The biggest element of most romance is timing and place, don't you think?) Add to that a tablespoon of rose oil (love, duh). Feel free to add dried or fresh rose petals and buds to the mixture. Stir it with a cinnamon stick to mix sex and lust into the potion. If you can get your hands on an orris root—it's frequently used in hoodoo traditions to draw love and sex—add that as well. Cut open an apple, remove two seeds, and drop them into the mixture.

  You now have your potion. Anoint the backs of your ears, the hollow of your neck, the insides of your wrists, between your legs, and behind your knees with this each day when you leave the house or otherwise come in contact with people. Enjoy!

- To use a crystal to pull love into your life, select a rose quartz, known as the love stone. Sleep with it under your pillow, carry it with you everywhere, meditate with it. Ask it to open your heart to love and to sharpen your intuition so that you can spot your soul mate. You can use it in conjunction with the potion by either letting the crystal sit inside the magic oil to become infused with additional power or anointing it each day with the potion as you do yourself.

The Three of Cups

The Three of Cups is one of the most potent love cards in the Tarot, but it is not about romance. This is the love of friends, community love, squad love. The three dancing maidens are toasting each other, each wearing a wreath of triumph on her head. When one member of our community wins, we all win, and we all celebrate.

If the Three of Cups has danced into your world, there is surely a celebration to be had. Maybe the achievement is not specifically

your own, but that of someone you identify with or support, and so you too can bask in the victory. Perhaps your happiness is so great over a friend's win that it truly feels like your own. Or perhaps the win *is* yours, and it is time to call your people to gather around you and toast your success. Recently I attended a gathering at the house of a casual friend whose television show was premiering. What a big deal! And how strong and positive was the energy in her small house as friends from every stage of her life arrived to help her welcome her success. As part of her community, I beamed with pride; one of our own had experienced an incredible achievement, and our shared values were evident in the work. I knew that even people who weren't there and didn't personally know her, but who identified with what she stood for, were also celebrating this cultural win.

There is the possibility that there is no real accomplishment to be toasted and that the Three of Cups has come into your life because it wants you to take a moment to celebrate your connections—the friends who inspire you, the friends who have stood by you and helped you through difficult times, the new friends who bring a freshness into your days, and the old friends whose cozy love is priceless. Any of us can take up the dance of the Three of Cups at any time because we all have something to celebrate—the people in our lives who bring their magic to our days.

Be the Three of Cups

- The realm of magic is overflowing with love spells, but how many *platonic* love spells are out there? If you're not feeling the

joy of the Three of Cups as vibrantly as you'd like, maybe it's time to call some new besties into your world. You will need a pink candle, three dried rose petals, and sweet pea oil. Before lighting your candle, anoint it with the oil. Then chant: *Bring me friendship, strong and true, open my heart to friendships new.* Burn the roses in the candle flame. Repeat the chant each time you relight the candle, burning it until it's gone. By the time it's spent, new potential friends should have appeared.

- To cast a spell of love and gratitude for your people, acquire a rose quartz for each of them. Soak them in saltwater and infuse them with your love. Sit with the bowlful of water and crystals on your lap and conjure all your feelings of love and gratitude, all your deepest and best wishes for each individual. Then give them the stones—a crystal embodiment of your love for them!
- If drawing the Three of Cups has inspired you to be a better friend to those around you, gather the following stones into a pink or white pouch and bring it with you wherever you go: rose quartz for the self-love you need to be a good friend to others; jade for generosity; amethyst to sharpen your intuition and allow you to relate to people on a deeper level; and green aventurine to build your capacity for friendship.

The Four of Cups

Look at little pouty-pants. Three lovely cups sit in the grass before this figure. Another cup is being offered by a magical cloud-hand, but even this otherworldly offer isn't enough to stir them from their extreme self-absorption; indeed, they may be so deep in their own internal hamster wheel that they can't even *see* this miraculous offering.

If the Four of Cups has popped up in your world, it is probably

time to pull your head out of your arse. In certain cases, the figure beneath the tree is not self-obsessed but contemplative, meditating; like the Buddha beneath the Bodhi tree, the figure is turning away from the things of this world in favor of a more spiritual path. It's possible this is what you're doing, but more likely you're being a baby, proclaiming that an imperfect situation, a disappointing person, the whole world maybe, just isn't good enough for you and withdrawing into a cave of sulky isolation.

How to tell the difference? Well, take a good hard look at how you feel. Do you feel inspired, hopeful, aspirational? Like you are not so much turning *away* from one thing but turning *toward* something else? Can you articulate what you desire, and does the desire make you happy? Congratulations, you are of the smaller percentage of Four of Cups drawers whose golden chalices represent illusion, materialism, and fake happiness.

But the rest of you: Are you feeling bitter, disenchanted, judgmental? Are your defense mechanisms hella inflamed? Are you turning toward nothing but yourself, folding inward, isolating, detaching from life because it just hasn't lived up to your expectations? Well, it is time to open your eyes. The things being offered to you are gifts, gifts that other, *healthier* people would die for. There is something wrong with your attitude, and it's time to really dig out what the problem is. I can tell you this—it's probably not what you think it is. There is a problem underneath your problem, and you need a reality check to get at it. Perhaps you are suffering from depression, a disease that makes great things look shitty. The aid of a therapist could be useful to suss out what is making it so hard to enjoy your life. Maybe you just need a

heart-to-heart with a friend you can trust to be brutally honest with you.

Often when this card comes up, the problem is you but you're too deep in your own bad feelings to see it. The most important thing to do if you've gotten this card is to be willing to look at the situation from a different angle. Be willing to really consider another point of view. Be willing to be wrong. We all have had the experience of letting our bad feelings color our experience; it seems so real, but feelings aren't facts. That final, magical cup being offered is probably a wonderful opportunity for love or growth or fun or abundance, and you run the risk of letting it pass you by. Uncross your arms and start saying *yes*.

 Working with the Four of Cups 

- *Don't let the perfect be the enemy of the good* is a good motto for working with this card. In the Four of Cups, emotions have gotten so heavy and soggy that they've weighed the figure down into a grumpy, isolated individual. What you need is some fire magic to evaporate some of the feelings and set the stage for action. Using blue ink, write down all of your problems, everything you're dissatisfied with, all the people, places, and things that have not lived up to your standards. Even if you can see how foolish some of them are, write them all down. Meditating before a red, orange, white, or black candle, hold your list in your hands and ask the Universe to remove them from you. Ask for the willingness to see things differently; ask for the

strength to be positive. Then, keeping a fireproof bowl or jar nearby, dip your list into the flame and let it burn. Set it into the bowl or jar and watch the fire transform it to ash. Ask the power of fire to come into you and transform your attitudes.

Take the ash and bring it to a place that resonates with your issue, a place linked somehow to what you have been resisting. If no such place exists, then go out into the natural world and scatter the ashes of your bad attitude. Keep lighting the candle for four weeks or until the candle has melted down, always asking the power of fire to keep you active, positive, and saying yes.

- Water energy might be dragging you down, but you can also use it to wake yourself up. This ritual requires that you seek out some cold water. Perhaps you live by a chilly body of water; a spa's cold-plunge feature would also do the trick. At the very least, a bathtub full of icy water or a seriously cold shower will do the trick. Get your hands on a carnelian, a fiery red stone that is good for courage; you're going to take it with you into the cold water and infuse it with ice-cold, red-hot *go!* energy. Your intention here—which you should at least pronounce clearly in your mind if not out loud—is to ask the power of water to shock you out of your apathy, and to ask the power of the carnelian for the courage to face whatever fears compel you to isolate and instead to say yes to your life. Count down from four—three, two, one—and jump in!

  You don't need to stay in the cold water long, but make sure you linger long enough to really feel its magic working on you. Keep the carnelian on or near you, and rev yourself up with it if old, soggy emotional habits threaten to overwhelm you.

- Another stone that is your ally when working to overcome Four of Cups slumps is fluorite. All fluorite crystals work to banish

emotional chaos and confusion. They promote harmony, and when you're in this card you are out of alignment with your life. Fluorite clears negative vibes, which you are probably a fountain of right now. A multicolored fluorite is the strongest magic for this card, but any color will be your friend. Meditate with it regularly, asking it to bring you clarity, to help you open up to your own life, to embrace your reality. Ask it to help you say yes.

The Five of Cups

This card possesses a heartbreaking simplicity. There is a loss, something is gone. You cannot make it come back. Love has been taken away, you've lost your house, money has vanished. Whatever it is, it is big, important, something relied upon. What has gone has taken with it your capacity for joy and hope; your vision of a happy future has vanished. All you can do is grieve in anxious

regret, mulling over what you might have done differently, as if any of that matters now. Your heart aches.

When the Five of Cups arrives, you are at an emotional low. Like the figure on the card, you are hunched over with emotional pain, covering your face because you can't bear to face your situation, turned toward your loss because it is all that you can see. You don't see the two cups standing behind you. That's fine. Now is not the time for clarity about how bad that relationship was for you, how incredible your new freedom will be, how a bigger, better love lies in wait for you. There are other homes for you, and you still have money in the bank—you are not destitute. Maybe family will rise to the occasion and lend you a hand; maybe the work you will have to do because of this setback will bring you into contact with someone who will change your life. There's no way to know what those two cups represent, and you certainly aren't being asked to figure it out. The Tarot only wants to tell you that they are there, and to ask you to tuck this knowledge into the back of your mind so that when you emerge from this period of grieving, you might open your heart to the possibility.

If you do not feel this extreme sadness in your life right now, it may mean that something you are expecting to work out will not. Prepare yourself however you can. It also might mean you have a grieving person around you. If so, allow them to feel their loss; don't attempt to cheer them up. If this person is a potential romantic connection, back way off. This person is in no way ready for a relationship, no matter what they may be saying to themselves or you.

Getting Through the Five of Cups

- Make a Five of Cups pouch. The color of the pouch can be white, black, blue, or red. The volcanic, black obsidian known as "Apache tears" is a strong stone for healing grief and clearing out negative energies. Likewise, jet, not a stone but fossilized wood, is used in mourning jewelry for its power of negative absorption. These stones will help to balance your sadness somewhat so that you can function better and begin to see a way out of your sorrow. Rose quartz, the most loving and healing of stones, will help you with self-forgiveness and introduce joy back into your heart. Herbs that can support you while you grieve include skullcap, hawthorn, chamomile, and rose. Place a mixture of these herbs inside your pouch, along with an image of an unbroken heart—a heart-shaped stone or figure perhaps, or your own drawing of a heart.

  Keep the pouch with you at all times, especially when you sleep. When you have emerged from this sad time and are able to see the two cups waiting for you, scatter the herbs to the earth and soak the stones in saltwater.

- The herbs in your pouch—skullcap, hawthorn, chamomile, and rose—can all be brewed into a tea that will help heal your broken heart. Add to the tea some valerian, if you can stand the stink, and/or some kava kava, especially if you find yourself at the mercy of your emotions.

The Six of Cups

The overarching message of the Six of Cups is one of sweetness; if this card is up for you, it is encouraging you to be sweet and kind, to embrace wholesome pleasures and things of innocence. It is time to be forgiving and generous, to offer aid to people who need it, always coming from a place of care. If you've been thinking of reaching out to someone who may need your help, do it. If you've been asked a favor, grant it. The scene in the card

evokes a pleasant day, even joy, but it is a strictly family-friendly type of good time. It reminds me of how, after I'd been sober for a while, all sorts of nerdy pleasures became appealing to me: proper dates, game nights, a cozy evening at home. After spending much debaucherous time with many debaucherous people, I found myself attracted to people who radiated a sort of wholesomeness. The Six of Cups was in my sphere.

This card also has a deep connection to the past—childhood and nostalgia, specifically. When it pops up, you are sometimes being called back to your hometown, or for a family visit. Maybe you've found some long-lost childhood friends on the Internet and are getting reacquainted. If your childhood was a rough one, it could mean that childhood issues are up for you; unhealed wounds are making themselves known, and you could be feeling triggered and vulnerable. If that is the case, seek the kind company of those who love you. The Six of Cups is set in the courtyard of a fortress; sometimes we need some safe space to sort out our past. The card might be telling you that such a retreat could be beneficial.

Our culture is so youth-crazed that it encourages us to believe that our best years are behind us by age twenty-five. Of course this isn't true, but if you've been feeling old before your time, this card is telling you to get off your ass and do something childlike. Play, run, dance, go rock-climbing, eat an ice cream sundae, dress inappropriately, go to a concert, make some sloppy art—do whatever it takes to pull yourself out of the mental doldrums. The children at the heart of this card encourage us to locate our inner child and try to see the world with their simple, innocent, joyful vision.

 Be the Six of Cups 

- To restore a lost youthful outlook and energy, make a garland of anise pods and hang it around your bedpost. Easy-peasy.
- Here's another spell to do when the Six of Cups card comes up: Take a bowl of pure spring water and float a rose in it. Next add two sprigs of fresh rosemary. If you can get your hands on a bloom of blessed thistle, do add that—it's great for renewing vitality. Sprinkle it all with catnip, which is sacred to youth and beauty. If you have a special wand you use in magic, take it and stir the bowl (otherwise use a stick or piece of wood) three times counterclockwise. Say this chant: *Six of Cups, innocence and beauty, bring your sweetness to me.*

  Let the rose and rosemary dry on your altar or someplace where you will see them frequently. Let them remind you to be kind and to love your sweet life. When the time comes that a loved one is struggling with emotional hardship, tie the flower and rosemary together, or place them in a box, and give them to your loved one.

The Seven of Cups

A figure beholds seven shimmering, glimmering cups emerging from a cloud as if by magic. Each cup offers a different and totally fantastic treasure—a pretty, androgynous lover; a veiled being glowing with spiritual mystery; a snake, classic emblem of sexy wisdom; your future dream home, a literal castle; a heaping pile of gems and baubles; a victorious laurel crown (just ignore the subtle death's-head shadowing the actual cup there); and an adorable, if

somewhat evil-looking, blue imp that would make an amazing pet if you were *out of your goddamned mind*. And that's the problem with the Seven of Cups. If everything is feeling like wicked big dream magic is right around the corner, you're not in touch with reality. And that is going to become a problem.

It took getting sober for me to understand that the Seven of Cups is a bad card. Alcoholics are magical thinkers, and this is the card of magical thinking. You can imagine, so clearly, how totally incredible it's going to be—that relationship, or getting that spiritual practice started, or really taking care of your body, or, like, accomplishing that thing you haven't even figured out how to begin to accomplish. Because accomplishing things is actually hard and takes planning and application and chutzpah and stamina. Dreaming about something takes you right to the finish line and all the rosy feelings of accomplishment without any of the work! Without any of it happening.

You aren't necessarily an alcoholic if you get this card, but you could be. Maybe you're not really a full-blown drunk, but you've been partying a lot, you're on a pill bender, it's not a big deal, it's just something you're doing right now. With the Seven of Cups's tempting, lazy, quicksand energy, though, right now becomes forever in the blink of an eye. Perhaps you're suffering from untreated depression or some other such condition that makes it very difficult for you to follow through on your dreams. Maybe you're a stoner in a little community of stoners who all support each other's great ideas and enable each other's total lack of follow-through. Whatever is holding you back—chemicals, fear, mental illness, procrastination—the Seven of Cups has arrived with an ultimatum. Get off your butt, clear the cobwebs out of your head, and make a first move toward something you want for your life. Or settle back into your metaphorical (or not) opium den and let life continue to pass you by.

Working with the Seven of Cups

- Get thee to a crystal store, and purchase the biggest, purpliest, sparkliest amethyst you can afford. This wonderful crystal is known as a sobriety stone. Its tremendous energy helps people who are working to rid themselves of any type of harmful addiction or pattern. It's also a visionary stone, so while it's helping you stay strong and clearing the bad patterns from your life, it's also essential in helping you formulate a plan that is both solid and inspired. The amethyst will clear the illusions that you've been nurturing and help you see your reality for what it is, but in a gentle way that supports as it reveals. Lean heavily on your amethyst; keep it on you at all times, sleep with or beside it, and clutch it when the temptation of the Seven of Cups comes slithering your way.
- Light a purple, white, black, or red candle, then clutch an amethyst and pray for clarity and the courage to face reality. Make a list of all the very real things that are holding you back. The majority of these blocks should be things you have influence over—if you are blaming external factors for your inability to move forward, you're still under the spell of the Seven of Cups. The real reasons might be hard to look at, but let yourself have your feelings.

  When you're done with your list, review it. Let each item

register. This is facing reality; after this and only this can things start happening. Dip the list into the candle flame and let it burn in a fireproof dish. When it is done, take another piece of paper and write down your heart's desire, the goal you haven't been working on, the dream you want to manifest. Fold the paper and seal it with a bit of the candle wax. Blow the ashes away outside, letting the air carry them away. Allow your candle to fully burn down, however long that takes. Keep your dream beside the candle until it's gone, and then keep it in a special place. Hold on to your dream. It is a pact you made with yourself. Know that the sealed paper is a talisman or amulet, and hold and meditate with it when you feel overwhelmed or tempted away from your dream.

- Make an altar dedicated to pushing yourself away from the Seven of Cups and into action. Your altar should have an amethyst; candles of purple, red, black, or white; feathers; clear water; a mirror; and images or figures that represent motion and action to you—arrows, wheels, whatever feels correct. Place anise pods and fennel seeds on the altar, and burn frankincense. Speak to your altar. Tell it your story. What was the illusion that you fell into? What effect did it have on you? What is the dream you want to pursue? What must you do to make it happen? Ask the Universe to support you in your efforts. Burn the candles until they are done, consistently in the sink or relighting, as suits you. If your candle burns up but you want to keep this altar going, get more. Keep the altar active until you feel solidly on your path to success.

The Eight of Cups

Okay, this card is a drag. A solitary figure walks along a jagged ocean landscape; at her back is a pile of golden cups, abandoned. The walker has literally turned her back on them, and even the emoji-esque eclipse in the sky is bummed out about it. But here's the thing—the mysterious walker is doing the right thing. And if you're called to turn your back on something and walk away from it, no matter how deep you're in it, you'll be doing the right thing too.

When the Eight of Cups comes up, it means that something we have put a whole lot of ourselves into isn't turning out as we hoped. Maybe the relationship you've nurtured (quite possibly with a person who requires a lot of caretaking) has finally proven to be too much for you. Recognizing that you're never going to get back all that you've been giving, you cut your losses and move on. Or the job you've tried to make work for longer than you should have is finally proving to be untenable. Or a friendship once precious to you has been too damaged to ever heal. Whatever it may be, the situation is totally tragic and there's no way around it. In your heart, you know there is no future in this situation; the change you fought for and hoped for is not going to come. The only thing more heartbreaking than all you've put into it is how much more you could lose if you stay. Time to go.

The Eight of Cups is ruled by Cancer, which, as a water sign, is intensely emotional; things aren't ever just a little bit important to a Cancer. If they invest at all, they invest totally. They're represented by the crab because it is very, very hard for them to let go once they've attached themselves to a person, place, thing, or idea. Yet this card calls them to do exactly that—to let go and move on—regardless of how difficult it is.

The Eight of Cups is not without hope, but that hope is directed toward the future—the person you'll be and the life you'll find when you put this situation behind you. This card is a travel card and a quest card. You are closing one chapter and opening another, and the adventures you'll have in the wake of this disappointment will be life-changing. I had the Eight of Cups in my life after a relationship I'd invested a lot in fell apart. It wasn't a particularly long relationship, but it was intense. Coming on the heels of the end of an eight-year relationship, it was obviously a rebound, but I fought that idea at the time. I was so distraught at the end of my LTR that I had concocted a story in my head about the rebound to make myself feel better—*this* person was actually my soul mate, and *thank God* that LTR fell apart or else we never would have met! I knew for a little while that this was just major magical thinking—not only was my new date *not* my soul mate, but he might not actually have been in possession of a soul—but still I clung. Our dynamics got darker, my days marked by whole new anxieties. Eventually, thankfully, it ended.

Once my troubled date was gone, I felt my unknown future before me, scary and exciting. I decided I would do something that's hard to do while in a relationship—say yes to whatever travel invitations came my way. The first offer came from a coworker, who offered me a week in his Mexican beachside condo for free. I invited my best friends along, and not only did we have an amazing experience, but we decided to start a writers' retreat in that very location, to ensure that we could return again and again and share the magical paradise with others. And we did it! For six years we fund-raised to finance free retreats for the low-income writers we supported, and in so many ways those retreats changed lives—validating these writers as real *writers*, enabling them to finish their books, engaging parts of their spirit that had gone dull in the urban rat race but that bloomed among the baby turtles and raw sunsets and scampering iguanas.

The golden cups in the card are stacked five on the bottom, three on the top. The five on the bottom signify the bulk of time

you've invested in the failed situation; it's a row of heartbreak. The smaller row of three cups represents more recent times, when you've had some insight about the futility of the situation and learned something about yourself; now this self-knowledge has ripened and grown and can give you the strength to move on.

You'll notice there's a cup-sized gap in that more enlightened top row. The gap represents your next cup, the one the cloaked figure is on her way to claim as her own. For me, it was that writers' retreat, born from the ashes of a bad relationship I let go on a bit too long. As sad as it was, such disappointments are common. It's what you do in the wake of them that is truly uncommon and can change your life.

Be the Eight of Cups

Oh, dear. This card requires a few spells, one for every stage. There's a spell for those who *need* the Eight of Cups—those stuck in a hopeless situation. These folks need the chutzpah and clarity to get the hell out *now*. Then there's a spell for the ones who've turned their back on something and are slowly but surely stomping away from that waste of time. They're likely to be all bogged down in the sadness of loss, not to mention beating themselves up for not having acted sooner. (Needless to say, acting sooner wasn't possible.) And finally, there's a spell for those who've shaken off the blues and are engaged in *Cup Quest!*

- Has your nagging higher self finally convinced you that the path you're on is a total dead end and you deserve *so* much bet-

ter? Great! All you need is a little courage, a little action, a fire under the seat of your pants. We're going to do a spicy candle spell, so get yourself to a place with much ventilation; open any windows you can. Red, orange, white, and black candles work best for this. Raid your spice cabinet for cinnamon, ginger, and cayenne. Chili oil works too, but make sure those windows are open! Sprinkle your candle with the spices. Use the cayenne sparingly; you can always add more if you want. I don't want your spell called off because the pepper smoke is stinging your eyes and catching in your throat!

Ask the Universe and all the creatures of fire to lend you their bravery so that you can instigate this great change. If you have a hard time envisioning fire-creatures, look deep into your gut and summon all your strength and daring. In fact, do that either way. Talk to the Universe and talk to yourself to gather all the spiritual help you can get. Sit with it for a while, envisioning it all going down the best way possible for you. After a bit of time has passed, snuff the candle. I recommend doing this right before bed and asking the Universe to bring you dreams of courage and valor. The next day, make your move.

- If you're deep in the sorrow and loneliness of the Eight of Cups, wait for a full moon and make a tea of peppermint and rosemary. Put a whole bunch of honey in it. As it steams, whisper into the cup all of your sorrows, all of your regrets. Tell the tea the story of what happened and share with it any bad feelings you have about yourself as a result. When the tea knows your story, bring it outside and leave it in the highest place you can reach.

  The next day, fetch your tea and take it to a patch of earth. Draw a circle in the earth with a stick. Beneath the full moon, thank the tea for this experience, express your gratitude for it having ended, and ask the tea for its help in assimilating its les-

sons. Then pour the tea into the circle. You should feel markedly better by the new moon.

- You've walked away from the disillusioning experience, a lot of the sadness has worn off, and you feel ready to begin the new stage of your life. Set up an altar somewhere. Arrange eight cups, each filled with water, leaving a visible, cup-sized gap in the lineup; hold your hands over them and thank the essence of water for your emotional intelligence. A black or white candle will represent fire; as you light it, thank it for giving you the will to change your life. To stand in for air, bring in a knife or dagger, a fancy pen or a feather. Hold this item and thank it for giving you the clarity to see what needed to happen. Any stone can stand in for earth, but garnet would be especially nice for this spell. Hold it and thank the earth for your unshakeable core, your strength and grit. Add something to the altar to represent you, like a mirror, a happy picture of yourself, or an item that you identify with.

  Gaze out at the altar, breathing, feeling all the energies coalescing and finding their way into you. Close your eyes and speak out loud your intention to begin a new cycle of your life. Something like: *As this chapter closes, let another brightly begin. Grateful for my past, grateful for my present, bring me into my future with power, grace, and joy.* Then sit quietly, eyes closed, and imagine all the things you'd like this next chapter of your life to have. The things you'd like to do, the places you'd like to visit, the people you want to be close to. Think big. Life has a way of scaling things down, so start as large as possible! When you feel like you've really hit on the many wonderful possibilities your future holds, you can stop. Let the candle burn as long as you're comfortable, and keep the altar arranged for eight days (or until your roommates want all their cups back).

The Nine of Cups

This is a gorgeous card. A person sits before a presentation of nine shining cups, wearing a plush white robe and a fancy little hat. Their smile seems to be biting back a larger, uncontrolled smile that would probably swallow their face if set free. This person has just seen a wonderful dream come true, and if the Nine of Cups has popped up in your life, hopefully you will too!

The Nine of Cups is known as the "wish" card; it's one of those

cards you really, really hope comes up. It heralds a great big good time. Something you have worked very hard for has paid off marvelously, and now it's time to party. Throw a celebration (unless one is being thrown for you—totally possible with this card), take yourself out to dinner, book some time at a spa, or just pack a book and some snacks and plant yourself in a park for the day. The twin vibes of this card are achievement and luxury; it's about seeing what you've made of your life and yourself and truly savoring the goodness of it.

Sometimes this looks like a wild accomplishment, and the payoff you're celebrating is material, like my friend who bought herself a motorcycle after publishing a book she'd worked very hard on. Sometimes it's simply a moment where things have calmed down and you're able to take a breath and really feel the love you have for your life. I remember a particular moment when my son was an infant and I was propped up in bed nursing him. The sunlight from the back door was sort of cascading onto the bed where we were relaxing, and out that window I could see the brilliant green of the moss and trees in our backyard. I felt such a simple, content joy—for my son and the love I felt for him, for my body, for the sweet home I'd made with my wife. The Nine of Cups rules all these things, both triumph and the physical enjoyment of it.

If this card has come up for you, indulge! If you're wondering whether to splurge on a piece of jewelry or an extraneous vehicle or dinner at a Michelin-starred restaurant, the answer is yes. If you're not able to celebrate your victory at that level, then say yes to whatever indulgence means for you right now—the nicer cheese, the fancier ale, an extra item off the sale rack. What this card is really about, at its core, is celebrating where you're at and finding the victory in this moment. It's about being content with what you have and really basking in it.

If this card has come up for you but isn't quite resonating, then it means one of two things—either a wish is about to come true for you in the coming days or weeks *or* the Universe is calling you to take stock of what you have and celebrate it. I say go with the latter, as daily gratitude is something we should all be practicing. If a wish happens to come true in the near future, all the better! Whatever the Nine of Cups looks like in your life today, enjoy it.

Bring the Nine of Cups into Your Life

- There's only one real spell to bring the Nine of Cups into your life, but thankfully it works like a charm (oh wait, it is a charm). I call it Calendula Three Ways, but as with all of my spells, if you can't get your hands on everything, just use what you can access.

  First, take some fresh calendula flowers and put them in a vase on your altar. A yellow candle can be burned as a stand-in if the blooms are unavailable; you just might want to burn a yellow candle regardless. Brew yourself a cup of calendula tea, which can be found at health food stores but if you like you can find loose, dried calendula petals and steep them. Finally, light a charcoal and place some dried calendula petals on top of it; this is an offering to the goddess, a thank-you for all that the Universe has given you, so while you're doing this really access some gratitude and put it into your motions.

While you sip your tea, make a gratitude list. Come up with ten things in your life you feel truly thankful for, ten things that bring you happiness. Hopefully this won't be too difficult, but if you're currently in bad shape, you can be thankful for things such as *indoor plumbing* or *sunshine* or *sleep*. Take a moment with your list and reflect on how these things came about. Probably a lot of it was chance, the mysteries of the unknown, but certainly a good amount of what you have to be grateful for has come about because you worked for it. You made a good decision, and that decision was based on years of learning what good decisions are.

Come up with something little you can do to celebrate each thing on your gratitude list. If you're grateful for a friend, have them over and bake cookies for you both to enjoy, or, if you've got the funds, book a friend date at a massage joint. If you're grateful for your job, take some of your hard-earned money and treat yo' self. If it's something you can't quite take credit for, like the sun, offer something to it in thanks and worship. Maybe your body, lying on some grass in a park? Be creative with this. The point is to recognize how great you have it and to make it even greater by introducing celebration. That's what the Nine of Cups is all about.

The Ten of Cups

I learned to read tarot when I was a fifteen-year-old goth, alongside my similarly gothic best friend, Peter. We did the serious, ritualistic things you were supposed to do with our precious decks—wrapped them in silk and slept with them beneath our pillows. (It is very hard to get a good night's sleep with a hard chunk of tarot under your head, FYI.) As together we learned the vagaries of the Suits, the powerful forces of the Major Arcana, certain cards began to

present themselves to us as, in Peter's words, "coupons." A ticket from the Universe entitling you to some dazzling, much yearned-for experience. To be honest, most people who seek a tarot reading are hoping for a coupon: a get-out-of-jail-free card for bad behavior, a signed check if times are tough, a bolt of inspiration, or, in the case of the Ten of Cups, a promise of happily ever after.

The Ten of Cups is a glyph of familial fulfillment that is deeply profound yet totally ordinary. The couple depicted here—decked out in simple outfits they either sewed by hand or maybe dug out of the free box at the local farmers' market—aren't newlyweds beaming with the novelty of cohabitation. The Ten is the grand finale of the Cups' emotional ups and downs; this couple has been together through some crazy twists and turns, yet they wound up here, enjoying a pretty day, their arms wound affectionately around each other. Neither are they celebrating a big anniversary or marking another noteworthy occasion. This is a simple scene: two people taking a moment to enjoy the dazzling rainbow that has popped up in a clear blue sky. (Okay, I guess that's pretty special.) Their kids aren't fighting, possibly for the first time that day. The stream is lush and flowing, their house, surrounded by protective trees, is super-modest, but don't you bet it's way charming inside? Like one of the pair hand-batiked their bedroom curtains or built shelving out of driftwood or lined their cabinets with herbs stuffed into gleaming glass jars? The kind of home you come to for a dinner party and wind up staying all night, the beautiful children falling asleep by the fire as the grown-ups stay up late sipping homemade mulled wine and sharing stories. You want an invite to this family's gatherings.

When you get the Ten of Cups, it's time to pause and take the time to really enjoy this moment of peace and abundance in your family sphere, whether it's the family that birthed you, the family you birthed, or the comrades you pulled around you to create community with. Maybe even all three—there's that much joy packed into this card. Certainly such domestic bliss hasn't always been the case, and just as true is that the magical rainbow arcing over this moment will fade. Annoyances will creep up, someone will get on someone's nerves, and a spat will ensue, the bliss-busting realities of daily life will pull you away from this sweet moment. None of this makes the swell of beauty and happiness in this card any less authentic. Chances are its sweetness is available much more often than we realize; we'd tune in to it more often if we could only get out of our pesky heads and remain in this anxiety-free moment of pure love and gratitude for our lives and the people who fill them. For whatever reason, staying connected to the gift of the present moment is hard for everyone. When the Ten of Cups appears, it signals that this recognition is easier for you to tap into. Perhaps you've already noticed your rainbow. The Ten of Cups urges you to bask in it.

The Ten of Cups popped up in my life only this morning. After my seventeen-month-old son finished his morning bottle, he rolled around the bed where we lay, alternately growling and giggling, giving me spontaneous if painful kisses, his hard plastic binky still jammed in his mouth. He played with a stuffed tiger his nana had sent him for Valentine's Day, then pointed to the shelves on the other side of the room, stacked with books and toys. He made urgent grunting sounds. "You want something over there?" I asked.

"Go on, you go get it." He crawled over my legs and out of the bed and walked straight to the small Rider-Waite tarot deck I had given him the day before. We'd gotten into the habit of picking a card each day from my collection of decks, and realizing I had two Rider-Waites, I gifted him with his very first. He was excited to use it. I joined him, lifted the deck, and spanned the card for him to pick. Voilà, the Ten of Cups. "That's Baba," I said, pointing to the figure in the waistcoat, "and that's me." I pointed to the one in the skirts. "And that's you, dancing with a friend." He smiled hugely and grabbed the card.

Nothing special happened today. It's actually been sort of tedious. At breakfast my son rubbed porridge in his hair, getting it stuck with globs of oats and quinoa and chia seeds. I drew him a bath to wash it out, and as soon as I removed his diaper he peed on the bathroom floor. Then the whole family hopped in the car to retrieve the baby's birth certificate from the giant public records office, journeying cities away, only to find that it was not there. We drove back home and put the baby to bed, and he remains there, napping with my wife. Not the sort of day you'd expect to be defined by a glowing rainbow stuffed with a rack of golden chalices . . . but. Through it all we laughed and loved each other. Through it all we felt palpably grateful that we get to be together, that so many risks—the risks of dating and marriage, the risks of fertility treatments and pregnancy and birth, the risk of relocating our little family to a whole new city—paid off for us. The little home we rent doesn't look so different from the house on the card. It is a day like every other day, and as is true of every other day, we are incredibly lucky to have one another.

When the Ten of Cups comes up for you, expect to experience harmony. If you've had strife with anyone close to you, prepare for a resolution. Maybe the rainbow will inspire you to be the bigger person and make the first move toward reconciliation. Collaborations will be smooth and successful, dates may grow into much, much more. If you're already romantically involved, you'll probably be hit with a bolt of gratitude for what this romance adds to your life.

The figures on the card are standing in a pose that suggests pride; at the heart of this joyful, happy card is also a sense of triumph. It isn't always easy to get happy. Think about the work you and yours have put into it, and enjoy the feelings of triumph.

Be the Ten of Cups

- Chances are, you're already the Ten of Cups. But a great way to get conscious about it is to plunk a quartz crystal into a cup (filled with water) and set it outside under the full moon. The following night light a candle (blue, pink, white, or yellow is good), remove the crystal from the cup, and drink the energy-infused water slowly, consciously, asking the powers of the elements to help you wake up to your good fortune. When the water is gone, hold the crystal to your third eye and ask the Universe again to help you feel your life's happiness. Hold the candle, ask the power of fire to help you tune in to your life's awesomeness, and blow it out. Carry the crystal around with you; when you feel it in your pocket or glimpse it in your bag, it will trigger a moment of awareness of how good you've got it.

- But in case you need a deeper nudge, each night before bed make a gratitude list, jotting down ten things in or about your life that you feel grateful for that day. Gratitude lists are great abundance spells; they make what you've already got sparkle harder, and they draw more abundance your way. Keep the list going for ten nights minimum, and if you find that its spell is such that you want to keep it going, by all means do so.

Swords

The Ace of Swords

All aces represent the beginning of a new cycle, and the Ace of Swords comes bearing fresh ways of seeing the world. It might be a new vision of the wider world, or of life itself; it could be an inspired take on your own life, your work, your relationships, your spiritual journey, or a problem you may be wrestling with. The

crown topping the point of the double-edged sword symbolizes clarity and the victory inherent in figuring out a problem. The little yellow raindrops around the handle are *Yods,* from the Hebrew alphabet. *Yod* is the first letter in the Hebrew name for God, and its presence in the Ace of Swords signifies a beginning and also speaks to the divine energy present at this beginning. Though the double-edged sword famously cuts both ways—and as you will come to know, the swords are the most painful suit in the Tarot—this Ace is a most auspicious one to receive.

It requires some work, though. This isn't one of those simple, happy-day cards that affirm you're on the right path and encourage you to lie back and enjoy your bounty. The Ace of Swords is a mentally rigorous card. If it's come up for you, you might find your mind running a mile a minute; sleeping could be difficult. It's like you've had a revelation and now you're obsessed with the desire to put what has been revealed into practice. Perhaps you've realized how to mend a relationship, or, just as likely, you've come to know that you must cut a person out of your life. If something has been vexing and frustrating you, you'll finally find your way through it with this sword.

The sword often stands for justice; it points to situations that deal with right and wrong. If this is the case, you might find yourself needing to take a stand. Depending on your personality, this could be an invigorating experience, or it could feel really uncomfortable. Taking a stand for justice requires that you claim to know what the right way is, and that requires confidence in your heart and mind. By taking a side, you are inviting conflict into your sphere, and most people find conflict unpleasant. Still, if the Ace of

Swords has come up for you, it means it is time for you to dare to publicly express your ethics, perhaps by attending a rally, publicly supporting an issue or candidate, speaking up against something you are witnessing, joining an advocacy group, or maybe simply letting the people around you know that you don't share their opinion. No matter how intimidating this might feel, on the other side of it is the relief of having stood up for yourself and something you believe in, plus whatever good you might have done by lending your voice to a cause.

If you feel compelled to help settle a dispute or a conflict, the Ace of Swords says do it. If you are being asked to weigh in on something, you probably ought to—this is not a neutral card. If you are looking to shift your lifestyle to be more in line with your sense of justice, this card has your back. If you are thinking about entering a new profession, one that requires sharp mental powers, logic and reason, debate, communicating and clear writing, this card says *yes*. As an ace, it is only the start of a journey. The move you make now will have strong, character-defining results that will stretch well into your future.

Be the Ace of Swords

- Saying *yes* to something often means saying *no* to something else. If the Ace of Swords is asking you to make a change, to cut away people, places, or things that do not resonate with your idea of fairness or harmony, this spell will help you out. You'll need a piece of blank white paper. Make two columns. In one

column, make a yes list—a list of everything you are *for,* the energy you want to call into your life, the things you want to do or embody. On the other side, make a no list—a list of what you are *against,* the energy you want to cast out, the things you don't want to do anymore, the points of view you want to get rid of.

Take a sword—like, a pair of scissors or a craft knife—and cut the page in half. Then cut up your no list into the smallest bits of confetti you can. Take this pile to a high point—such as a hill, an outdoor stairs, or a roof—and scatter the confetti into the wind. Say good-bye to your old way of being. Let the power of the swords, which is the power of air, carry them away. Then take your yes list and keep it someplace where you can see it. Look at it often. You're engaged in the powerful, admirable activity of training your mind—which swords rule.

- If the Ace of Swords is an upsetting card for you to receive because it's requiring you to take a stand that is uncomfortable or unpopular, or because such declarations do not come easily to you, here is a spell to soothe and prepare you. Brew a strong cup of chamomile tea, preferably with loose flowers, though a tea bag is fine in a pinch. Sit before a black or white candle and sip your tea, asking for calm and clarity, for quiet strength and serene confidence. The Serenity Prayer is a good chant for this spell; feel free to replace "God" with the deity of your choice, as in:

Stevie Nicks,
Grant me the serenity to accept the things I cannot change,
The courage to change the things I can,
And the wisdom to know the difference.

I have made Stevie Nicks my own higher power, but feel free to sub in "Universe," "Creator," "Great Unknown," "Unicorn," or "Ace of Swords," or just omit that part of the spell entirely. The point is, you need serenity, you need courage, and you need wisdom. And you're going to sip your calming chamomile tea, gaze at the candle burning away fear and resistance, and ask for what you need to take your stand.

Make the action you are about to take a spiritual, magical gesture. Maybe you are going to begin volunteering at an animal shelter. Maybe you're going to be organizing with Black Lives Matter. Maybe you're going to help a friend by babysitting while they're in school, or maybe you're going to help quarreling friends sort it out. Or you're going vegan, or swearing off plastic, or decided you're going to come out to your family about that crucial part of yourself you've kept under wraps. Whatever it is, consecrate your actions in advance.

Build an altar—a glass of water, a candle, a crystal or flower or plant, and, to represent air, an actual blade if you have one; otherwise, use a feather or a pen. Light your candle, and light incense or sage if you've got it; smoke is ruled by swords/air. State your intention out loud: "I am going to put my body on the line for justice for black people." "I am going to go vegan because I want justice for animals and for the earth." "I am going to come out to my family as a gesture of truth and in order to be loving and fair to myself." Whatever you're doing, whyever you're doing it, state it loud and clear and then sit with it for a moment, watching the candles burn, holding a crystal or a feather. Know now that when you go forward and take these actions they are reverberating on a much deeper level. They are part of a pact you have made with the Universe itself.

The Two of Swords

When the Two of Swords comes, we've got ourselves a situation. And you certainly know which situation it's referring to, because it has been festering and growing and worsening due to your inactivity. There can be many reasons for your problematic hesitation. The worst is outright denial: you're pretending the problem isn't a problem, and by doing so you've allowed it to continue and to grow in magnitude. If the Two of Swords has come for you, it is to

force you to reckon not only with the problem but with the hows and whys of your unhealthy response to it. It's time to take the appropriate and long-delayed action, *and* it is time for some psychological soul-searching. Why couldn't you face this? Is denial a recurrent problem in your life? What are you afraid of?

As you will see, the swords suit has a tense relationship with the realm of emotions. In some readings of the Two of Swords, it represents a problem whose solving requires strict logic; you must not rule with your heart in this moment, but with what you know to be intellectually true. Perhaps you need to draw a difficult boundary with someone whose behavior is abusive or self-harming; perhaps you've got to get out of an uninspiring relationship but you are so conflict-averse you hate hurting feelings. In these situations, you must channel the cold, detached nature of the Two of Swords and do what must be done; to let it go further is abusive in its own right. Remember that it's not possible to simultaneously draw a boundary *and* take care of the other person involved. This is a moment for taking care of yourself.

Sometimes the Two of Swords shows up for a person who has shut off their emotions in a problematic way; in doing so, they've shut themselves off to love and the sort of joyful risk-taking that leads to a full life. If this is you, no doubt you've had your reasons for shutting down. But if this read on the card is feeling true to you, it means it is time for you to begin the healing work of cracking that cold heart open once again. Sometimes coping mechanisms that work for us in one phase of life become a problem later on if we don't cast them off.

Whichever side of the Two of Swords you're on—and I'm pretty

sure you know which it is—the common denominator is a need to act, and to act now. You've hesitated long enough, whether because of denial, emotional seesawing, feeling shut down, or honestly not knowing which option is the right one. The Two of Swords orders you to pick a path and take it. If it turns out to be the wrong course, you'll have an opportunity to change direction.

✸ Working with the Two of Swords 

- Flip a coin. No, I'm serious. Some people really love to make difficult decisions with the use of a pendulum, a pointed stone hung from a chain. I find pendulums aesthetically attractive, but ever since one wrongly predicted the sex of my child, I feel like their magic isn't for me. But, a penny! I keep a dish of them on my dresser because I frequently find it really taxing to make even simple decisions. Here's the thing about a coin flip: if you truly don't know what to do, you get a directive, and you just do it and you see what happens. But lots of time you *do* have a preference buried under all that anxiety, and that is revealed through the relief or disappointment you feel when the coin is flipped. If this happens, it means the coin has helped you sort out your real desire and now it is your duty to follow it, regardless of how scary or lousy or intimidating the path might be.
- Or get a pendulum. You begin this ritual by asking it questions you know the answer to is yes, like, "Is my name Madame X?" or, "Am I alive?" or, "Is Beyoncé unstoppable?" This establishes which movement denotes yes in your interaction with the pendulum. It's different for everyone, so if you use your pendulum

to help others make decisions, they too have to establish their yes and no directions. You can make a pendulum by hanging a crystal from a chain or string, using a crystal necklace you might have, or buying a pendulum from an occult shop. Go toward the crystal that speaks to you, though white, clear, and black crystals are always solid, and red crystals and the courage they impart are particularly good for working with the Two of Swords, which comes up when fear has so often been immobilizing.

- To get clarity on an especially tough decision, try Sage Three Ways. Burn a bundle of sage to purify your space and your mind. Meditatively drink a cup of sage tea, asking it to fill you with its magic decisiveness. Finally, carry a pouch of fresh or dried sage with you throughout your decision-making process and into the period when you are implementing your decision. When all is done, thank the herb and bury it in the earth.

The Three of Swords

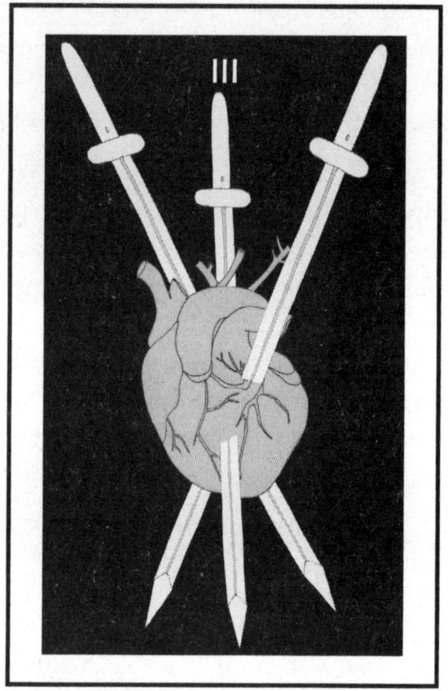

When the Three of Swords pops up, it's like life has sucker-punched you right in the jaw. Someone you like very much has crept up behind you like an assassin and stabbed you in the back. A bit of malicious gossip, started by someone you trusted, has made its way back to you. Someone has sabotaged you at work. Your beloved has been cheating on you or stringing you along for some painful reason. Your family has turned their back on you. You've fought

with your best friend, saying terrible things, the type of things an apology can't undo. The Three of Swords is a big card, and it's a bad card. There is no way through it but to accept that something awful has happened, express your deep and justified hurt, and begin moving on.

Sometimes the Three of Swords has a very thin silver lining: at least you know you're not crazy. Coming on the heels of the Two of Swords, where indecision rules, now something deeply decisive has occurred, something no one can deny. No more battling your creeping intuition, that sinking sensation that something is amiss. Everything is pretty much as bad as your most paranoid suspicion said it was. Time to have a pity party.

I'm quite serious. Why not throw yourself a pity party? When something this destructive occurs, it's best to mark the occasion. Holding your head up in pride and acting like you don't care will only turn this sadness and anger into a boil to be lanced further down the line. You must purge the toxic feelings the event has generated, and what better way than unabashedly, among friends? Invite the people closest to you, the folks who will feel your pain alongside you. Ask them to bring you some comfort food, if you have any appetite at all. Drink if you drink, unless drinking is somehow involved in this situation; then you may want to step back and keep your head clear for a bit. Once everyone is assembled, cry and shit-talk and repeat the same flabbergasted commentary as many times as you feel compelled.

My mother once survived a very violent hurricane, one in which she first believed she would die, and later mistakenly thought that her home had been blown away. Though she had been spared these terrible outcomes, she lived amid the devastation for months. It was deeply traumatizing, and she talked about it constantly. She had to. It's how our minds make sense of and move through situations that would otherwise destroy us. So talk your head off. As time passes your friends will get a little tired, understandably, of hearing about it, but right now it is so fresh that they will indulge you. They want to be there for you.

A warning that comes with the Three of Swords is that, although something horrible has happened to you, you are at risk of marrying this pain and nurturing your resentments and carrying on until it is really you, not whoever did you wrong, who is to blame for the present misery. This is why it's recommended to get all your initial pain out as thoroughly and flamboyantly as you must. You want to purge it so you can carry on with your awesome life.

If the Three of Swords has come your way and you're *not* devastated, take a good, hard look at your behavior and make sure you are not knowingly or unknowingly hurting someone. Maybe you've been a little bit of a bitch, but you don't think it's too big a deal. Guess what? It is. You might want to eat some humble pie and offer some apologies. If you are in denial about the way your behavior is wounding someone, stop and ask for forgiveness if appropriate. If you're wondering if something you're up to might have a negative consequence, the answer is yes. And if you really don't have any idea why this card popped up for you, investigate your habits to see if they are having an inadvertently difficult effect on someone. Perhaps your loud parties are tormenting your sad old landlord, or your best friend is secretly madly in love with your new date, or your habit of compulsively checking your phone is sending a deep message to a child that you're not interested in them. It could be a little thing with a surprisingly big consequence. Search your heart and mind, have a difficult conversation, make some changes, and carry on.

Getting Through the Three of Swords

- Construct an altar to the Three of Swords. Although this is not the type of energy you want to feed and nurture, when the wound is fresh it is absolutely helpful to build an altar to this event, with the intention of showing respect to the power of your emotions and to stimulate healing. Have the image of the card itself on the altar, as well as three daggers or knives, three pens, or three feathers. Bring to the altar something symbolic of your heart, your emotions. Perhaps a puff of cotton, or a flower, or a drawing of a heart on paper. Arrange your sharp things in imitation of the Three of Swords. Light a candle—white, black, or purple. Fill a cup or bowl with saltwater, and to represent earth bring out your crystals, a dish of salt, or a dish of soil. Finally, put a mirror on the altar.

  Sit before your altar and freak the fuck out. Cry, rage, wail. Take a pen and write down all of your terrible feelings. Write down your angry revenge fantasies. Call the person who betrayed you every name in the book. Express yourself until you feel fatigue set in. Then take your heartfelt, heartbroken rant and allow the elements to destroy it. Cut the paper into smaller pieces and dip them in the candle flame. As they burn, extinguish them in the water. Do this until you are done.

Then take the bowl of water and ash outdoor and give it back to the earth. Thank the earth for accepting your pain, for its constant, healing energy. Prepare a fresh bowl of saltwater and return to your altar. If you have crystals that promote healing—and most all of them do—sit and meditate with one. Lie down and let it rest on your heart chakra; ask it to heal your heart. Place it on your third eye and ask it to bring a healing vision to you, to heal your upset mind.

When you are calmer, write again, this time a list of things you will do for yourself in the wake of this calamity. Maybe you will travel, or book a massage, or get serious about meditation, or get a new hairstyle. Make a list of five activities, big or small, shallow or deep, that you can do to focus on yourself and bring yourself pleasure in the coming months. Fold the paper up and keep it on your altar. Return to it as necessary for reinspiration or to check an item off your list. Keep your altar up as long as necessary, but remember: it is a healing altar now. Come to it for that purpose only, for as long as you like.

- Give yourself a flower blessing. You'll do this in the shower, for a few reasons—though you are working with a mind card, it is your emotions that are roiled and unwell right now, and water rules emotions. Showers bring negative ions, those invisible particles that bring good vibrations, the reason you feel so at peace after a day at the beach or frolicking by a waterfall. Finally, showers are purifying, and this is a spell for purifying your heart, for helping you let go of the pain that has accumulated as a result of the Three of Swords, for reminding you that you love life and beauty and that life and beauty are waiting to receive you.

  Gather as many of these fresh or dried flowers as you can: orange blossoms, jasmine, chamomile, rose, elder flower, and lavender. Add some sage to the mix. Boil water and pour it onto the flowers; let them steep for a bit. If you have the oil of any of these flowers, add some drops to the mixture. Take a shower as you normally would, but let your mind linger on the sweetness of life, the things you appreciate, even if all you can come up with is the love of an animal or a blue sky. When you are done washing up, take the flower infusion and ask it to help open you to the beauty and love around you. Make sure it has cooled to skin temperature. Pour it over your head. Let yourself air-dry—do not wipe the infusion off or brush the flowers from your hair. Let them fall away on their own. Repeat as necessary.

The Four of Swords

If there is a tarot card that acts as a prescription for a vacation, the Four of Swords is it. This card gently insists that you turn off your devices, power down your computer, and go off the grid. You badly need some downtime to refresh your energy. Whether you've recently suffered a trauma, your schedule is insanely hectic, or it's just that time for you, the directive is the same: relax.

While to many people this sounds like a lovely invitation, to others it's an incomprehensible demand, one that simply cannot be fulfilled. My wife comes from a family of relaxers. They all work hard, and when the day is done they like to kick it. This is most apparent on holidays—or anytime we all get together. People nap. They lie around on couches, or in front of a fire, maybe reading a magazine, more likely not. They just, like, *lie* there. It's called relaxation, and if you're like me, it's a hard state to achieve. As a work-from-home, self-employed type who says yes far too often, I always have a lot that needs to be done. Also, like many of us, I'm addicted to my phone. I can feel the dopamine surging in me when I receive text messages and emails or even when I stumble across an interesting blog. The pull to check my screen is deeply physical.

The Four of Swords has probably never been a more important card than it is today. Originally meaning a retreat from battle, it now pushes us to retreat from our hectic lives and our even busier minds. If relaxing is hard for you, it's all the more important that you figure out a way to do it. Lying idly on the couch might not be your thing (though seriously, no judgment); maybe you'd rather go contemplate nature, or sit at an outdoor café watching the river of life stream by, without a phone or a copy of *The New Yorker* to distract you. If you can afford it, treat yourself to a day at a spa. Get a massage and soak in a tub and lie in a quiet room being quiet. Lie and tell your friends you're out of town and unreachable, and stay at home lying around, meditating, taking baths, and mindfully eating something delish. Sign up for the silent retreat you've always imagined doing; silence is big with this card.

However you spend your time-out, it's only crucial that you take it. The repercussions of pushing yourself too hard can be

alarmingly physical, taking a toll on your relationships and overall happiness. If it feels too weird to take a break from working your fingers to the bone, if it triggers feelings of guilt or anxiety, spend some time with that. Write about it. Where does that feeling come from? Remember that the way people work in America and other industrial countries is seriously out of whack. There are other ways to live. If the Four of Swords is up for you, take stock of your resources and go on the biggest vacation you can afford.

Be the Four of Swords

- The Four of Swords is a card of meditation and contemplation. When we're excited, our breathing can get fast or shallow. To facilitate relaxation, try some smooth, deep breaths. For this card, I recommend mullein magic. Before bed, prepare yourself a cup of mullein tea. Mullein is a primary ingredient in many herbal teas that promote lung and respiratory health, and it can be found at herb shops. Add some honey to your cup if you like; this spell is about bringing sweetness into your life. Light a white or black candle, sip your tea, and . . . relax. That's the spell. No busywork or writing or chanting. You are only to sip your tea and focus gently on your breaths, being mindful that they are deep and relaxed.

  I see this not as a onetime thing, but as a practice to integrate into your life for a month or so. Who knows, this sweet downtime, with phones and all other screens turned off and in another room, may become such an enjoyable part of your day that you continue the practice long after a month has passed.

If so, try adding a bit of meditation to your ritual, just five minutes or so of sitting with your eyes closed, maintaining awareness of breath. An extra bonus of mullein is that it is wonderful for sleep magic and guards against nightmares. So if this foray into relaxation brings up issues for you, it won't plague your sleep. Mullein also brings about prophetic dreams, so pay special attention to what you see at night and consider keeping a dream journal.

The Five of Swords

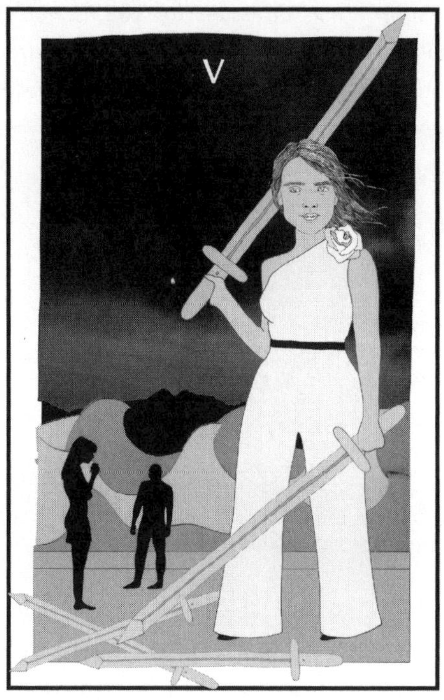

Perhaps at first glance the Five of Swords isn't so bad. After all, the fellow in the foreground, the one you're meant to identify with, is smugly collecting the swords of his enemies. You won! Those two figures in the background, the one retreating and the other seemingly sobbing, holding their face in their hands? Screw those losers!

The swords represent air, and in this card we can almost *see* that

element—in the form of an ill wind blowing through the landscape. Jagged gray clouds mar the sky, and wind whips the hair of our so-called hero, rippling the water in the background. This scene lacks the glowing glory that the Tarot bestows on scenes of true victory. In this card, the winner appears to have won the battle, but winning the war is not in their destiny, perhaps because there are no winners in a war.

If the Five of Swords has come to you, you're probably considering a full-on Joan Crawford *Don't fuck with me, fellas!* display of your strength and power. And guess what? It will almost certainly work. You'll get what you want in the short term, but only because you have not given enough thought to the long term. How will this situation persist, in spite of your small victory? Will your showy performance make your opponent double down in a way you can't compete with? Will there be fallout from an unforeseen quarter? Who will turn on you because of this power play? And then there is the question of your own well-being. Is it really good for you to be engaging in such negativity? Is this fight bringing out the worst in your personality? How does it wear on your body and your mind, on your spirit and emotions, to be in war mode?

When the Five of Swords comes up in your life, you are either already embroiled in a messy conflict or on the edge of tearing something down. There's a bad situation going on that feels untenable to you. You're sick of putting up with someone's shit. You're observing something unethical and it's time to blow the whistle. Whatever it is, this card suggests that you will succeed. If you feel like someone needs their comeuppance, well, they will get it. But what you need—really need—to do is examine what the outcome will be, not for them but for you. Is it really on you to expose your coworker as the lying, lazy phony he is? Or could you back off and allow him to downwardly spiral into his own consequences?

Perhaps you really *do* need to make a power play. Maybe you have a bad relationship to get out of. Well, do it, but with a minimum of damage. It might feel great to release all those rotten text messages you've been sent to the Internet, exposing your cad of a soon-to-be-ex, but when the Five of Swords is at play you can bet that you're going to look like the crazy one when the dust settles. The Five of Swords is telling you to keep your head down, put on your cloak of invisibility, and get out of the conflict with a minimum of damage.

Get the Five of Swords Out of Your Life!

- When the Five of Swords is around, chances are you're riled up and full of steam. And you're obsessed. The conflict is living at the forefront of your mind. The first thing you need to do is get to some moving water. If you live near an ocean, get there, pronto. A waterfall is amazing, if you're lucky enough to be in proximity to one, or the rough part of a river, where it crashes into rocks. These places are sites of negative ions, and they will give you a calming, balancing charge. For my landlocked or urban readers, a shower will work. Showers give off negative ions too! If you have only a bathtub at your disposal, grab a wide cup, tip your head back, and pour the water onto your head, being sure to hit your third eye. Do this fifteen times.

Whether you are sitting by the ocean or bathing in your tub, close your eyes and breathe. Count your breaths, one to six and back again. Do this until you can feel a palpable relaxation in your body. Ideally, have a rose quartz crystal with you. Rose quartz is the crystal of love, love for yourself and love for others. Hold the crystal to your heart for a bit, breathing. Next, hold it to your third eye. Feel the cooling energy of love coming from the crystal into your body. Abstaining from unnecessary drama is an act of self-love. Ask the crystal to give you the strength to prioritize peace.

The next level of this spell is to imagine the rays of soft, pink love the crystal gives off entering the third eye of your enemy du jour. This may ruffle your feathers, but think: If this person had adequate love in their hearts, for themselves and for others, probably *you* wouldn't be in the pain *you're* in right now. Am I right? Take the high road, and wish for them to feel the same calming love in their hearts that you are feeling in yours. If this feels absolutely impossible, then simply ask the Universe to bring this person what they deserve and trust that the Universe—not you—will see to it.

For the next five days, abstain from talking to others about this person and the situation. Whenever you feel the urge to shit-talk, hold on to your rose quartz and allow it to soothe you. Hopefully, at the end of five days your hotheadedness will have become tempered with wisdom, and you will be in a different place with this issue. If not, repeat the ritual. Repeat it until the conflict's hold on you has lessened.

The Six of Swords

In the Six of Swords, what appears to be a family is taking off by boat. The figure in the front is hunched and weary; you get the vibe that they have recently endured something, that the trip itself may be a source of sadness. The water in front of the boat is choppy, but the wide expanse of sea behind is calm, even welcoming.

When the Six of Swords comes up, you are making the best of a bad situation. This probably involves making an uninspiring or even painful choice; still, it is the best choice available at the time, and your eye should be on the long term. Even though the immediate repercussions of your decision are difficult, you know that it will ultimately bring you to a better situation.

One consolation of this card is that, when all choices bring some heartache, you can trust that you're making decisions with your mind and not your emotions. This being the suit of swords, being rational and prioritizing logic is often the way out. In the Thoth deck, the artists named this card Science and illustrated it with a fencing map that pinpoints where a fencer might stand to be invulnerable. This is a card about applying the powers of the intellect to protect yourself and get yourself out of a bad situation. It is probably not an overnight solution. The hardship feels large, like one you've been in for a while. Perhaps it is a committed relationship or family issue. Or maybe it concerns your livelihood and basic security, and the change you're taking must be slow and promote stability. Maybe you have been bogged down with depression or a habit that is taking a toll on your happiness and it's time to begin mapping a plan of care. The Six of Swords often portends a literal move or a journey; if so, there is a sadness at leaving, but where you are headed will open up a whole new life for you.

And that's the crux of this card. When you are done grieving whatever is abandoned, when you're done hashing out your best strategy, what you have is a path to a whole new chapter of your life, one that will be infinitely better than where you're at now. The promise of the Six of Swords is a bright and strong one: The worst is behind you. With every step forward you put distance and energy between you and whatever mistake you're correcting or problem you're solving. Your future is guaranteed to be calm and happy and new.

 Working with the Six of Swords 

- A protective bath would be a good spell for someone who just pulled the Six of Swords. You are probably reeling and healing from whatever bad situation has you making these moves, *and* you're having to devise the best plan for your future and carry it out. A lot is going on. This relaxing bath will ground you, connect you back with the calmness at your core, and offer protection from negative energies as you go about building the next phase of your life.

  Dump some Epsom salts into the bath. In a bag or loose, add to the bath lavender and orange peel, chamomile and cinnamon. Most crystals have some property of repelling bad vibes, but rose quartz, black tourmaline, and jet are especially good for this. Bring what you have into the bath with you. As you soak, envision your future—what you want it to look and feel like when this chapter is through. Imagine yourself surrounded in a clear, bright bubble that no bad energy can penetrate. Carry one of the crystals around with you as you make your changes.

- If you are stuck in your bad situation and haven't yet begun letting go of what you must leave, here is a spell that will call Six of Swords energy into your life so that you can begin moving on. Make a bath bag of eucalyptus, bay leaves, and rose petals, or sprinkle them loose into your bath. Put a generous helping of Epsom salts into the water. Also helpful would be a chunk of

pink salt. Crystals that help with letting go and moving on include charoite, red calcite, serpentine, and smoky quartz. Bring white and/or black candles into the bathroom with you, and as you relax into your bath, cast your spell. State aloud what you intend to let go of. Pledge yourself to this process, no matter how tough it will be. Ask the Universe, all the elements, and your crystals for energetic support. End with an affirmation of love for yourself, your life, and the Universe. You are making these changes to bring you to a place of increased joy and abundance. Let that stay foremost in your mind as you set about letting go and moving on.

The Seven of Swords

The Seven of Swords is a paranoiac's worst nightmare—or dream come true, as it will allow you to indulge in and engage all of the plotting and planning and scheming that usually begins and ends in your head. When this card pops up, *something* is up. Secrets and tricks are the name of the game. The big question is, are you the trickster or is someone tricking you?

Look at the mug on our little thief, looking totally smug for

scampering away with a pile of stolen swords. They've left behind a couple of swords because it's time to skedaddle—the troops in the way-back have spotted the situation. No big deal, though, this person has gotten what they wanted, and the stolen swords are their secret weapons.

Before we talk about you and your secret weapon, the card begs for a bit of soul-searching. You are almost certainly about to take some underhanded action. You're going to be sneaky and possibly deceitful; you will tell lies, at the very least via omission. The Tarot understands that there are times in life when you just can't be honest. Sex workers often can't be honest about their jobs for fear of arrest and other traumatic social punishment. Sometimes queer and trans people have to pretend to be other than who they are for their own physical and emotional safety. The world is full of creeps and tyrants; perhaps you are having to deal with one and must keep your victory plan secret. Maybe you are in an occupation where political scheming makes or breaks careers, and you've got to play ball or lose hard. If these situations ring true, the Seven of Swords has your back. Keep your plan to yourself, trust no one, make sure your strategy is foolproof, and then strike! Victory is yours.

But. If you are feeling a desperate, angry, clawing sensation and feel that the only way to get what you want is through deceit and dishonesty, you might want to question that philosophy. Where did you learn this? Is it possible there is another way? As the street artist Seth Tobocman boldly proclaimed in a piece of stencil art I passed by for years in San Francisco, YOU DON'T HAVE TO FUCK PEOPLE OVER TO SURVIVE. If you disagree with this statement,

the Seven of Swords has come as a warning that your motives and methods are going to bite you on the ass. It's time to develop a new way to live.

There is also a socially withdrawn component to this card. Our little shoplifter is turning their back on the brightly colored tents of civilization. Everyone needs a time-out from social activity every now and then. Solitude is soothing and allows for self-focus and relaxation without distraction. Getting offline can be crucial to maintaining a serene brain space. But if you are all huddled away, licking your wounds, feeling superior, and generally hating on the human race, the Seven of Swords has arrived to coax you back out into the land of the living. Pick a preferred human and schedule a hangout to remind yourself that not all humans are bad.

Working with the Seven of Swords

- A complicated card like the Seven of Swords needs a simple, all-purpose spell. I think a soothing, clarifying bath is in order. Of course, dump a bunch of Epsom salts in there. When this card comes up, detox is mandatory, and the purifying element of salt is crucial; whatever the Seven of Swords is bringing to you, your response must be pure. If you have a piece of clear calcite—a great stone for clearing energy blockages—bring it into the bath with you. The following herbs will stimulate clarity and healing and help to balance chakras, which is essential for the kind of work the Seven of Swords brings: lavender, sage, fennel, rosemary, basil, sandalwood, cinnamon, and

mint. Either make a bath sachet or toss the herbs loose into your bath.

Meditate on your problem. If you are going full-on James Bond, ask for the stealth and wisdom to make good, clear judgments. If you need to stop acting like the world is against you, ask for the Universe's support. If you are taking a well-deserved time-out, enjoy your bath! If it is time for you to enter the world after a period of isolation, ask the Universe to give you the courage and the trust to be among humanity once more.

The Eight of Swords

When the Eight of Swords arrives, you are so deeply stuck that you have given up any hope of fixing the situation. Or maybe you delayed fixing a situation until it swallowed you whole and now you've lost hope. Either way, here you are: bound so loosely that you could totally escape, but you don't; imprisoned by a half-assed fortress of swords you could actually walk right out of; and blindfolded, but making no effort to pull the blindfold off your face.

If you did allow yourself to see, you'd have to acknowledge that this miserable situation is at least partly your own doing. You have tremendous personal power, but for some reason you are choosing not to use it, or you have handed it over to someone else.

The reality is that you got yourself here and only you can get yourself out. If you are waiting for a rescue, an apology, or an about-face from someone other than yourself, you're going to be stuck down here in gloomy Swordsville for a lot longer. At this point it hardly matters who else was involved or what drama or circumstance got you here. The problem is, regardless of how you got here, you chose to stay here. It's now up to you to quit the job, end the friendship, file for divorce, offer an apology, begin to make amends, or stand up to your parents. However, the Eight of Swords is shaking down in your sphere, and it's time to claim your power and get on with your life.

 Get Past the Eight of Swords 

- Plant a seed. Any seed, for any kind of plant or herb. Gather the things you need to plant something—soil, a container, water. Before planting the seed, ask it to impart to you its magic and wisdom. Ask it to be your familiar and to share its slow, steady, fearless plant magic with you. Bury the seed and tend to it every day as you would a pet. On the day when it bursts through the soil, take a moment to marvel at the big strength of this small energy; it has pushed its way up through heavy, wet soil that weighs much more than it does; intuitively, it knew to go toward the light and it did, bursting through the dirt.

It is now time for you to do the same. It's going to take a minute for that seed to germinate, so spend the time doing something each day that stokes your power. Journal your truths. Take a bath and meditate on your strength. Walk in nature and synch yourself to its power. Pummel yourself with positive affirmations. Know that your time to move is growing near, and you get stronger and more capable each day. On the day the seed sprouts, take one major action to remove yourself from the bad situation you've been lingering in. Like your plant familiar, go toward the light. Continue to care for your plant as necessary.

If your plant sickens or doesn't sprout, this is not a sign! Sadly, I kill plants all the time. Instead, get yourself the biggest clear quartz crystal you can afford and meditate with it daily as you begin breaking free of your oppressing circumstance.

The Nine of Swords

There is no way around it: this is a terrible card, as confirmed by a glance at its drama—a person sitting up in bed, holding their anguished head in their hands as a wall of brutal swords pierce the night behind them. The person is traditionally said to be female, and this card can be connected to violence against women as well as the insomnia and unstable moods that are known to accompany menopause. But fear not: the Nine of Swords brings its doom and

gloom to all genders and ages and physicalities. If it's popped up in your life, it's safe to say that things are, at the very least, uncomfortable, but quite likely hitting the high notes of panic, anxiety, depression, and full-on despair.

The first thing to suss out when the Nine of Swords comes for you is whether you really have a problem or the dark drama is unfurling its three acts in your mind. Of course, this can often be a difficult question to answer. Maybe you don't know if something terrible is going on, but your bitch's intuition is ringing bells and sending up so many red flags that all you see is crimson. Outside manipulation may have you feeling gas-lit. You may be suffering from a mental glitch that's made you unable to discern mundane reality from your paranoid fantasies about it.

Whether or not you can figure out if your distress is real or imagined, my tarotly advice is the same: talk about it. Talk about it with your favorite nonjudgmental listener—maybe your best friend, or someone you know less well but whose good vibes and generosity have always impressed you. Maybe a therapist or a spiritual person whose wisdom you can trust. If the cause of your anguish is rooted in reality—you've done something you're ashamed of, you've made a mess of things—you need solid advice on how to put the pieces back together. If you have run yourself into a deep, scary rut with the mechanisms of your own mind, it will be useful to have that validated, and you could probably use some advice too. Perhaps it's time to do something about recurring bouts of depression or anxiety. Perhaps you have already taken action, but it's not working and a new strategy needs to be developed.

Regardless, when the Nine of Swords comes calling, you need

help. This might be horrible news to you; maybe you hate asking for help, or truly don't know where to start. Maybe you're so ashamed that the thought of sharing your situation with another cripples you. There is nothing easy about this card. But to get through it you need to deal with the source of the daggers, either in the real world or in your mind.

Here's some good news: it's often not as bad as you think. Fear often magnifies the truth with this card, and you very likely didn't mess up half as bad as you think. Or the others involved are super-forgiving. Or a dumb misunderstanding triggered preexisting trauma and nothing is wrong in the here and now. Alas, the only way off your internal hamster wheel of fear is to bring the light of day into the situation, and that's telling the truth, talking about it, reaching out.

For most of my teenage years I had a terrible suspicion that a family member was secretly spying on me, a violation that was devastating in its consequences. I was deeply afraid to confront this person, so instead I existed in a state of fear, anxiety, and guilt. Like the woman in the card, my sleep was plagued with grueling mental equations: *Either this person who I love is doing this horrible thing to me and is awful, or I am awful enough to think that this person who loves me would do something so horrible.* It's the kind of loop ruled by the Nine of Swords, and one that does not get interrupted without a drastic move. At the end of it, you're left at the Ten of Swords—devastating, yes, but over, with peace on the horizon.

If the Nine of Swords card comes up, it's time to take action. My guess is that in your gut you know what has to be done. You just don't want to do it, because it's terrifying or heartbreaking or dev-

astating. It might be helpful to know that inaction is not protecting you from any of these negative experiences. The badness is already happening. Don't be afraid of the tough steps you may need to take to free yourself from this emotional prison.

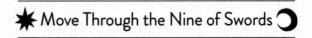

Move Through the Nine of Swords

Anyone sparring with this card needs some help. Here are some energies you might like to call your way, and a way to summon them.

- For a problem so potentially large, let's call all the elements to your aid. First, to represent the earth in which it grew, take a quartz crystal, selected for its quartzy clarity. Hold the crystal to your third eye and to your belly, asking in both places that the crystal help your thinking become clear and wise. Ask it also for the wisdom to trust what you know.

  Immerse the crystal in water. You're going to freeze this water, so make sure you will be able to neatly extract the block of ice; sealing it in a plastic bag would work. Before you freeze the crystal, work with the water in its liquid form. Give respect to the power of emotions. Yes, they can cloud things and bring suffering, but they are also our alarm system, letting us know something is wrong. By placing the submerged crystal in the freezer, you are asking the cold, clear air-power of the intellect to make the hard-to-grasp nature of emotions something solid that you can handle and inspect. So freeze it!

  After the crystal is solidly frozen in ice, begin melting the ice over a candle. This might take a sec, and you need to take

care to not burn yourself and to not douse the flame with the drippings. The element of fire is what's going to get you out of your situation, so this is a crucial, if awkward, part of the spell. The fire is your will—it's your bravery, your boldness, your inner fire. It's the part of you that would rather face down anything than be imprisoned in some stagnant loop of fear. You need to call that energy into your heart, summon it from where it lies inside you. Hold that block of ice and look clearly, honestly, fearlessly at your predicament. Dare to trust yourself, your intuition, your analysis.

As the ice begins to release the crystal and the frozen emotional layer melts away, let the burning desire to take charge of the situation rise inside you, melting away soggy fears and hesitations. Keep the crystal around like your best friend. It holds all the energies you need to stay strong, calm, and focused and to take action to end this holding pattern once and for all.

The Ten of Swords

Okay okay okay okay okay, take a deep breath. Yes, you did just get a very bad card. It's a dead person with, not one, not two, but ten long swords jammed into their back. This sad sack is a bloody mess, and if you've plucked this card, chances are you are too—but like a British "bloody mess," not literally. The realm of swords begins and ends within the confines of your mind, so even though it might feel like blood is trickling from your ears, you are physically fine. Inside, however, is a whole other story.

The Ten of Swords makes me flash on one of the darker nights of my soul, which has endured some doozies. An eight-year relationship had disintegrated. Being a ten, this breakup was long in the making (and I bet whatever tragedy you're experiencing has been building for a while as well). In an attempt to let some steam out of our volatile relationship, my ex and I had opened things up; unsurprisingly, it backfired. We were done. Not long after he moved out, I went dancing. It is what you do when you are newly single, is it not? A sober person, I abused my body with sugar-free Red Bulls instead, and made it home around 2:00 A.M. roiling with hypercaffeinated angst and anxiety. I literally collapsed beneath the weight of my sorrow.

Sobbing and insane, I phoned my ex. We were so recently broken up that he still felt obliged to take my calls, even when they came in the middle of the night, even when he had a cute girl in his bedroom. I kept him on that phone, crying and sobbing and accusing and lashing out, playing the victim one minute and the attacker the next. Our tumultuous relationship, which I had spent so much time trying to control, was now totally beyond my reach and I didn't know what to do with myself. Eventually someone hung up, and I slept for about two hours, got on a plane, and flew to a university to give a reading. My face was so red and puffy that it looked like I was having a dangerous allergic reaction. I could now add a feeling of deep shame to my volatile stew of emotions.

If you've picked this card, you are most likely experiencing a loss. Something has ended. Maybe it's a breakup, or you've been fired. Maybe you've been nurturing a hope (or delusion) and something has occurred that requires you to face the painful fact that what you want so badly isn't coming your way. The pain you feel is probably overwhelming, and the situation is probably complicated. Though your suffering is sincere, part of you had to know it was coming. I mean, I did. My relationship had been unhappy for years, a ribbon of angst interrupted here and there with some good sex and honest tenderness. But though it hurts to have a relationship end, much of the venom I was spitting at my ex was misdirected. I was really mad at *myself*. Why did I spend so much time codependently caretaking a connection that wasn't feeding me? A hard question to answer. Much easier, much more glamorous, was playing the mad victim, the late-night martyr. I ached for the world to sob along with me, for my friends to shun my ex, for my ex to shun himself in the face of *what he'd done to me*!

If this card is up for you, take a good, possibly painful look at just what you might have done to play into this situation. Maybe it was just an overload of optimism—*This is gonna turn out great!*—in the face of a million red flags. Maybe it was something more complex. Hey, you're human. Relationships—friendships, collaborations, family, marriage—are tricky. I don't suggest that you do this searching to have yet another thing to feel like shit about. I suggest it so that you can pull yourself off the ground and start yanking the swords out of your back.

When the Ten of Swords comes up, you've bottomed out. But the good thing about a bottom is that there's no place you can go but up. The card itself suggests this. Ten is the end of a cycle. If you release the idea of yourself as someone who's been massively fucked over and instead begin to let go of the drama, you are that much closer to the start of a healing new cycle. You also are closer to the hard-won knowledge this situation will provide you with. Swords, after all, represent the intellect. Also, beneath the blanket of night a golden sun is rising. Now that the worst has happened, it's time for you to get on with your life. Who is the person you'll become now that you're free? *Free* is a great word to keep in mind as you traverse the Ten of Swords. Whenever you start to feel sorry for yourself, your anger starts to rise, and those one-sided arguments take off in your rattled mind, just breathe and think, *Free*. Keep your mind on the future, not the past. This will all be a story you tell over drinks someday.

Get the Ten of Swords Out of Your Life

- You'll need a great big apple, some mint, ten skewers, and a pretty ribbon. Cut the apple in half through the middle, so you can see its secret star. Take one half of the apple and rub it with a mint leaf. While you do this, think hard about the energy you want gone from your life. Ask for the removal of self-pity, of blame, of attachment to the past, and of anything else that you're haunted by. You might feel a lot of emotion; it hurts to give up your attachment to such things. Let yourself cry, let everything out. You are at the end of a cycle.

  When you have exhausted yourself, put the apple back together and stab it through with the ten wooden skewers. Secure it further by tying your pretty ribbon around it. Now bury the apple. If this is absolutely impossible, I suppose you could simply toss it into your compost, or the garbage. Although you may feel lighter and more hopeful when you finish the ritual, it will take a little longer for your upset to subside. This was a serious blow. As the apple slowly returns to the earth, however, so will your issues and problems. Have some patience, and remember that you are free.

- Get yourself some jet. Though jet is often sold in crystal stores, it isn't actually a stone; it is a piece of a tree that lived on earth millions of years ago! Jet is believed to absorb negativity and heartache, hence its use in mourning jewelry. And aren't you mourning something right now? Give your jet all of your sadness. Sit with it each night before bed and send your sadness into this hardy little fossil. Carry it on your person to soak up any bad vibes. Do this as long as necessary, burying it in sea salt every ten days to clean it. (Don't use that salt on your popcorn after, obvi. Throw it down the drain.)

Pentacles

The Ace of Pentacles

You guys, we're living in a material world! As in, we are not ghosts, we are not made of ether. We may be having spiritual experiences, but we are having them in our bodies. We eat, we have sex, we poop, we create things using our hands, we use money or trade. When the Ace of Pentacles comes around, one of its

messages is that we are embodied humans existing on a material plane—enjoy it! There is no way of knowing how common or uncommon life on earth is, but chances are that even if embodied life exists elsewhere, it probably isn't *exactly* like this place, or the creatures exactly like us. This Ace offers us this information as if a revelation. Allow it to strike you like a gong and fill you with the appropriate inspiration.

If the Ace of Pentacles has come for you, it's time to treat your body. Have some orgasms, eat delicious foods, go swimming, climb some rocks, play sports, lie in the sun, get a massage, just *feel* yourself. Literally. Smell flowers or perfume, buy yourself something beautiful that really indulges your senses. Decide today is the day you are going to begin taking care of your body the way it deserves. Play with your crystals. Not in an *I need this thing to heal me right now!* sort of a way, but like how my toddler son plays with my crystals—like they are delightful chunks of earth candy meant to be eaten by fairies. Just admiring and touching and whatnot.

The Ace of Pentacles has additional promise. It often suggests an opportunity is being offered to you, something that will bear fruit at some point down the line. *Big* fruit. Delicious fruit. Big, delicious fruit. I hope you are in a yes state of mind because the Ace of Pentacles—which holds within itself the complete potential of the material world, from utter wealth to total destitution—wants to take you on a joyride. There's bound to be some work involved—quite literally if, as is likely, it's a joblike opportunity, and emotionally if it's a romance or other personal connection—but you'll be into the work. It will be rewarding, and where it is taking you will be apparent and deeply desirable. Say yes to your body, say yes to the material plane, say yes to life, and yes to the Ace of Pentacles.

 Be the Ace of Pentacles 

- Basil, a serious prosperity herb, is sacred to the Ace of Pentacles. Make yourself a batch of enchanted pesto. For serious! The spell is in the preparation of this savory potion; understand that you're not simply cooking, you're making magic. The basil is for wealth and prosperity, and pine nuts also attract money and prosperity. Olive oil strengthens the spell and adds protection, as does garlic. Black pepper banishes negativity, and salt summons positivity. A perfect and healthy offering to the Ace of Pentacles. Feel free to share with loved ones. Freeze what you don't consume right away—do not throw away this batch of magic pesto.
- Acquire a piece of petrified wood and dedicate it to the Ace of Pentacles. Part wood, part stone, petrified wood is as earthy as you can get. It supports the physical body, so any changes you are looking to make—including the mandate to increase your physical enjoyment—are supported by this stone. Petrified wood also helps bring out your highest self and helps you manifest your best life, something the Ace of Pentacles wants for you too.

The Two of Pentacles

A toe-tapping figure in an eccentric chapeau deftly juggles a couple of pentacles, the symbol for infinity winding around and containing these motions. This is a great card. It pops up when you've got *a lot* going on, and a lot of uncertainty, but you're handling it all with stunning aplomb and even enjoying the high-wire derring-do of it all. Not only that, but you are managing all this intense activity while being totally, unabashedly yourself. Twos

are only the beginning, but with this card you are setting up a dynamic of self-love and positivity that you will take far into the future.

The main point of the Two of Pentacles is flexibility. The more flexible this dancer can be, the more elegantly they can handle their pentacles. It's challenging, but deeply rewarding. Whatever you're working your butt off on right now should feel meaningful, even enjoyable, to you. If it doesn't, ask yourself if it's the work that isn't moving you, or if it's the fast pace that is stressing you out. You will be able to adapt to the breakneck speed and multiple moving parts of the work, getting the hang of it and even coming to enjoy your mastery of it. But if the work itself is a bummer, you're in for a rough ride—so get out now.

The cartoony way the ships in the background are bouncing on the waves encourages you to cultivate a sense of humor about the inevitable ups and downs. The blue skies promise all is going well. The kooky hat the dancer wears is a mandate to be your weirdest, most authentic self. This is your life/work/project/relationship/vacation/etc., and it's up to you to give yourself permission to be thoroughly, totally yourself. If you're not, the situation's stressors will get to you much more easily and your crucial sense of humor will be eroded.

I relate to this card a ton. I'm always juggling a million projects, as any working artist / freelancer / Aquarius often is. To some people, working like this sounds stressful, but I find it invigorating and inspiring. It keeps me busy and future-focused, like our dancing juggler. If I focus too hard on any one aspect and begin to fret about end results, I could throw myself off and drop the many

balls I have in the air. But if I just focus on staying flexible, doing the next right thing, and maintaining my creativity, the mess of it seems to come together like a mosaic.

Be the Two of Pentacles

- If you find that you're having a hard time balancing all that you've got going on, whip up this magical smoothie spell. Yes, a smoothie spell. Here are your ingredients: aloe, to help bring success to your endeavors; avocado, to help you see the beauty in the madness; a pinch of cardamom, to keep you loyal to yourself and your vision; tangerine, to keep your energy high; strawberry, to bring about situations that benefit you; maple syrup, to prevent burnout; lemon, to remove blockages (in particular anything that might be blocking your sense of humor); a bit of (preferably fresh) ginger, for confidence; and grapefruit, to keep you pure of heart as you manage your wild, exciting life. Toss a bit of echinacea in there just to strengthen the whole thing. I can't promise it will be the most delicious smoothie you've ever drunk, but it is super-good for your body and your magical spirit.

The Three of Pentacles

A young apprentice—or, in modern terms, an intern—shows their work to a couple of monks—the suits of yesteryear—who regard the youth with respect and approval. Hooray, they want your stuff! If the Three of Pentacles has popped up, you might be getting a significant career win. Perhaps you sold a story, a pitch, a design. Or you scored an account, or were accepted into a prestigious program. Perhaps you got some great feedback from a men-

tor or a superior, or got a great write-up, or a stellar review. You're beaming, and your belief in your abilities has increased threefold.

If the Three of Pentacles comes up, you should know that you've got what it takes to succeed at what you're pursuing. It also suggests that you won't be satisfied unless the work you're engaged with is close to your heart. Everyone has a different relationship to how they earn their money, and different requirements; for you, it has to be meaningful and keep you inspired. The Three of Pentacles is suggesting that this is how it is with you, or is about to be. If you're looking for a job, aim high and pursue your passion. If you've been offered a job someplace where they seem to "get" you, go for it.

The Three of Pentacles could represent, not a paid job, but an internship. If you're offered an internship that's at a venue you really value or that gives you a chance to work alongside individuals who matter to you, do it. But if it's unpaid slogwork you're hoping might lead to something you're more passionate about, don't waste your time. The Three of Pentacles believes that you have talent, and that your talent will find the home it deserves. Try not to settle for anything less.

If this card represents a romantic situation, it could be a workplace affair. Tricky as those things can be, this one just might work out. Common interests and mutual admiration can take this connection far.

Be the Three of Pentacles

- To call your dream job to you, mix benzoin, frankincense, copal, and dragon's blood resins to create an incense. (All of these are

available at your local magic shop or on the Internet.) Light a small charcoal and sprinkle the incense onto it, saying, *I have the power, so mote it be, bring my dream job here to me.* Repeat nightly until your job is secured.

- If you are lacking the skill, confidence, and direction that the Three of Pentacles exemplifies, the following spell will explicitly call all that this card represents into your reality: Arrange to take a class that will give you the skills necessary to better pursue your dream vocation. When you're attending the class and doing the work, know that you are actively making magic and changing your destiny.
- Get a black, white, or red candle. Light it and sit before it. Write down everything you believe stands between you and having the career that you want. When you are done, read what you've written out loud and then dip the paper into the candle flame, letting it completely burn in a fireproof dish. Take the ashes and flush them down the toilet.

  Return to your candle and take up your paper again; make a list of all you can do to make your dream job a reality. Place the paper underneath your candle. In the morning, take your first significant step toward making this happen. Continue burning your candle until it is gone, and repeat the ritual as necessary, watching your list of what stands in your way shrink.

The Four of Pentacles

Stability is the name of the game with this card. Depicted in the Four of Pentacles is a person who prizes stability over everything else, and up until now it has paid off. Literally! If their solid crown and rich robes didn't tip you off to their material wealth, you can't miss the giant golden coins they're clutching. With one coin clamped under each foot, one held to their breast, and a fourth

balanced on top of their crown like the cherry on a sundae, this person is making sure that nobody is taking off with their cash. There's just one problem: they're not taking off either. A beautiful town beckons in the background, but this figure is so dedicated to staying glommed onto their money that they can't make a move.

When the Four of Cups pops up in your realm, it means scarcity issues are running the show. Sure, you should be prudent with your spending. Absolutely, you need order and structure to build a fine life. But these concepts have been blown out of proportion, and you're valuing them at the expense of other important things—joy, flexibility, risk, generosity.

It doesn't matter how much or how little you have in the bank—anyone can fall prey to economic fears. When I was flat broke, broker-than-broke, I feared something terrible would happen and I wouldn't have the funds to take care of it. In my early twenties, newly on my own, with no safety net, I feared homelessness. When I started making some money I feared spending it—surely extreme poverty was right around the corner, I couldn't go and spend $40 on a *skirt!* Why, I'd get used to wearing $40 skirts and then what would happen? *Homelessness!* Now my family has more money than I've ever had, and I still have the occasional panic attack checking out at Target. I can speak about this card from deep inside its fearful guts. You've *got* to loosen up.

Whether you're on food stamps or managing a stock portfolio, the crux of the Four of Pentacles is control. People on government assistance are afraid to get a job because they'll lose their paltry paycheck; people rolling in dough are afraid to make a charitable contribution because the feeling that their money is slipping away brings on survival terror. I've known or been these people. Holding on tighter doesn't solve the problem—you've got to do the opposite. Trust that the Universe is taking care of you and relax your grip on what's yours. Buy yourself something a little splurgy, or a lot. Give spare change to someone begging on the street, or cut a check to an organization doing work you admire. Take your friends out to dinner. Buy the organic produce, the nice cheese, the top-shelf whiskey. Money is a part of life, and life is to be enjoyed. There are lean times and times of plenty, and this card counsels being flexible as these times come and go, loosening your grip, and always choosing to enjoy your life—and maybe even help others enjoy theirs a bit more.

Working with the Four of Pentacles

- Aragonite is a great stone to help combat a scarcity mind-set. Part of its magic is helping to change perception. If you meditate with aragonite, it can guide you out of your fear-based state and into a way of thinking that is more trusting and less controlling. This stone corresponds with the earth element, so it's useful for getting you out of your anxious mind and grounding you in reality. It also brings tolerance and flexibility, qualities that run counter to rigidity and control. Plus, aragonite is really cool-looking, little red clusters of chunky crystal squares.
- Sit with your aragonite, meditate with it, ask it to help you think differently about money. Ask it to help you be generous,

with yourself and with others. Ask it to remove your scarcity issues and to help you trust that you will be taken care of. Carry it on you when you're on the move, and keep it by your side when you're working or sleeping. And be sure to bring out your aragonite when you are shopping, paying bills, or doing anything that triggers those scarcity fears.

The Five of Pentacles

No way around it—this card is tough. Two extremely down-on-their-luck individuals struggle through unforgiving weather—toward what? It's as if the very elements are against them. The full range of material possibility has played out negatively for them; they hobble through the snow, risking frostbite and a worsening of their terrible overall condition. However—and this is a significant detail of this card—a church glows with warmth right beside

them. This is a place where they could step out of the cold and get some help, but they are either too oblivious—too stuck in their pain—or too proud to ask for help. Regardless of the reason, they are bypassing salvation and trudging deeper into a worsening condition.

The Five of Pentacles, while acknowledging that you are hurting, possibly experiencing significant loss, wants you to take a hard look at the way you are living and see where and how you are playing into your own unfortunate situation. Have you been ill for a while but refuse to seek care, whether out of financial fear or bureaucratic ignorance? Have you known for a while that you need to treat your depression but instead have let it fester and progress until now you find yourself in a deep mental, spiritual, and material hole? Have your spending practices finally blown up in your face? Have you resisted help out of controllingness or pride and now find yourself overwhelmed as things fall apart? Have you been in willful denial about the character of the person you're dating and now things have gone too far? Whatever it is, the point is not self-blame or recrimination. The point is to pick yourself up and seek the help you could have sought in the past. Things are in bad shape, but all is not lost. There's a lot to recoup here, not least your sanity and sense of peace.

Perhaps the misfortune that has befallen you could not have been prevented, no matter how vigilant or proactive you were. The Five of Pentacles's message for you is that help is available. Do not be so consumed by your problems that you are blind to the help that is nearby. Look around. Reach out. Make a call. Take action. The only alternative is to trudge deeper and deeper into your devastation.

Get Through the Five of Pentacles

- Such a bitter card requires the sweetest magic. You shall prepare for yourself a magical chocolate cream pie, sans dairy. There are dozens of recipes for vegan chocolate cream pie on the interweb, penned by people with far more culinary expertise than me, so I will just direct you to a search engine and tell you that, whatever vegan chocolate cream pie recipe you decide upon, it should have the following ingredients: cocoa, as an offering to the gods, the goddesses, the spirits, and the Universe, to make the help that is available to you abundantly clear; salt, to bring about actual material abundance and aid in manifesting assistance and success; almond milk, to bring money into your realm, as well as those fortunate circumstances known as "luck"; coconut milk, to offer protection and to purify energy that may have gotten a little negative during this stressful time; and finally, the great consolation of vanilla, to sort of psychically pet your head and murmur, "There, there."

  Cook up your chocolate cream pie and eat it ritualistically and mindfully, while saluting these ingredients and offering gratitude for all they offer. Eat the whole damn pie. Either all at once or gradually. Don't share—this isn't normal pie, it's a spell, don't forget it. When you're done, help should be clearly on its way.

- Take a green, white, or black candle and dedicate it to the Five of Pentacles. Write down exactly what you need help with, as well as exactly what your dream assistance would be. Dip the paper in the candle flame, and let it burn in a fireproof dish while asking out loud for the Universe to please send help.

When the paper is nothing but ash, take it outside and scatter it into the wind. Let the candle burn until it is out. Your help should appear by then.

- Another candle spell is to take five candles, ideally golden if you can find them, though white, black, or yellow works too. They should all be the same color. On five small pieces of paper, write down five things you have in your life that you are grateful for. Place each piece of paper beneath a candle and light the candle. Say aloud, "Thank you for these five blessed things, I ask you kindly five more please bring." This will increase your abundance and help you out of the scarcity and fear of the Five of Pentacles.

The Six of Pentacles

The Six of Pentacles is a very deep card, far more complicated than it looks on the surface. In the image, a Richie Rich is doling out some ducats to a couple of lucky beggars. Or are they unlucky? They're still beggars, after all. Though one theme or promise of this card is of welcome financial gain—you'll get that job, that check, that grant, that inheritance—the crux of the card, and the worm in the apple, is the dichotomy of haves and have-nots.

It is said that what the Six of Pentacles will mean for you depends on who you identify with in its image. Maybe you're feeling flush and you identify with the generous individual tossing coins to the poor. It's a great moment for you financially. You have enough and then some. Perhaps you were born so lucky and you've made a practice of devoting some of your money to charities. Well done. Or perhaps this level of income is still new for you and you don't quite trust it. As understandable as this is, a schism between your mind and your purse will make you a lousy caretaker of your cash. You've got to get right with your fear of financial insecurity so that you'll not only enjoy your wealth but feel confident enough in it to spread it around. For those in good financial standing who receive this card, the mandate is clear—give some away. Money is energy, it is to be shared, recycled, let go of and allowed to return. And when you give the money away, do it without strings. Turn that loan to a friend into a gift. Give a spare-changer a twenty in spite of the fact that you don't know what they'll do with it. Make a contribution to an organization without taking credit for it. Do not use money to control the people you are intending to help with it.

A note on identifying with the Richie Rich on the card: take care that you are not living above your means. The images plastered all over the media of the extremely wealthy and the way they use the world itself as their playground can provoke jealousy, longing, and compulsion. It's perfectly understandable to yearn for nice things, or a better standard of living, but make sure you are going about your acquisitions honestly, not feeding a shopping habit or maxing out a credit card you'll have to deal with down the line.

And for those of you who identify with the beggars—I feel you! Maybe you are legitimately broke. You're freelance and your income depends on scoring jobs (or not) and having clients who are willing to pay you swiftly (or not). As the head of a nonprofit, I was *always* begging for money in the form of grants, which often required standing before a panel of the people holding the purse strings and telling them how awesome my organization was. It was exhausting and demeaning. If this is you, the Six of Pentacles is telling you to expect some windfall to come your way. Make the most of it.

More deeply, this card asks whether there is anything you can do to get out from under your dependence on other people's money. Maybe you're living off your wealthy parents, but their control over your life feels bitter. Maybe you're mooching off friends or dates. If you are, you probably have a great story as to why it's okay that you're doing this, and you might have convinced them of it too. Well, you have not convinced the Tarot. It's time for you to make your own way in the world and to start taking whatever baby steps necessary to get yourself on that path. Maybe you are like an ex of mine whose scarcity issues were so far advanced that he couldn't get a job for fear of losing his food stamps. Your life gets very small and vulnerable when you are that stuck in a poverty mind-set. The beggars in the card aren't going to go from kneeling for handouts to running their own small business in a week, but the Six of Pentacles promises that the road to self-sufficiency is before you and that you can make it there, step by step.

More important than the image of the rich person or the beggars is the presence of the scale. All of the Six of Pentacles's complicated meanings can be distilled into that single image: balance. Do you have too much? Or too little? Are you being controlled by money? Or are you controlling with what you have? Seek to create some balance in your financial sphere, whether that means giving some money away or getting some for yourself, no strings attached.

 Work with the Six of Pentacles 

- Perhaps appropriately, the crystal known as morganite is a bit on the expensive side. It is possible to find beads or small gems at affordable prices, so see if you can get your hands on one of those. And for those of you legitimately identifying with the one-percenter in the card, treat yo' self! Morganite is *literally* named after the banker J. P. Morgan, who was a real crystal nut. This Richie Rich made whopping donations of his own cash to support the arts and sciences, and he donated a bunch of his rocks to the Museum of Natural History in New York City. When this pretty pink beryl stone was "discovered" in the early 1900s, scientists named it after their benefactor—a nice example of each party being generous with what they had to offer.

  Morganite is known to be helpful in all matters of money and business. It protects businesspeople from rip-offs and aids in fair dealings, and for the moneyed it encourages generosity and promotes justice in the realm of money. No matter what side of this card you're on you can make this stone work for you. Simply meditate with it daily, holding it in your hand and speaking to it, asking it for the help you desire.
- A ritual to aid you as you seek to break free from fear-based stinginess is to take two cups, ideally identical, and fill one of

them with saltwater. Go someplace where it's all right to spill a little water. Begin passing the water back and forth between one cup and the other. The longer you do this, the more meditative you will feel it become. Understand that money is energy, and as liquid as the water moving between the cups. One cup is having nothing, one is having everything. As you pass the water between them, feel the cups switch. Which is which? The demarcation between them fades. This is the middle path you are looking for. Everyone has more than some and less than others. What you have is both enough for what you need to accomplish and enough to share. You will feel when the meditation is complete. Bring it to a stop and pour the water down a drain or into the earth. Make this part of your practice as you continue to work with scarcity issues.

- In magic, the humble herb alfalfa is one of the most powerful for warding off poverty and assisting in the lifting of individuals out of poverty, real and internal. Prepare a pouch or sachet of dried alfalfa and carry it with you throughout your day. Also, keep a jar of dried alfalfa in the room in your home where you do most of your interacting with money. Hold your pouch and your jar in your hands and consecrate the alfalfa, asking it to support you in your efforts to move from poverty to abundance. And I suppose it couldn't hurt to toss some into your salads and sandwiches too.

The Seven of Pentacles

When the Seven of Pentacles appears, it's break time. The figure on the card has stopped working and is deeply considering their garden's progress. In this image, it appears that all is going great—the leaves are green and plentiful, and the golden pentacles are rolling all around the gardener. If this card is up for you, chances are you've been working hard and are being invited to rest a moment and enjoy the fruits of your labor. Perhaps you're receiving an accolade or promotion; the card is urging you to really take it in and enjoy the moment, don't rush over it with busywork. Since the Pentacles represent the material world, this card may signify that it's time to take some of the money you've made and get yourself something. Each time I finished a series of mermaid books I was writing I bought myself a piece of mermaid jewelry. Though those accomplishments are behind me now, whenever I wear the pieces I feel a little pride that I followed my inspiration and committed to the stories. What can you do for yourself in this moment of accomplishment? It can be big or small, but it should bring you pleasure and pride at your hard work and skills.

If your efforts aren't generating any fruits, the time-out the card advises is quite a different one. Step back from your project and suss out whether it's worth your while. Perhaps you've been working for free and it's starting to feel bad. Perhaps your wages are too low and it's time to advocate for yourself and walk away. Is someone else taking credit for your work? Figure out what you might be able to do to rectify that situation.

Even if the Seven of Pentacles is heralding a problem, it still wants you to step back from your work. If your work is stressful, that's all the more reason to take a break. Call in "sick" if you must, but give yourself a needed break. It might be tempting to spend your downtime vegging out, but do use it to formulate a plan for getting what's yours, even if it means walking away.

 Be the Seven of Pentacles 

- The figure on the Seven of Pentacles might be looking at his crop wondering if he made the right choices to bring about the best harvest. All of us have moments when we wonder if we're on the right path; when I hit these junctures, I turn to the Tarot.

  For guidance, shuffle your cards nine times, in any style you like. While you shuffle, ask where your current path is leading you. Pick three cards off the top and lay them face down. Then shuffle the deck another nine times, now asking what it would look like to change course. Pick three cards off the top and place them face down. Flip your first row first, the one that illuminates the results of the choices you've made. If they are mostly positive, it looks like you're on the right track. Sometimes you get two good cards and a bummer, and that's often how life goes; it doesn't mean you messed up. But to be sure, flip the next row. If it is significantly better, you might want to consider your options. Can you do something over? Head in a new direction? Walk away? Make a list of possible new directions you might head in, and pick three cards for each possibility.

  You should have a new plan by the end of this exercise. If you don't, it could mean that there is an option that hasn't occurred to you. Talk to the people around you about your predicament, and see if they have any illuminating suggestions.

- A good use of the time-out prescribed by the Seven of Pentacles is to make sure you are staying focused and meeting whatever goals you've set. Cherry blossom is good for refocusing the mind. Take a magic tea break with a cup of cherry blossom tea, and as you sip it think about where you were when you started this project. What were your thoughts, your hopes, and your fears? What did you intend? Have you gotten off track? Is that a good thing or a bad thing? What sort of energy should you summon in order to bring this project to fruition? Take this magical tea break as often as you need, until a strong plan has become clear to you and you're inspired to take action.

- Start a meditation practice and dedicate your time meditating to the health and viability of your project. That doesn't mean you have to sit there and dwell upon it; it's still meditation, and its goal is to clear the mind of thought (aka fistfight with your brain for twenty minutes or so). Inevitably, some of the thoughts that arise during your meditation will relate to your project; take note of them before brushing them away. After your meditation is done, revisit those thoughts. What can you learn from them? Were they fearful? What are you afraid of, and are your fears working against your efforts? Maybe you had a flash of insight, or a hunch to follow. If you don't remember your thoughts, or if nothing that significant occurred to you, no matter.

  The real purpose of the practice is to promote mindfulness and come to understand that 85 percent of what your brain churns out is utter garbage. The longer you stick with a meditation practice, the more you will see its positive effect on your project and on all areas of your life.

The Eight of Pentacles

If the Eight of Pentacles has arrived, you can be sure it's all work and no play. Or it better be—the Eight of Pentacles demands nothing less than total attention to the work at hand. No slacking off, no cutting corners, no daydreaming. The type of work the Eight of Pentacles is engaged in can be tough for a lot of us. Look at the image: the worker is hammering out coin after coin after coin, working like a machine, with no room for creativity or whimsy, just with rote attention to detail and endless repetition.

Even creative work has its drudgery. If the Eight of Pentacles arises, you're probably drowning in it. There's bound to be a good reason you're required to work so hard—there's a deadline, you're rolling out something new, your collaborators are relying on you. Depending on your temperament, this phase of your project is either a tad soul-crushing or oddly meditative. So much the better for you if you can find a way to enjoy it. For those who are struggling, remind yourself that drudgery or not, this is an essential part of the process and you won't be doing this task forever.

Unless you are. Sometimes the Eight of Pentacles comes up when we are trapped in a job we hate, one that does not draw on our skills and interests, that makes us feel stressed and unappreciated. If this read on the card is speaking to you, it's time to go. Begin looking around and talking to friends to see what's out there and start planning your exit. Even if you take a job that has you working at a lower level or accepting less pay, as long as you can make it work it will be worth it to get out of the employment that is crushing your heart.

Working with the Eight of Pentacles

- This earth spell is doubly good with an earth card like the Eight of Pentacles. To work this plant magic, simply plant a seed of any kind and watch it grow! Before you sink the seed into the

soil, ask it to be your spirit seed. As your seedling begins the hard, slow job of busting out of its casing, sprouting up through the dirt, and turning the sun's rays into energy, so will you be hustling at work, plodding away at your task, helping your project grow. Eventually your seedling will be out of this phase of growth—it won't be a seed anymore, but a flowering plant or tree. And thanks to the hard work you are putting in now, your project will likewise blossom and you will be happily going on to the next phase of your work.

- To get yourself out of your current drudgery and into a job that suits you better, procure a green candle. Some of you are so magical that you only have to burn the candle and a job will appear. An ex-girlfriend of mine once left one casually burning on top of the television set while she played video games, and soon she was hired at a great job she stayed at for decades. She was a Pisces. If you are too, feel free to be this casual about it. For the rest of us, some focus on what we are trying to attract is helpful.

  First, light the candle. You know that your current job is something you *don't* want. But what *do* you want? Take the time to articulate what elements your next job should have. Make a list of them. Carve them into the candle if possible; otherwise, write them on paper. Read them out loud, asking the Universe to please bring you your dream job. Fold the paper and seal it with wax from the candle. Keep this list with you, especially when you go on job interviews or pursue job-related activities.

The Nine of Pentacles

The Nine of Pentacles is traditionally illustrated with the image of an elegant woman hanging out in her garden, her pet falcon perched on her gloved hand. Behind this lady, a luscious vineyard blooms, with grapes ripe and heavy on the vine. Golden coins are stacked behind her, and she rests her hand atop the pile casually, as if taking the bounty for granted. Beyond her fruiting landscape we see healthy trees, a mountain range, and a bit of a castle that we can only presume is this privileged woman's crib. Also noteworthy is her attire, a cascading robe marked with flowers that look suspiciously like the glyph for Venus, also known as the woman's symbol. It's a picture of peace—the kind of peace that money can buy.

The Nine of Pentacles is associated with pristine Virgo, a sign of refinement, a sign of editing and careful decision-making. Though this babe looks decidedly *old-money* and certainly never worked her fertile land with her own tender hands, it's clear that she's made choices that encouraged the steady growth of her good fortune. This card also belongs to the planet Venus, whose rule over the land of beauty is often overlooked because of its association with love, sex, and passion. But Virgos, while skilled in the arts of love, are not wildly passionate creatures. Their attention to detail fosters a minimalist, careful, pared-down aesthetic, one that always has a practical component. It's not a flower garden this woman presides over, after all, it's grapes, a crop with a multitude of uses—wine, of course, but also juice and fruit and edible leaves. And she's not frolicking with a cat or petting a horse; her spirit animal is the falcon, a bird associated with intense focus, planning, and opportunity.

Once upon a time a happy confluence of incomes—a grant, a teaching gig, a book deal—allowed me to stand in front of the mirror in a dressing room at Barney's trying on and peeling off a variety of outfits that previously were *waaaaaay* out of reach for me. With a trip to Paris Fashion Week on the horizon and an assignment to cover it for a brainy magazine, it basically felt like my *job* right then to pick out a decadent dress or two to wear to shows and parties. This was a full-on Nine of Pentacles moment. I'd worked hard and, amazingly, made some good choices to wind up in that dressing room with enough money on my ATM card to walk out with my purchases in a chic black Barney's bag. But like the woman posing before her land, I was lucky too. She lucked out, as many do, by being born into wealth. I lucked out in ways I can't always discern, tangled as they are with my efforts, but luck is always present at the site of any good fortune.

When the Nine of Pentacles pops up, perhaps she is reassuring you that you're going to be *just fine*. The bottom isn't going to fall out, you're not going to wind up in the poorhouse, you will not experience financial ruin. I don't know about you, but I have needed such reinforcement throughout my whole adult life and will probably keep seeking it out now and again until I croak. If you've been having financial fears, allow this stately lady to remove them. If you were wondering if you can afford something—something basic or something luxurious, something practical or something frivolous—she says yes, yes you can, and you owe it to yourself to splurge on this treat.

If you actually, completely 100 percent for reals *know* you can't afford anything extra right now, then the lady has popped up to urge you to look around at what you already have and *enjoy* it. Let this be a balm to the sting of real financial struggle. Cook yourself a delicious, low-cost meal. Ransack your closet for whatever finery you have and wear it proudly—even more proudly if it renders you overdressed. People in this world don't dress up enough! And when money is scarce, fancy times tend to be also, so it's up to you to make an occasion for donning your loveliest robes. Raid your refrigerator for the makings of an at-home spa treatment and go relax in the tub. If money isn't tight, feel free to pay a professional to cook you some five-star grub or rub the soreness out of your muscles. The entire suit of pentacles is played out in our material world, where money, sadly, determines access. But the sweet underbelly of this card promises that wherever you currently fall on the income scale, you can take a moment to enjoy the fruits of your precious life.

Be the Nine of Pentacles

- To bring Nine of Pentacles energy into your life, take a handful of coins and bury them at the base of a fruit tree or flower garden. Ask the forces of nature to help your abundance grow.
- Go to the fanciest store you can think of and try on a bunch of clothes in the dressing room. Take your picture in the mirror. Print the pictures out and make them the centerpiece of an altar of beauty. Add flowers and honey and crystals and coins. Meditate before it nine minutes a day for nine days in a row, visualizing yourself having *more* than you need, having everything you can dream of.
- Adopt an animal. A bird or a lizard, a snake or a dog, a hamster, cat, guinea pig, or goldfish. (Find your familiar at your local animal rescue, please.) Let this creature be a living reminder to you of your abundance. Your abundance of resources—you have enough that you can spare some to help this animal also live. You have enough love that you can spend some on caretaking something smaller and more vulnerable than you. You

have enough wisdom that you know how to keep this little pet alive. You have enough intuition to form a connection with this beast and enjoy the exchange of energies that is so sweetly particular to human and nonhuman relationships.

If it is truly impossible for you to move a small animal into your home, cultivate a relationship with animals in another way. Spend some time at your local shelter, if not volunteering then at least dropping by now and then for an exchange of affection. Go to the park or a beach, someplace where ducks or gulls or pigeons gather, and bring some food for them.

Emergency Pigeon Intervention

You guys, pigeons are birds. They're actually doves, rock doves. They're related to those cute, slender mourning doves that probably squeak around your neighborhood. If you have any bad feelings toward pigeons—and I know many of you do, simply because such attitudes are terribly popular—I urge you to investigate and drop them, to heal your relationship with our world's most resilient bird. Really, what have pigeons done except find a way to not become extinct in the face of massive habitat destruction and infinite human encroachment? What do we do to congratulate them on their wisdom and strength? On the more harmless end of things we call them "rats with wings." (But hey—what's so bad about rats anyway?) The more violently opposed leave out all types of poisons and chemicals trying to knock off pigeons. And what do they do, in spite of this bullying? They thrive. These animals are heroes! They can *fly*. Can you fly? Didn't think so. Show some respect.

You can't practice magic, even this low-key, personal type, and harbor an unprovoked hatred of one of the goddess's hardier children. Befriend the pigeon. Show it compassion. Seek out the illustrations of old-fashioned children's or nature books and see how pigeons are included in the regular pantheon of lovable animals, their nests tucked away in a farmy alcove just above the chickens and the cows. If you detest the pigeon's sooty feathers, bemoan instead the grunge of our cities and perhaps take action to make your corner of the world a little spiffier. For those of you willing to take the Extreme Pigeon Challenge, look into adopting a bird from Palomancy, a pigeon and dove adoption agency. For real! http://www.pigeonrescue.org/.

The Ten of Pentacles

What a pretty, satisfying card. In a prosperous village, people of all generations gather, casually taking part in daily life. An elderly person sits, well cared for, wearing a long, gorgeous robe. Some younger people stop to chat while a toddler plays with a couple of Italian greyhounds. The sky is clear and blue, and all around the scene golden pentacles are hung. This village is that cluster of buildings depicted on the horizon in many tarot cards. With the Ten of Pentacles, you have finally arrived.

With the Ten, we've come to the end of an earth cycle, and we finish on a high note. When this card shows up, it is affirming that you've done the right thing, taken the correct actions, and made the best decisions, and the proof is in the very life you're living. This isn't a victory card with a tickertape parade, or a whopping success card with popping bottles; you've had those experiences already. This is the card that comes when you've actually integrated your past achievements and their material payoffs into your life. You've accumulated enough emotional and material security to trust that it's not going anywhere. You are acclimating to this new normal of increased stability in many arenas. You're not worrying that you've overdrawn your account. You don't walk on eggshells with your partner because you're sharing your abundance with someone emotionally healthy. You can see how this situation of material and emotional wealth could last well into the future. You are not in survival mode. You are able to enjoy the many fruits of your labors without anxiety or guilt.

When this card comes up, you have a lot in your life to enjoy. Hopefully, you know it. Throw a party or a barbecue, have your closest people over and treat them. This is not a moment to rock the boat or strike out in a radically new direction. This is a card that enjoys keeping things as they are, because everything is so damn perfect. If you are considering upsetting the apple cart, check in with yourself and make sure you aren't having a hard time just letting all this goodness into your life.

If you find yourself at a crossroads and needing to make a decision, this card counsels you to make it conservative. This is a great card for buying a house, investing your earnings in something secure, getting married, having children, or welcoming an elderly family member into your house to lovingly take care of them. It would also be cool to get a couple of rescue dogs, if that's something you're considering. Any action you take should have the intention of bringing about increased material security and family joy.

 Be the Ten of Pentacles 

- To pull into your life the lush prosperity enjoyed in the Ten of Pentacles, you'll need loose chamomile, fresh strawberries, and a chunk of orange citrine. Bury the crystal in salt for twenty-four hours before this spell, to purify it. Fix yourself a strong cup of chamomile tea. The flower is good for drawing prosperity, specifically money. Take a handful of strawberries and a little bit of water and cook them on the stove to release their juices. Once the berries are soft, mash them through a sieve and add their juice to your tea. Strawberries are known for bringing fortunate circumstances to those who invoke their magic. Finally, take your orange citrine and put it in the tea. Orange citrine is beautiful and wonderful not only for attracting money but also for giving you the energy and intuition to go out into the world and generate it for yourself. Cast your spell upon this brew: *Prosperity, money, come to me; success and riches, come to me; wealth and abundance, come to me.*

Remove the crystal and enjoy your tea. When you are done, carry the orange citrine with you wherever you go, and sleep with it under your pillow or beside your bed at night.

- Banishing poverty consciousness is a radical thing. Letting go of personal identification with poverty might feel like a betrayal of your family of origin, your clan, or your politics. But to hold on to poverty consciousness is to allow your body, mind, and spirit to atrophy. If the Ten of Pentacles has come up for you, something within you—or maybe the Universe itself—is pushing you to let go of this consciousness, which is no longer serving you. To bring the bountiful energy of this card into your life, you need to welcome it.

  Meditate with either a citrine herkimer or a smoky citrine, asking these strong crystals to rid you of poverty consciousness and help you invite prosperity into your life. Sit with the stones at least once a day, and keep them on or near you at all times.

- There is a notion that in order to hold on to a beautiful energy you must release it into the world. In this spell, you will dedicate all of your actions to the prosperous energy of the Ten of Pentacles. It is a gratitude spell, and all of your movements will be in thanks to the abundant Universe.

  First, take money out of an ATM. You're going to be cooking a beautiful dinner for the people you love, so take however much you can spare. Don't pay for the meal with your card; you want to feel the vibrations of the money itself, the paper that has come from living trees, the metals dug up from the earth. Go to your nicest grocery store and splurge as you are able. Select the nicest, most fun, interesting, and decadent ingredients. At home, prepare the meal with conscious joy, giving thanks for what you have. As everyone sits down to eat invite each guest to share something they are grateful for. Yes, it's cheesy, and people might feel a little awkward, but make them do it anyway. Such things are little spells, prayers to the Universe. Take this ritual all the way through the end: as you mindfully clean your home, thank the Universe for continued prosperity for you and your loved ones.

The Court Cards

Wands

The Page of Wands

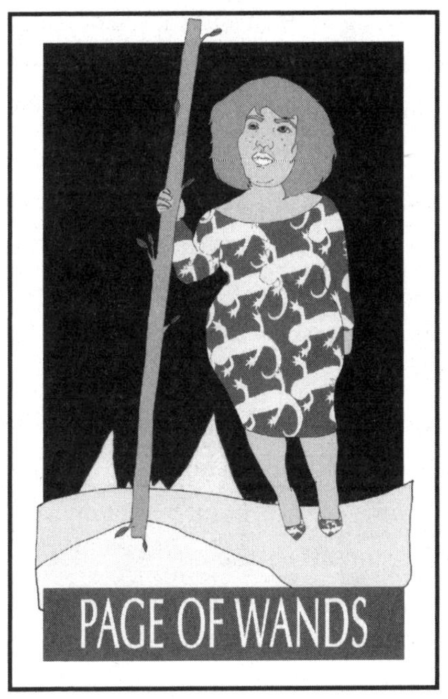

What a wonderful, creative card. The Page of Wands comes calling with a notebook stuffed full of ideas—art projects, travel routes, start-ups, nonprofits, guerrilla theater ideas, urban planning, a new invention, sketches for clothing that you've never seen the likes of. Which ones will the Page decide to sink her energy into? For now,

that is a mystery. The Page of Wands generates ideas and the fiery, electric inspiration that makes everything seem possible. But with her youth comes a slight lack of confidence; she simply does not understand how to make things work yet. But since she's a member of the court of wands, you can be sure that she will.

This card makes me think of myself in high school. I wanted to do *everything*. I wanted to be in a band, of course; pleas for a drum set were ignored and instead I got a bass guitar with better volume control. I didn't enjoy learning to play it, so I gave it to a friend and wrote song lyrics instead. But I didn't have the courage to front a band, so the lyrics turned to poetry and stories and scripts. With my friends, I made ridiculous horror movies—it would be rad, I was thinking, to be a filmmaker along the lines of Russ Meyer or John Waters. Or an actress—that I would love. Think of the costumes! I did think of costumes every day when I dressed myself in intense gothic regalia—widow's weeds and clown white worn as foundation, black lipstick, and boots imported from England. I tried making my own clothes, but it wasn't my skill set. Instead, I skillfully thrifted vampire-esque clothes and wrote short stories about, well, vampires and other ghoulish things. All the time—*all the time*—I felt the life around me crackling with possibility. I couldn't wait to grow up so I could finally do—*something*.

If the Page of Wands shows up as a person in your life, it's probably a pretty delightful individual with a spark about them. They aren't short on ideas, and they become inspired very easily. Allow their inspiration to become contagious. If you're expecting this person to follow through on their designs, however, you might be let down. They will eventually acquire the focus, confidence, and know-how that makes for solid follow-through, but right now they're like a child, regardless of how old they are. This person could just as easily be an older person who has swapped careers and is starting out at square one once more, as a young intern in your office. What's great is that this person is embracing their circumstances with beginner's mind, an excited humility. If you are in the position to be a mentor to this person, do it. They'll do you proud and remember you with gratitude forever.

If this person is a friend, there'll be no end to the hijinks they dream up. As long as you're cool with making the first move, expect tons of fun. And if this is a romantic relationship, it's likely to be with a person younger than you. Perhaps they simply have a young spirit; if that is the case, you should be able to expect a bit more out of them. Relationships with such folks often don't make it because they tend to be enamored with as wide an array of people as projects. Polyamory suits this person, so if you're down for that, you can expect lots of pleasant, fun, sexy times with this Page. But if you're looking to settle down and pop out a kid or rescue a cat, maybe try again in a few years.

If you're the Page of Wands, hurrah! The big, big world is so available to you. So many things attract you that you might feel true despair wondering how you'll ever pick just *one* project to spend your time on. Of course, you don't have to pick just one, not ultimately. Keep playing around and trying your hand at what inspires you, and if something comes along that you both like and excel at, why not spend a little time racking up some experience?

It's not forever, and whatever you learn you'll be able to take with you to your next venture. Still, if the only thing that matters to you right now is playing the field of life, go for it. Your enthusiasm is contagious and a delight to be around, and you're bound to find lots of supporters.

If the Page of Wands represents a situation, it's one that isn't fully formed but has lots and lots of potential. Do you take a chance on it? Yes! The Page of Wands has *yes!* written all over it. It's true that the promising situation might not lead to what you're hoping for; try to keep your expectations loose and stay in the present. Something magical is happening and you have the opportunity to get in on the ground floor. Who knows where it will take you?

Be the Page of Wands

- Standing in what appears to be a desert, the Page of Wands's magic is evident in the way her energy causes shoots to bloom on her stick. If, like our Page, you feel creatively pulled in multiple directions, go to your local nursery or plant shop and purchase an array of herbs. Whichever ones strike your fancy—this is the rare spell that is not about the properties of the herbs. The point is that they are growing things (and relatively inexpensive). Buy one herb for each possible direction you're considering.

  Bring the herbs home and write down your various options; stick one piece of paper under each plant. Now care for your plants. Watch their progress carefully. Are some blooming and

others withering? Have some made no discernible movement? Take from this spell that the plants that flourish represent the path that will serve you best. The sick plants are standing in for projects that will ultimately leave you cold, and the ones that are growing steadily but not dramatically represent occupations that you'd get something good out of but that might not be your ultimate destiny. Now take those herbs and make a salad.

- Create a Page of Wands pouch. The star of this pouch should be a piece of rhodonite, a cool-looking light or deep pink stone, often shot through with streaks of black. This is a great stone for helping you unearth hidden talents and interests and for guiding you toward your destiny. Pair it with a quartz crystal for extra power and clarity, as well as some chunky salt. Take a single leaf of lettuce, dry it out, and chop or crinkle it into bits. Throw some of that in your pouch—lettuce, which we chomp without thought, is actually great for divination, and we are working to divine your true calling. Add a star of anise and your bag is complete. Wear or carry it with you, sleep with it near your head, and take out the rhodonite whenever you wish to meditate or bond with it. Ask it to make your destiny known to you.
- Build an altar to the Page of Wands. Candles can be white, black, yellow, orange, or red. Any blooming branches or twigs are welcome, and place the card itself where you can see it. Let air be represented by a windblown leaf or feather. For earth, any crystal is fine, but rhodonite is especially great for Page of Wands magic. Bring fresh water in a pretty bowl.

  Kneel, sit, or stand before your altar and address the Page of Wands, asking her to lend you her inspiration, her sense of

adventure, her ability to take charge. Ask her to blaze the trail for you to follow, and ask for the courage to follow it. This altar is great when you feel that a certain spark has gone out of your life; if you are looking to be more spontaneous and outgoing, to focus less on outcome and more on the journey, this is a fantastic altar to keep you fired up.

The Knight of Wands

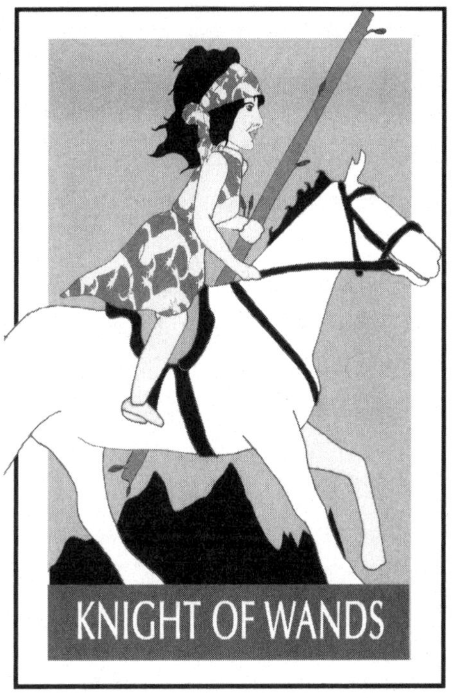

I *love* this Knight. Knights are fire, and wands are fire, so this character is fire on fire, burning up the landscape with endless ideas and schemes, dreaming big dreams and not stopping for a *second* to ask if said dreams are good, prudent, or even remotely possible. If you are foolhardy enough to step in the path of this Knight's horse to, say, check in, be prepared to get trampled—this Knight does not have the patience for processing. The Knight of Wands responds

primarily to yes. If you have a no, or a maybe, or even a "let me get back to you tomorrow," forget about it. The Knight will be a million miles away, concocting something outrageous with whoever was smart enough to provide the required yes.

I shouldn't say "smart"; to be fair, the Knight of Wands is not everyone's cup of tea. He has a lot of strikes against him. He doesn't always finish what he starts. He can't be bothered to clean up after himself. He's definitely on an ego trip. Good luck if you want some alone time with him, or hope to do something mellow like share a cup of tea. And if you were looking to get into a traditional, monogamous love situation with this joker, forget it. Obviously, a lot of people are not going to abide by this person's nonsense. But if you're like me, someone perpetually charmed by those who fit this profile, here's what you *do* get out of them:

Someone who makes shit happen. Some people believe it's best to be well rounded, proficient in many different arenas. This is not our Knight. He is good at pretty much one thing—getting a project off the ground. He's not good at much else. Frankly, who cares? He is *so good* at being inspired, at brainstorming, and creating sparks, that everyone needs to just let him do his thing and back off. Same goes for having to clean up after him. Comes with the territory. And the same goes for the ego trip. His ego is bound up with his electric chemistry. And plus, wouldn't *you* be feeling yourself if you were this awesome at making shit happen?

The life of the party. No, this is probably not the person to sit down and share your secret childhood shames with. This is a person to party with. To travel with, to have an adventure with. Maybe, during the downtime between hair-raising thrills, you'll find yourself sharing a philosophical moment wherein childhood shames are shared. But he'll be off and running to the next good time before long, so don't get too deep about it.

Hot sex. This person is not quite ready to settle down, and possibly never will be. If you want to sign up to be part of his poly pod, go for it. But if you have a jealous or possessive streak, or if the idea of sharing your beloved with others just makes you sad, enjoy this wild horse for what he can offer you: a string of wild nights that will make you sigh with longing in your old age.

The Knight of Wands coming up can mean a few things, as all the court cards have triple meanings. It could be that a person with many of the Knight's characteristics has popped up in your life. Enjoy them and let them go. If you are entering a collaboration, know that you will have to do most of the heavy lifting while this person generates ideas, makes helpful connections, and acts as the charismatic public face of your project. If this person has emerged as your nemesis, don't waste your energy fighting them—I guarantee they have more energy than you. The good thing is, if you sit tight, stay out of their way, and let other people deal with them, they'll eventually go away. These folks do not stay in any situation for too long.

What if the Knight of Wands is *you*? Well, firstly, congratulations on living your best life! This Knight settles for nothing less. Your essential nature is up for some reason right now; possibly you're feeling like your best self, or you're in a situation where your core qualities are able to thrive and you feel psyched. Or, conversely, you are having some problems and it's your basic nature that is causing the trouble. Know your limitations and be clear about them. If you're not up for settling down, don't lead someone on. If you're not pulling your weight in a project, own up to it and strive to do better, but also consider renegotiating your responsibilities to better fit your strengths. If people are upset with you because you're not fulfilling their expectations of what a friend should be, there's not much you can do. Maybe you guys are not destined to be BFFs. If so, they're likely to take this harder than you, as they're probably more charmed by you than you are by them.

In a situation, the Knight of Wands represents a big, fast, shiny, fun opportunity that you should say yes to without a minute of thought! Indeed, this Knight urges you to live by your wits, to make rash and intuitive decisions knowing that if things don't go the way you hope, well, you'll cross that bridge when you come to it. If you're feeling inspired, either creatively or romantically, or driven to travel, or to drastically change your life, then the Knight of Wands is here to say *Do it! Now! Yes! Go! Wheeeeeeeeee!*

Be the Knight of Wands

- Fire is the only element you need to create some Knight of Wands magic, though bringing a fiery stone or herb into the mix is great too. More is always better with this one!

  Find a red, glass-enclosed candle. Drop into the wax a small carnelian stone if you have one. Sprinkle some cayenne pepper on the candle, or throw a whole fresh or dried chile pepper in there. Now light it on fire and let it burn. For strong Knight of Wands magic, light and relight it each day until it burns

to the bottom. Ventilate the area to guard against the chile smoke that might occur (although the pepper is likely to stick in the wax and you can breathe easy). Meditate before your candle, locating the place within that sparks all your best ideas, your lust for life, your fire. Ask the Knight of Wands to keep it all burning.

The King of Wands

The King of Wands is the king of fire. His blooming staff signifies how extra-alive he is, and how creative. His totem animal is the salamander, which legend holds was able to hang out in actual fire and slither away unscathed. Salamanders decorate his cape, and one scampers by his throne. This guy is a born leader, not in a pushy-grabby way but because he radiates a certain capability. People get the vibe that he can take care of business, and he does.

His creativity isn't necessarily artistic; he is more a solutions person, able to solve problems, prone to flashes of insight.

If the King of Wands shows up in your life as an actual person, you'll probably find this person pretty impressive. They're often in leadership positions; if you find yourself working for or studying under this character, you'll learn a lot. They tend to be good teachers, eager to share what they know, at ease with the subject. If the King is more of a peer in a work situation, you might want to step up your own game; they tend to raise the bar without even trying. They have a lot of energy and are driven by curiosity. These people make great friends, helpful and caring and exciting to be around, and if you're romantically involved, they'll put a ring on it. They'll hold your interest for years to come, and you'll hold theirs so long as your mind and energy can match their own action-oriented inquisitiveness.

If you are the King of Wands, it probably means you are being called to take a leadership position. Hopefully, this is a pleasant situation—the King leads quite naturally, so the card does suggest that this role has developed very organically, it's made for you, and you'll slip into it easily and with lots of excitement. If you feel out of sorts about it, ask yourself if it's the role that makes you uncomfortable or the work. If you don't find the work stimulating, get out of it. You're made to shine, and you have so many interests that you're bound to find an arena that inspires you. If the work is great but the leadership role is challenging, rise to the occasion! Summon your inner King and greet your people. This position would not have come to you if you weren't ready and worthy. If your confidence is a little low, it might be a fake-it-till-you-make-it sit-

uation. When you experience how skilled you are, and see others appreciate your leadership, you'll become more self-assured and be grateful that you didn't let that initial worry sabotage such a great experience. If this is a romantic situation, you are probably in a dynamic that requires you to take the lead. Hopefully, this is enjoyable to you—the King of Wands is a dominant personality, so even if it feels a bit unusual, if you're having a good time, go for it! Likewise, if a romance isn't getting off the ground, it's probably because it's up to you to make it happen. Similarly, if you have your eye on someone, it would be a great moment to make a move.

If the King of Wands represents a situation, it is one that will very much engage you, make great use of your plentiful energy, and give you room to grow. Depending on the nature of the situation, you may find yourself eventually making a good amount of cash, running the show, hooking up with a serious life partner—whatever sounds like a great end result to you. This King represents scenarios where you are the leader. If you are in any situations that feel stagnant or confusing, it's telling you to take control.

Be the King of Wands

- I'm calling this spell Breakfast of Champions. It is a magical dish for you to start each day with as you summon the fiery, confident leadership qualities the King of Wands is known for. I hope you like oats, because that is the base of the dish. Oats are good for drawing money, which I don't necessarily think is the point of this spell, but hey, money is rarely unwelcome.

Cinnamon ramps up your inherent fire power, so that is a main ingredient. Bananas are good for potency and will strengthen your abilities. Also good for increasing powers are flax seeds, so toss some of those into the mix. Lemon is helpful for longevity, and as you want these King of Wands qualities to be integrated into your personality for the long term, shave some zest into your breakfast. Finally, throw some nuts on top. All nuts are good for prosperity, and we want you to summon this energy in order to prosper. If you need a sweetener, use maple, and add it knowing that you are calling down further prosperity.

Eat your breakfast mindfully, knowing that you are enacting a ritual. Keep the King of Wands card by you and meditate on the image. If possible, your breakfast should be silent, thoughtful, respectful. Know that the food is nurturing not just your body but your spirit. When you finish, wash out the dish by hand and leave it to dry. Eat this breakfast for as long as you need to while channeling this card.

The Queen of Wands

All hail the Queen of Wands! Everybody loves her—and what's not to love? Her good vibes are infectious. She's always got something cool up her sleeve, she runs with an interesting posse, and her outfits are bewilderingly excellent. She seems to have energy to spare, so if you're looking for inspiration, she's a great card to come into your world. The key to this queen's infectious joy is that she's incredibly ambitious, but deeply noncompetitive. She's always hustling, but she wants to know about your hustle too, and if there's ever anything she can do to help, she will. The Queen of Wands has a serious abundance mind-set—there is more than enough to go around, and it's our duty to assist others working to make their dreams come true.

If the Queen of Wands has come into your life in the form of another person, get ready to meet your new best friend. These people have irresistible energy. They're often funny and charming, the life of the party. If you've noted the lions on her throne and wondered if she has any affiliation with the astrological sign Leo, you're spot-on. This person—a strong female, or a person with a radiant feminine flair about them—loves to be the center of attention. But like most cats, they reward their pets with nuzzles and purrs. The Queen of Wands is so charismatic that you can't help but give her lots of attention. Her propensity to give great attention in return guarantees a mutual appreciation society. If this person has arrived in your world, count yourself lucky. They're almost certainly not competing with you, so check whatever competitive vibes their overall glow and accomplishments might have triggered in you. The Queen of Wands wants to be your friend. This is a fantastic person to have on your squad—friends, coworkers, teams literal and figurative. If this person has come to you for romance, I hope you are also a high-energy person because they are a lot to keep up with. The payoff, though, is a lot of passion and an exciting life, so pop some ginseng if you have to—this person is worth it.

If the Queen of Wands in this picture is you, how fabulous! You must really be enjoying your life right now, meeting friends, being

social, following your dreams in a way that feels invigorating. If that's not the case, she is here to assure you that all this is within your reach—you only need to drop your apprehension, boost your confidence, and put yourself out there. If you are suffering from the idea that to be confident and self-assured is to be a conceited bitch, the Queen is here to help you drop this outmoded, anti-feminist way of thinking. Loving and believing in yourself is the way to be—the better to help you love and believe in others! But I hope, if this card has come your way, it's because you already live that way and today you're reaping the benefits.

If the Queen of Wands represents a situation, it is one that will really support you getting whatever it is you want. It's a dream job come true, it's a party you'll shine at, it's a performance you'll captivate your audience in. This situation will help you live your best life, so say yes to it. But then, if the Queen of Wands is around, *yes!* is probably the word of the day.

Be the Queen of Wands

The Queen of Wands is a witch, as symbolized by the black cat, her familiar, resting at her feet. So just by practicing magic at all, you are well on your way to embodying her spirit. But if you are looking to amp up your positivity and confidence, there are a couple of spells that do the trick.

- The sunflower the Queen of Wands holds in her hand demonstrates her allegiance to the sun and all that the star represents

in magic—magnetism, outgoingness, vitality, self-love. Sunflower magic is a great way to channel her vibrations.

- Keep a single flower, or a bouquet, on your altar or someplace where you can see it regularly. Pluck some petals and a leaf and put them in a pouch (red, orange, or yellow, preferably) along with a handful of sunflower seeds. Wear or carry the pouch with you as you seek to wear and carry the Queen's magnificent vibes.
- Consecrate a pile of sunflower seeds to her and ritualistically snack on them (who doesn't love snack magic?), taking the time to be mindful of her energy and your own—you are literally taking sunflower magic into your body. Feel it nourishing your magic body as well as your physical one!
- The Queen of Wands is a fire queen. Light candles to her—some combination of red, orange, yellow, white, or black is great. As the fire of the candles maintains their energy—their luster, their warmth, their helpful, illuminating light—ask it to help your own energies rise and burn strong. Ask the fire to help you be radiant, to be kind, to be confident and diligent, to be inspired and inspiring. If you want to create a fuller Queen of Wands altar, you can also offer a sunflower, sunflower seeds, a cat icon or the shed whisker of a cat, a branch or twig with green on it, and a lion icon or a glyph of the zodiac sign Leo.

Cups

The Page of Cups

When the Page of Cups arrives, you can expect the unexpected, much as the Page herself is startled by the fish popping out of her cup. The Page of Cups rules the depths of our emotions before they have risen to our consciousness—dreams, the uncanny, strange impulses, wild creative bursts, love at first sight, feeling like you've

met a person in a past life, a wave of emotion that suddenly shifts your perspective. The Page is likely to take you on a bit of an emotional roller coaster, but it is ultimately a positive experience that brings you close to beauty, love, and the sensation that there is so much more going on beneath the surface of our daily lives than we know.

If the Page swans into your life in the form of a person, it has probably happened suddenly and you probably felt an instant connection: spontaneous BFFs and those who sweep you off your feet belong to this page. Such experiences heighten the joy and wonder in our lives, even though they may be short-lived. If someone around you has captivated your attention, either romantically or platonically, dare to make a connection. If someone has approached you in an unusual way, don't fear it. The Page of Cups is loyal to the unconscious and allows the world to be colored by all sorts of fantasy and imagination. Allow a brush with this person to loosen the floodgates of your own deep creativity. This person may be young and not yet have their feet firmly on the ground, but that's okay. There's a place for dreamers, and the Page of Cups is inviting you to dream alongside her.

If you are the Page of Cups, you're probably having a pleasant but topsy-turvy time of it! This would be a great time to keep a dream journal, study lucid dreaming, and read or write poetry. Writing letters professing love or asking forgiveness is another activity that benefits from the presence of this page. If you find that people are nudging you to get more organized and be more responsible, take a moment to check whether your behavior is truly hurting anyone. If it's not, float away from these folks. There are plenty of people who value what you have to offer right now; your way can be an inspiration to people whose lives have gotten a little stodgy. Seek out beauty, indulge in emotions, and take a first step toward making a dream come true.

If the Page of Cups represents a situation, chances are it seems a little murky or not fully formed. If the situation concerns beauty, magic, the occult, the arts, or love, take a chance and wade in. You're likely to be surprised and inspired. If it is something more practical, having to do with business, contracts, home, or work, and it doesn't seem to have all its pieces in place, it probably doesn't. Walk away. The Page of Cups rules art and magic workshops, dating sites and matchmaking parties, social gatherings (especially with strangers), and actions that make you feel more beautiful. Entering into psychoanalysis or therapy of any kind would also be a good move, as it brings you closer to the subconscious realm ruled by the Page of Cups.

Be the Page of Cups

- Build a lunar dream altar to the Page of Cups to get closer to your unconscious and more comfortable with the unknown. Cups and the element of water are the primary focus, so a nice vessel of water should have pride of place. Use images of fish or fish bones, as well as anything that has come from the sea—shells, seaweed, rocks and sea glass, driftwood, and sand. Candles should be black, white, and/or any shade of blue. Feathers from seabirds or images of them are a good way to represent

air. Amethyst is a great crystal to bring into such an altar, as is moonstone.

Holding either the crystals or the water, sit and meditate on the Page of Cups. State your intention to connect deeply with your unconscious mind and all the unseen energies that move through your life. Sit with your altar especially before sleep; have a dream journal beside your bed and write down your dreams immediately upon waking. Also sit with your altar in the morning and carry one of the crystals with you throughout your day to keep you linked to it. Be open to synchronicity and coincidence; with this altar activated, these moments are pointing to something more significant. Be open to talking to strangers. This altar is strongest if built during a new moon and kept throughout a full moon cycle. Take care to note what astrological sign the new moon is in, and bring something onto the altar to honor it.

The Knight of Cups

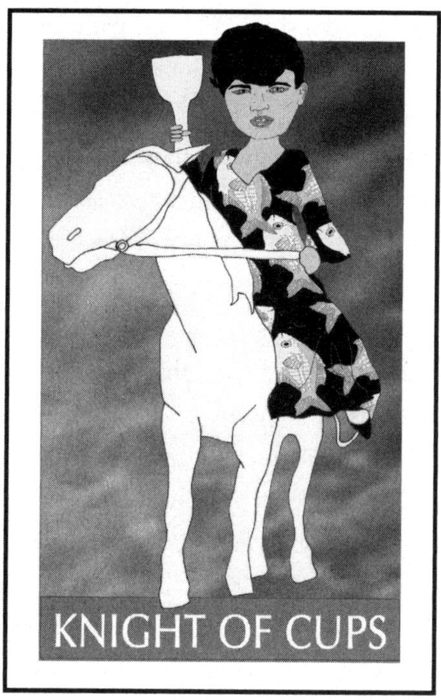

When the Knight of Cups struts in on horseback, I guarantee you things are about to get interesting. The things that are great about this person are *great*, like really, really great—they're funny and polite and dress awesomely and are super-romantic and very artistic and creative and sensitive and easy on the eye. But here's the bad side: they are often too good to be true. The Knight of Cups is in love with love. They enjoy the heady rush of falling for someone, they enjoy doting and doing sweet things, they play a mean game of seduction, and they are a good time in the sack. However, they have a hard time sticking around for the deeper, more challenging aspects of relationships. Indeed, with many a Knight of Cups, things rarely progress to relationship after that dizzying first explosion of dopamine.

If the Knight appears as a person, they are ardent, pleasant to be around. You will almost certainly get a crush on them. Whether or not the affection is returned, you will for sure think you have a chance, because these knights are such flirts. They can be the coworker who makes the workday just a little more exciting. They can be the friend you always have that little bit of energy with. And if they do represent someone you're actually involved with, you are certainly swept off your feet by now.

The emotional energy of cups as held by the fiery Knight tells a story of love and sex gone out of control. Your knight may be totally legit and 100 percent smitten with you, but your pacing and the intensity of it all may end up burning everything out in spite of your feelings. If you (or your friends) think things are moving too fast, they probably are. Put the brakes on if you can. You probably won't want to because it feels so amazing to be swept away by this Romeo, but just know that you are trading intensity for longevity. It all may be beyond your control anyway. Until the Knight of Cups matures and learns how to manage the intensity of their own feelings, they'll be leaving a trail of broken hearts behind them.

If you are the Knight of Cups, try to take a breath from your latest fling to catch coffee with your friends, touch base with your family, maybe even spend a minute or two *alone*. Romance makes you feel alive; it is the source of so much of your inspiration and motivation, it makes everything more vibrant, and if you are artistic it's probably your muse. But getting high off other people can be damaging for everyone. Try to go a little slower, nurture your other relationships, check yourself out of love jail for a day or two. And pay attention to the object of your affection. If you don't really see this going anywhere but, thanks to your pro seduction techniques they are ass over heels for you, maybe it's time to cut them loose, regardless of how rad the sex might be or how delicious the ego and dopamine boost you're getting. It is truly special to be gifted with such a sensitive, romantic, artistic temperament, but you must learn to handle yourself in a way that is more balanced for everyone.

If the Knight of Cups shows up as a situation, it's a nice one. Something glamorous is on the horizon, something you must say yes to. This could be a social activity or a job or a promotion that increases the glamour in your life. It also could represent a period of intense artistic inspiration. If so, do what you can to devote as much time as possible to producing work. Take advantage of this time; even if the work itself isn't your best, getting out such a wide range of material will ultimately be beneficial to your process and your career. This is also a great time to go on a shopping spree, especially if you have a fancy event coming up. A full-on makeover might be called for, and with the Knight of Cups, you won't sweat the splurge. You know you're worth it.

 Be the Knight of Cups 

- For all the shit I just talked about the Knight of Cups, I really do like the card. They are ruled by their heart, for better or worse, and often have a very dreamy, visionary quality. They can inspire us to take more chances, live more imaginatively, take risks, and prioritize beauty. If you are looking to draw this energy into your life, set up an array of blue, white, and black candles; a variety of shades of blue would be really nice. Set them up in an area where you can recline, and then—recline!

  With a notebook and pen. But don't begin writing right away. Lounge about and daydream. Let the candles hypnotize you and put you in a dreamy state of mind. What does your most glamorous life look like? Not your best life—specifically your most glamorous life. Does it include travel? Where to? Now is the time to start writing. Make an outline of everything your most glamorous life would include. What does your love life look like? Committed to one single international spy? Playing a field of playthings? A stealthy don't-ask-don't-tell arrangement? Would you dress differently? How would your style change? What are three items you can acquire to set your wardrobe on its way? What about money? How do you make yours? In your most glamorous life, what would you do for money? What do you have to do to get there? Make a list of steps you could take that might bring you closer to this ideal. Do you have creative aspirations? What are they? How can you make time for them? Can you keep a diary? Begin painting in the mornings in a nightshirt, drinking coffee and smoking a single Nat Sherman? Are there any vices you're thinking of adopting? How do you think they would enhance your life? Make a case for it. How can you change your living space to increase the glamour? Should you move? Where to? What experiences are totally glamorous to you that you haven't yet had—what's on your glamour bucket list?

Write all this stuff down. When you're done, take your notebook and do eeny-meeny-miney-mo. It feels silly and random, but you are allowing the Universe and the power of the Knight of Cups to guide you. Whatever you've landed on will be your first step toward fulfilling your glamour potential. Get started. Keep your candles around and continue to burn them; keep your list folded beneath them or in a nearby drawer. Each time you hit one of your glamour milestones, cross it off and eeny-meeny-miney-mo yourself your next assignment.

The King of Cups

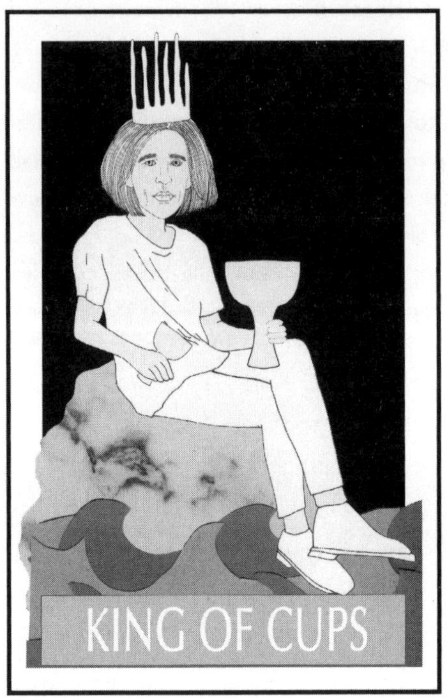

Who is this dreamy soul, chilling by the sea? Look at what a gentle, noble face he has! The face of a poet! Well, the King of Cups may never have penned a verse in his life, but the way he flows through life, spreading compassion, care, patience, and love, is truly poetic. This king has made tenderness an art. He knows that softness is not weakness, and by offering loving understanding to the people around him—and himself—his personal power grows, rather than shrinks. If this king cared about such things, he could probably be a mad self-care guru and make a bazillion dollars, but that's not his shtick. He's not looking for world domination; his kingdom is his community, and he serves rather than rules.

Like all Court cards, the King of Cups can be a person, a situation, or you yourself. If the card is appearing in your life as another human, lucky you! This individual truly has your best interest at heart. If you are wondering whether this person is too good to be true, the answer is no. They are genuinely good-natured, emotionally wise, and here to help. Don't be afraid to reach out to them if you need counsel or a sympathetic ear or even just a hug.

The King of Cups reminds me of someone I know—a real poet, actually—who exudes a wide, nonjudgmental radiance and has a true desire to support people and show them love. Once I spent a week at an oceanside artists' retreat with him and watched each morning as he sat on the shore, day by day moving a little bit deeper into the water, communing with the fish, soaking his giant crystals in the seawater, writing poetry. Total King of Cups activity. My poet friend, for all his serenity, is fiercely interested in justice and will not hold his tongue if something unfair is happening. Likewise, the King of Cups often represents a person who has dedicated much of their time to charity, volunteer work, work in the nonprofit sector, or activism. It's not a yelling-in-the-street path they've taken, however, but more like delivering meals to hungry people and fostering sick animals.

If the King of Cups has arrived in your life as a situation, you are probably being called to show compassion. Perhaps you are in a position to mediate between warring friends or family members; because you truly can empathize with all sides, you're in a lovely place to do so. Maybe you've been moved by a social problem and are feeling inspired to volunteer your time; with this king in your corner, you'll do work that truly matters and will gain a lot emotionally from the experience.

If this is a love situation—whoa. Congratulations! You are probably having the experience of being really, truly seen and loved and accepted. Super-beautiful! Say yes to the situation and return the favor. With this card up, it means your own powers of love and empathy are strong right now, and the Universe wants you to use them, for the benefit of yourself as well as others. This also can mean it's time to remove from your life any people, places, or things that are not loving or that force you to tamp down your loving nature.

And if you are the King of Cups, more congratulations are in order. It suggests that work you have done to allow yourself to be more forgiving, more open, less scared of people, less scared of pain, more patient and tolerant, and more giving of what you have—all of it has paid off. You have hit a serious emotional milestone. If you are considering it, work in the healing realms would be a great use of your emotional talents, as well as an opportunity to continue to grow them. You would excel right now working as a doctor, massage therapist, shrink, or witch, or working in any of the many ways one person can help another.

Be the King of Cups

- Here is a very sweet milk-and-cookies sort of spell to help you cultivate the type of compassionate spirit the King of Cups is known for. The first step would be baking some simple poppy-seed cookies. If you're vegan- or gluten- or sugar-free, you probably know how to alter the recipe to work for you, so please do. The important ingredient here is the poppy seed; poppy is a known magical aid to compassion, love, and tranquillity.

    - ⋆ Cream a cup of butter, a half-cup of sugar, and two egg yolks.
    - ⋆ Add two cups of flour, a quarter-teaspoon of salt, three tablespoons of poppy seeds, and one teaspoon of vanilla extract to the creamed butter mixture. Stir to combine until it's well mixed and refrigerate for one hour.
    - ⋆ While the dough is chilling, take a bath. Relax. Get yourself to a place of tranquillity. Wish that all people could know tranquillity.
    - ⋆ Preheat your oven to 375 degrees and grease some cookie sheets or lay parchment paper on them.
    - ⋆ Drop the dough onto the cookie sheets by the teaspoon. Bake for nine minutes.

  While your cookies are baking, fix yourself a cup of pine needle tea. You can make this yourself by grabbing a handful of fresh, green pine needles from a tree. Get rid of the brown bits at the end, chop up the needles, and put them in a teapot or tea ball or tea sock—whatever you use to brew loose tea. Let it steep, covered, for five minutes. Feel free to add a sweet-

ener. For those of you who are like, listen, I live in the heart of the urban jungle, there aren't any freaking pine trees for me to go harvest needles from—voilà! There is the Internet! You can order pine needle tea. If that is too much a pain in your ass, I understand. You can also make a tea from basil for this spell; just substitute fresh basil for the pine needles. Okay okay, you can use dried basil if you need to. But really, try to use pine needles, freshly harvested, if at all possible. Pine tree magic is strong and constant.

Take your tea and cookies and sit before a white, black, red, or pink candle. Burn myrrh. Sit comfortably, nibbling your cookies and sipping your tea, and think about all the people you know and love, the people closest to your heart whom you adore without complication. Let your heart be filled with these people, feel the love they inspire in you, notice how that love energizes your body. Groove on it for a bit.

Next, think about some people you don't know enough to like or dislike. The person who delivers your mail, someone you see a lot at the coffee shop, the person who rang up your groceries, a classmate who sits on the other side of the room from you. As you meditate on them, work to bring those feelings of love you had for your besties into your body. Know that, like your closest people, they have had tragedy and wonder in their lives. All of them strive to be loved and strive for happiness; all of them have known pain and have cried. The Universe created them just like it created those you adore. Send them love and well wishes.

Once you've gotten the hang of this and you're feeling pretty lovey, select some people you can't fucking stand. Frenemies, outright enemies. Home-wreckers and gossips, liars and Trump supporters. If holding so many of them in your mind starts to stress you out, just select one. Know that this person, like all the others, has had tragedy and wonder in their life, has strived to be loved, and for happiness, has known pain, and cried. The Universe created them, just as it created those you adore. Send them love and well wishes. Summon the feelings and goodwill you have for those you love and for those you don't know and feel it for these people too. Stay with this part of the meditation until you feel you've made some kind of breakthrough.

This spell is actually a lifelong practice, or it can be. You don't need to bake cookies and harvest a mug of tea (though why not). All you need is the practice of sitting and generating love, first for those who already have it, next for people you feel neutral about, and finally for those you are biased against for whatever reason. Compassion can sound like a flimsy buzzword in our culture, but it is actually tough work. The payoff, however, is the quiet power of the King of Cups and the ability to know his mysteries and work his magic.

The Queen of Cups

Half in our world and half in the world of intuition, love, and psychic phenomena, the Queen of Cups sits on her throne. She is happy and beautiful and almost certainly communicating telepathically with the anima of her ornate cup. The Queen of Cups is in touch with a deeper, emotional knowledge and is thus brimming with compassion. She exudes a deep serenity and is always guided by her intuition.

If the Queen of Cups has come to you in the form of a person, what a magical person they must be! Possessing a feminine energy regardless of gender, this is the sort of person you get a psychic vibe off immediately. Maybe you don't need to resort to vibe-level communication; maybe they come at you with crystals hung around their neck and a tattoo of a crescent moon on their third eye. The Queen of Cups might wear her spiritual proclivities on her sleeve, and perhaps in quite an eccentric manner. What does she care? She's a *queen*. Not only that, she is such a compassionate, caring, and nonjudgmental soul that she's not thinking that anyone is going to look at her askance. If anyone did cast a judgy glare at her overt witchiness, she'd respond by doing a spell to open their hearts to what they fear in the world.

Please don't expect this friend or lover or coworker or family member to get their head out of the clouds. If we were living in another society, there'd be a clear role for them—the village seer or town bruja or cul-de-sac conjure. In our modern world, shot through with cold capitalism and disproportionately influenced by science (and don't get me wrong, I *love* science!), there can seem to be no place for these dreamers. Nonetheless, they're generally quite happy with wherever their life has landed them, as they understand that the point to being here isn't accumulation or ambition, but feeling and connection.

If you are the Queen of Cups, it might be time for you to work on strengthening your spirituality or any psychic abilities you may possess. You may find yourself experiencing a lot of déjà vu, having vivid or lucid dreams, and feeling powerful connections with animals. Probably it's not the first time, but if it's come up for you right now, there is a certain meaning behind it. The Universe is trying to communicate something to you; I have no doubt you'll know what it is. Also, you might find yourself in a situation where you don't have the type of boundaries that others—or even you yourself—think you should have. As you know in your gut, this is okay. For now. It might be okay for a long time, but right now the merging that comes of your looser boundaries is as it should be.

If the Queen of Cups is representing a situation, it is one that you will need your intuition and gut instincts to guide you through. Follow your heart. If you are not capable of merging into the event, you probably should walk away from it. It is something that will consume you, something that will take up much of your heart and mind, something that you will no doubt bring a lot of positive energy to. But if you are unable to offer so much of yourself, better turn back. If not, you'll get sucked in despite yourself and the results could be anything from serious resentment to the type of burnout that manifests itself physically.

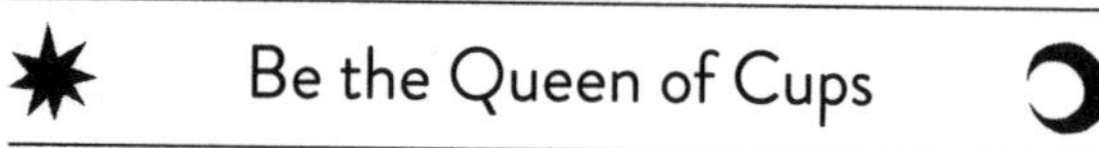

Be the Queen of Cups

- To raise your frequency in the direction of the pure-hearted, ever-loving Queen of Cups, we've got to wash that film of negativity off you. Everyone gets it; like the grime that coats our skin from living in a world full of air pollution, the world also pelts us with spiritual pollution day in and day out. This simple bath will wash away not only outside toxins but the internal toxins we so often conjure in an attempt to protect ourselves.

Take three bottles of beer (alcoholics, you can make it nonalcoholic beer, or if that is still too triggering, three bottles of kombucha) and dump them into a tubful of water. Add a heap of Epsom salts. Lie back and relax, envisioning a toxic layer, internally and externally, melting away. Without these grimy screens, your heart has a clear view of the world and you can begin to let that part of yourself lead you through life a bit more.

- To strengthen your intuitive powers and get closer to the psychic realms, try this jasmine dream spell. Before bed, fix yourself a cup of (decaf) jasmine tea. If jasmine grows fresh around you, bring some to your bedside. Finally, anoint yourself with jasmine oil before sleep. If you have the right hair type for it, throw a bunch of the stuff in your hair. You can also anoint your temples with the oil, as well as behind your ears, your throat, and the back of your neck. Keep a preferably unlined notebook and a pen by your bed. Now go to sleep.

  Upon waking, before you sit up or even open your eyes, write down what you dreamed. No matter how useless or expendable a detail might seem to you, write it down. It's amazing the types of things I think aren't interesting in that moment when I'm still half asleep—the most outrageous details seem blasé! Get everything down, and once you're awake, transcribe the dream if your scrawl is too illegible. Track your dreams, the symbolism, the feelings they give you. Regard the night world as another world you are living in, one as real as your daytime world. Make offerings to it on your altar. Really engage with it and watch your intuitive self blossom.

- Dedicate one day a week to volunteer for a cause that challenges your compassion. If you have a hard time with humanity but love cats, volunteering at the animal shelter is not what I'm

suggesting. More like volunteering at a homeless shelter. The idea behind this is to shock your compassion into growth, to push your comfort levels so that you can expand your heart outward in the style of the Queen of Cups. An alternative action would be to begin a course of study that focuses on compassion, such as the heart sutras in Buddhism. Whatever you decide to do, consecrate your efforts to the Queen of Cups, who is nothing less than the merciful goddess herself. Strive to be like her. Make it a ritual.

Swords

The Page of Swords

The Page of Swords is a whirlwind of ideas and excitement. Look at the blustery clouds in the background, the wind-whipped trees, the rough waters. All of this is being moved by the power of air, the sword power of our young, idealistic friend. If the Page of Swords has blown into your world, prepare for much action and energy, some of it not very well planned out but bound for execution anyway.

If this Page has entered your realm as a person, they are likely young or younger than you; at the very least they lack a certain amount of experience. Or they may be an older person who has never quite managed to grow up and retains the idealism of a much younger, less tempered person. Hopefully, you find their energy invigorating and inspiring; these people can help you reconnect with beliefs or energies that you nurtured when you were younger, but that have fallen by the wayside as other, more mature situations took up your time and attention. In the best situations, these people reignite your idealism while you lend to them the wisdom of experience; in such a collaboration, truly wonderful, innovative projects can take root and grow to fruition. In some situations, however, the Page of Swords represents people with no grasp of reality, whose stoner visions and resistance to reality are supremely annoying. If you find one of these types close by, avoid arguing with them; they've got more bluster in them than you and will keep the debate going until you pull your hair out in aggravation. Try to keep away from them and pray to the goddess that they grow up or move on.

If you are the Page of Swords, it is very important that you find people who believe in your visions and are willing to support your spirit, no matter how wacky your plans might be. You are in possession of beginner's mind, and in this way your lack of experience is actually great. You don't actually know all the things that can go wrong, so you're not weighed down with doubt and hesitation.

This card is giving you the green light to move forward with your dreams, outrageous as they may be. Make the leap! What you need is people who will catch you if you fall, not people trying to stop you from jumping. Your ability to take risks and follow your heart is being called upon right now—perhaps a project needs a leader, perhaps people around you need inspiration. Follow your gut and your heart. If something goes awry with your plan, you'll simply stop, tweak it, and keep going.

If the Page of Swords represents a situation, it might take the form of a zany scheme that fills you with excitement but has no proven track record. You may fear that you're signing on to a losing team or getting in over your head. The Page of Swords says, take a chance! Whether you are instigating the project or joining a team, you may have the opportunity to get involved with something innovative at its start—and yes, the road is sure to be excitingly rocky. Challenges and setbacks aren't signs that you're on the wrong path, they *are* the path. Any problems that need solving will be mentally stimulating to you. Say yes!

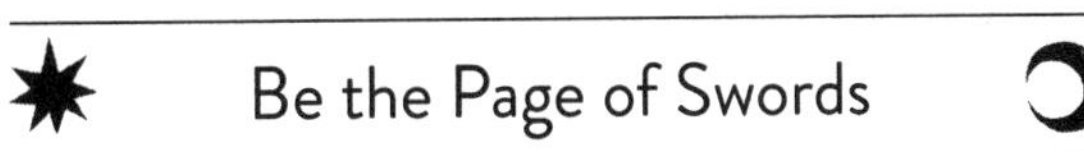

Be the Page of Swords

- The Page of Swords is able to take on visionary projects because of their idealism. To revive your own flagging idealism and bring about a positive attitude and practical hopefulness, create a magic pouch (which should be white, black, or yellow). The main ingredients are apple seeds and vanilla beans. If you have

nothing but these, you have enough to work with. Apple magic promotes friendship, and the heart of idealism is the belief that people are essentially good. Apple magic also is pro-healing; most of us lose touch with our idealism as it's beaten down by the harsher parts of life. Vanilla bean is wonderful for restoring lost energy.

Together, these two magical allies will conspire to brighten your belief system so that you can take more chances, trust your dreams, and have an overall sunnier day. To fortify your pouch even more, get your hands on the following herbs: hawthorn, for rebirth; lily, also for rebirth; willow (any kind), to help move past sadness; and best of all, yarrow, to drive out negativity and fear and build courage. A nice stone to add to your pouch is sodalite, a crystal that promotes idealism and is sacred to philosophers.

Meditate with your pouch, asking the Universe to work through these herbs and crystals to revive your idealism. Visualize what it would look and feel like to be more idealistic. What would you do? How would you behave? Ask the pouch to support you as you take steps to embody a more idealistic nature. Bring the pouch with you and sleep with it nearby.

- The Page of Swords's energy is always high, magnetizing wild ideas and the ability to carry them out. Give your own energy a boost with a ritual bath. If you have any white, black, yellow, blue, or red candles, bring them into the bathroom with you. Make a bath sachet from a cloth or paper tea filter; fill it with lavender, fennel seeds, fresh rosemary, and fresh basil. Tie it closed and toss it into a warm bath. You can throw the ingredients in loose, but you'll have more of a mess to clean up! (Sometimes it's worth it to feel like you're marinating in a magical stew).

Take three carnation blooms into the tub with you and scrub your body with them, from head to toe. Imagine the flowers—known for increasing strength and magical powers as well as healing whatever wounds your energetic body has sustained—exfoliating your aura, washing away a layer of grime that has prevented your energy from shining its brightest. The flowers will fall apart as you do this, which is fine. Linger in the tub afterward, meditating on rising energy. Don't use a towel but air-dry after you leave the tub. Let your magic bath stay on you. This spell works best before bed; expect to rise the following morning feeling renewed and optimistic.

- If you find yourself creatively frustrated, unable to locate an outlet for your Page of Swords energy, make this road-opener tincture. This is longer magic—it takes a while for this potion to come together—but once you have it, the potion will be on hand for whenever you're struck by energetic blockage.

Get some lemongrass, preferably organic, and after washing them, give the stalks a good pounding to open them up. Place them in a jar, fill the jar with vodka, and place it in a dark cupboard for one month. At that time, your tincture is ready. Put three to five drops of it in a glass of water or tea and welcome its blockage-busting energy into your body. If you'd rather not ingest any alcohol, simply bring the tincture mixed with the water or tea to a boil, and then let it sit; after five minutes the alcohol will be burned off. It is also possible to make tinctures with vegetable glycerin, apple cider vinegar, distilled white vinegar, or distilled water (*not* tap water). With the glycerin or vinegars, you should also steep the tincture for one month. With water you need to let the potion sit for two months. For *all* non-alcoholic tinctures, you must steep and then continue to store them in the fridge to avoid spoiling.

The Knight of Swords

When the Knight of Swords hurls itself into your world, prepare for things to get shaken up. Whether it's a person, a situation, or you yourself, the energy is bound to be jarring, confusing, off-putting, and intense.

Take a peek at the image. What we have here is the heavily armored Knight in battle mode, sword drawn, apparently dueling with the air itself. The horse he rides seems to have an *Ohhhhh shiiiittt* expression on its face, but the Knight is pulling hard on the reins, oblivious to—or more likely not caring about—the horse's experience. The clouds in the sky are jagged with wind, and the trees are resisting the blustery onslaught, fighting to stay straight. Everything about this card is forceful, unpleasant, conflictual. The Knight himself is totally checked out about the effect he's having on his environment: he has decorated his horse with butterflies and birds, and birds also adorn his cape. It's as if he thinks that because his intentions are swell, or his rationale is solid, his is a sweet presence in the landscape. Not true.

If this character has entered your life, keep your psychic first aid kit ready. Few emerge from a tango with this guy unscathed. He may be attractive at first, as many fanatics are. So passionate! So unafraid to take action! So confident in his theories, so hyperintelligent, so sure that his way is the best and only way! It can be heady. But his complete lack of heart, or emotional intelligence, leaves him dangerously unbalanced. This is the type of person so ill acquainted with feelings, so grossed out by vulnerability, that they believe logic should rule all, even intimate relationships. If this person is a coworker, try to stay detached from their poor bedside manner and focus on the good job they undoubtedly are doing. If they can be removed from any task that has them interfacing with the public, damage will be minimized. If you're doing political work with this person, they could be a real boon, as they believe in the cause with all their heart—if they have one. Science is also a great occupation for this person—any situation where it's more or less okay to pretend you're a brain in a jar. They're possibly great teachers, because they truly do know so much. Their critiques of students would be true, but delivered without an ounce of sensitivity, they could also be damaging. And they're the biggest mansplainers of the Tarot—even the ones who are women.

When I was young and discovering radical politics for the first time, I'm afraid I was the Knight of Swords. It was my way or the highway; you either agreed with me or you were part of the problem. There was a right way and a wrong way, and I knew what was best. For instance, at the punk rock queer club I danced at I had decided it was *not* okay for the punk guys to dance, well, punk. I hated them knocking into girls; it felt like total male privilege to hurl your big body around and not give any thought to who you might be inconveniencing or hurting. (This would be a good time to point out that the fragile females I had decided to protect were *also* dancing like crazed punk rock monsters, slamming into and spinning each other with centrifugal force.) So I decided that I would start kicking any guy dancing in a manner I deemed unacceptable. How horrible! Many, many years later, when I had come to my senses, I ran into the boy I kicked the most and apologized. He forgave me, but made sure to let me know how distressing my behavior had been to him. It hurt, but I needed to hear that.

If you are the Knight of Swords, it might be time to wake up to the people around you. It doesn't always matter that you're right, or that you're smart. At the end of the day, most people want to be happy, and if you aren't balancing your intellectual rigor with the bare minimum of emotional sensitivity, you're causing strife. At the end of it all it won't matter what a genius you are; nobody will want to talk, work, or have sex with you.

If this is a situation, it's incredibly fast-paced and may have come into your life out of nowhere. It will require you to tamp down your emotions and not take care of the emotions of others. A razor-sharp mind will be required of you, and a stomach for methods that push the boundaries of what is ethical. If all this sounds good, then by all means jump in; there is surely a lot to be gained—knowledge, adventure, stories, possibly some wealth and glory. But be aware that there might be a time limit on this sort of situation. If you don't burn out right away, you'll achieve longevity only if you twist your personality in fundamentally unhealthy ways. It might behoove you to create a system of checks before you hurl yourself into the mix.

Be the Knight of Swords

Wait, why would I help you be more like this card I just talked so much shit about? Well, in some cases the Knight of Swords is a welcome sight. Maybe you are painfully shy. You have a terrible time sticking up for yourself. You have a hard time believing in your intellect, valuing your own opinions, validating your experience of the world. The Knight of Swords has a special magic for you.

- Get yourself a pile of bay leaves. If you can harvest them yourself, that's amazing, but chances are you don't have bay leaves growing in your yard. If you can find some that are fresh, awesome, but if you're plucking your bay leaves out of a spice jar,

don't worry—your magic will still be magical. Take a strong, dark marker, maybe a Sharpie. You're going to write on each leaf a quality that is holding you back, one that you want to get rid of. Have a fireproof bowl or jar nearby, as well as a red, blue, white, or black candle. After you've written down all the qualities you're ready to let go of, dip the leaves into the candle and let them turn to ash in the bowl.

When you're through, speak to the Knight of Swords, asking him to endow you with bravery and conviction, swiftness and confidence, action and energy. Leave the ashes at the base of a tree, or sprinkle them into flowers or shrubbery.

 Stop Being the Knight of Swords 

- I'm glad you're taking the wake-up call of this card seriously! Now, assemble a magic pouch to help you snap out of your toxic know-it-all-ness and cultivate a mellower, more compassionate way of life. Your pouch can be blue, white, or black. Its most important ingredient is yarrow, for exorcism; you need to drive this demon out! Keeping yarrow on you can bring insight into what your demons are—what is the underlying issue causing you to act so intolerantly?

  Other herbs that can go into your pouch include chocolate, to soften your heart; cypress, to calm stubbornness; crystalized honey, to bring sweetness; lavender, for friendship; milk thistle, to break the negative spell you inadvertently cast upon yourself; peppermint, for healing; sandalwood, to cure confusion; a pinch of valerian to reduce conflict; and some echinacea to bring power to the spell. Sleep with this bundle under your

pillow, meditate with it regularly, and talk to it, asking it to bring you the qualities you need.

Protect Yourself from the Knight of Swords

- I recommend hematite. It offers strong aura protection, and can help ward off that icky, toxic feeling you can get from spending time with icky, toxic people. Obviously, you just want to get as far away from your Knight of Swords as possible, but if for the time being you're stuck with them, ask the hematite for protection, sleep with it under your pillow, and carry it on your body whenever you're interacting with this person.

The King of Swords

The King of Swords totally has a staring problem. Look at him looking right into your soul! If you think there's something judgy about him, you're right. He is sizing you up, and his eye is as sharp as his double-edged sword. The King of Swords is a straight-shooter; as stern and intimidating as he is, he is deeply ethical and very trustworthy. The plainness of his clothes indicates that he's not putting on airs and has no ulterior motives or hidden agendas. He is looking for the simplest piece of logic, the most economical collection of words, the most merciful yet ethical ruling. His golden crown is his only bling, and it's there to let you know that for all his simplicity, he's still a king: he rules, and he rules well. The crescent moon and the butterfly etched onto his stone throne suggest that although logic rules the day, he does allow mercy to influence his decisions.

If the King of Swords has popped up in your world, he might be an authority figure who is a traditionally masculine, sometimes even too macho, man. On the good side, he is truly fair, works hard, and wants to be in service to the greater good. On the downer side, expect some serious mansplaining. He is great at legal issues and leadership roles, and his grasp of language is incredible—he could be a professor or a writer or both. If he is a friend, he's probably someone who inspires you, who perhaps you have a friendly rivalry with, who pushes you to be smarter à la Lenu and Lila in Elena Ferrante's Neapolitan novels. But this person can also be a know-it-all and isn't necessarily the best shoulder to cry on. They're not very connected with their emotions and are too focused on solving problems to hang out and share a cup of misery with you. If this person represents a love interest, you're probably feeling frustrated. You will have to accept a certain style of communication and a detachment that all the snuggles in the world will not warm up. If you can embrace this person's character, they will be very loyal to you and very intellectually stimulating. But if you keep yearning for something they're not offering, walk away. It's not going to change.

If you are the King of Swords, your diplomatic skills, razor-sharp thinking, clear communication, and fairness are probably being requested. Perhaps someone is seeking your advice. Maybe you are being asked to take a leadership role. Of course you should say yes to all that is asked from you. Some people around you might be frustrated by your aloofness and your apparent lack of emotion in a situation. Depending on how important the person or the event is to you, it might be worth your while to sit down and explain, with your clear and marvelous linguistic skills, that you do care, even though you express yourself in a way that might not reveal that. That is, if you do care. If you don't, regardless of how painful it might be to the other, be clear. As if you could be any other way.

As a situation, the King of Swords represents a scenario where emotions just aren't welcome. Perhaps it's a science-y scene, or a traditionally male realm where emotions are seen as a sign of weakness. Bummer, but it's not necessarily a bad situation, just one whose code you need to adopt in order to join in and thrive. In spite of the coldness, it is not a hostile environment, just quite serious and intensely logical. If this suits your temperament, or if you can assimilate into it, say yes, as the situation will enable you to acquire and flex great skills and prepare you for further leadership down the way.

 Be the King of Swords 

- If you are looking to bring the bracing, intellectual yang energy of the King of Swords into your life, brew a cup of this King of Swords tea: a sprig of fresh peppermint (though a peppermint tea bag will do in a pinch), a half-teaspoon of fennel seeds, and a single bay leaf. It will taste interesting, but that's the King of Swords. The bracing freshness of peppermint reflects the King's airy nature; the fennel seeds are sacred to yang, or masculine, energy, and bay leaves bring wisdom and intellectual prowess. I hope at this point in the book it goes without saying, but yang, or masculine energy, can belong to people of all genders, as can yin, or traditionally feminine vibes. Everyone is welcome to channel the King of Swords; sometimes we all need to run a bit of paternal, mansplaining energy!
- The King of Swords is the airiest of the air cards—he's air upon air, dry and logical. If you are looking to bring these vibes into your life, get an air plant or two or three or five (they're small). How strange these plants are: they grow and thrive without roots and with hardly any water. So like our emotionless, heady King! Dedicate your air plant to the King of Swords and take care of it. Meditate with and befriend your air plant, and let it be your touchstone as you go about channeling detachment and logic and work to get your emotions under your control.

The Queen of Swords

All hail the Queen of Swords. With her mighty sword, she is ready to cut through whatever bullshit you or the rest of the world try to offer her. This Queen's royal BS detector is top-notch; she is quite skilled at sniffing out deceit, falsity, exaggeration, and denial. If you're not being honest with her—or with yourself—she knows, and she's unafraid to tell it like it is. This Queen is in service to the truth. She wears clouds on her cape, not because she has a

stormy personality—very much the opposite, she's got a keen sense of humor!—but because clouds, so high in the sky, offer her a bird's-eye, godlike view of the earth and its petty inhabitants with our silly squabbles. Clouds are her elemental throne. The mass of them billowing on the card are deliberately low in the sky, on their way out. The Queen brings clarity, conciseness, honesty, and clear skies. And despite her stern expression and serious know-it-all attitude, she's not judging you. This Queen has lived too long, been around too many blocks, to call out a human for being human. Because that's what she chalks up all the bullshit to—human foibles. She's understanding and forgiving, even as she calls you out on whatever nonsense you were trying to get away with. In this way she is a great friend. She's not at all emotional, so if you're looking for a hug or a cry-buddy, look elsewhere. But if you want some wisdom that pulls no punches, if it's tough love you're seeking, she's your man. She'll probably lessen the blow with a witty wisecrack, but she's not going to hold your hand or wipe your tears. You have other friends for that anyway.

When the Queen of Swords comes up, it's telling you that a situation, a person, or you yourself have taken on her attributes. If it's a situation, you can trust it. Things are as they appear. It's also a scenario that will require some real emotional IQ—meaning, knowing how to bite back your tears, cool your temper, soften your sharp tongue, and curb your enthusiasm. The Queen of Swords represents rational pursuits and styles of expression. If you can Zen yourself down and approach the situation with quiet competence, you'll find the payoff to be pretty awesome.

However, the Queen always warns against self-deception. If

you're getting into a job, a living situation, a relationship, telling yourself it's gonna be great in spite of that nagging feeling in your gut and the parade of red flags in the distance, you won't last long. Better to wake up now and get honest about your doubts. The Queen of Swords is an amazing ally for drawing boundaries. She can help you see clearly and unemotionally how boundaries make sense and show you how to construct them, how to communicate them clearly, and how to *not* take care of whoever you just drew a boundary against. The Queen of Swords holds this wisdom: you can't simultaneously draw a boundary and be a caretaker for the person or situation you need space from. It's not an emotional thing for the Queen—it's simply not possible. This is clear, rational wisdom from the literal *Queen* of such things.

If the Queen of Swords has popped in your life as a person, lucky you! This is a top-notch individual. They'd make a great therapist, or other adviser, because they're great at detecting what is *really* going on, and they know how to communicate it to you in a straightforward manner.

This person is never going to tell you a lie. If they're a romantic partner, you might find yourself a little frustrated by their lack of emotional expression. The Queen is not a mushy, huggy, sentimental person. But you can trust that this person is with you because they really *want* to be with you. You can trust that if they say they love you, they really, truly love you. It might not be enough for you; some people can't exist without cuddles. The Queen of Swords is actually wise enough to understand this, so before dumping your lover out of frustration, have a clear, calm talk and see if you can't get them to simply agree to cuddle you every once in a while, for Christ's sake. They understand and are sympathetic to human desires, even as they seem to have very few, personally. Chances are they'll grant you your request, and you'll get to have some cuddles *and* keep this friendly, funny, honest, and intelligent person around as your date.

If *you* are the Queen of Swords, then life is asking you to draw on the powers of your intellect and not lean on your emotions right now. Maybe someone around you needs some help and your frank assessment of the situation could really change things. Maybe you need to offer some brutal honesty to someone close to you, whether they care to hear it or not. Maybe you're finding yourself overcome by emotions in a way that is hurting a situation; the card is ordering you to access the part of yourself that can see beyond emotions and operate from there. Whatever it may be, if you are embodying the Queen of Swords, then it's time for your honest, clearly communicated take on some situation to be offered, *sans* emotions.

Be the Queen of Swords

- The Queen of Swords's ability to see everything clearly is enviable; who among us isn't shuffling away in the dark half the time? If you truly can't see your way out of a cloudy situation—or if you do sort of know what you need to do but feel powerless against the force of your own denial—here is a helpful spell. Get one blue candle and two red or orange candles. As you light the blue candle, state your intention to see the situation with clarity. As you light the others, ask for the

courage to see the situation with clarity. It's often our own fears that blind us to what's really happening.

Next, write down what the situation is—the person, place, or thing that it concerns. Drip wax from all three candles onto the center of the paper, and then fold it together. If you have a beautiful, clear quartz crystal, now would be a great time to grab it and sit with it, asking it to impart its clarity to you. Keep sitting with these candles for seven days, and keep your waxy paper with them. At the end of the seven days, dispose of the paper in running water or bury it at a crossroads (in contemporary terms, the corner of any intersection).

- One of the Queen's gifts is her ability to override her emotions. Truthfully, she may not even have any to override, but that is surely not true of *you,* dear reader. For a spell to help you gain some mastery over problematic emotions, light a white or black candle. Into a pretty glass pour an ounce or less of water. Project into it all of your emotions. Get really soggy with it! Reflect on the various emotions that are causing you problems at the moment.

  Next, sit holding a natural sea sponge in your hand. Like the Queen of Swords, the sea sponge does not have emotional issues. Project into the sea sponge the ideal, emotion-free demeanor you wish to have. Visualize yourself seeing clearly, communicating clearly, feeling calm and balanced and stable as you go about doing whatever it is your emotions have been getting in the way of. Then put the sponge into the water and let it absorb the water/your feelings. When it has scarfed up all of your figurative emotions, gently remove it and bury it in the dirt somewhere. Return to your candle and sit there, ideally with a quartz crystal, to recharge the spell for as long as the situation requires it.

- Much of the Queen of Sword's knowledge has come from living life and being observant, something you hopefully do every day. But some of it has to do with her strong intuition. To strengthen your own intuition, I have an herbal spell you can do two ways. The ingredients are the same for each: nutmeg, ginger, garlic, rosemary, thyme, vetiver, sage, cinnamon, clove, and mint. It's okay to omit some of these; using a minimum of three should be sufficient, but using as many as you can is optimal.

  In the first version of the spell, collect the ingredients in their whole form in a little pouch. Wear the pouch or carry it on your person every day, taking care to give it a deep sniff every so often. At night, leave it on your bedside table or sleep with it beneath your pillow.

  If you only have powdered versions of the ingredients, the second version is to combine them well in a jar and keep it on your altar or desk by day, huffing it occasionally. At night keep it on your bedside table and give it a good sniff before drifting off. Be mindful throughout the day that you are working to build your intuition, and keep a dream journal at night, recording your dreams the moment you wake up, while you're still in bed, if possible before you even open your eyes. Each night, before sleep, review the previous night's dream.

Pentacles

The Page of Pentacles

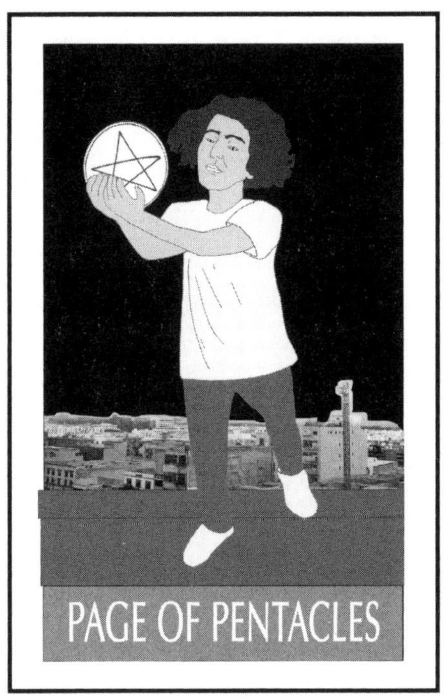

Look at this young person, walking slowly, even meditatively, transfixed by the beautiful golden coin in their hands. Extreme focus is the way to go when the Page of Pentacles pops up. Pages all represent youth, and youth in the Tarot represents newness and learning. Youths are the students of the Tarot. This Page, repre-

senting earth, is dutifully learning the ways of the material world. Earth signs are known for their dependability, and it is this Page's mission to prove their worthiness and reliability. They will have to work hard at it—they have no track record, after all—but success is implicit in this card. It only takes time and perseverance.

If the Page of Pentacles is appearing in your life as a person, you can depend on them. There might be something about this person that raises a bit of skepticism—their youth, their lack of experience, perhaps their very sheltered life. Regardless of that, their wish to apply themselves and make up for these deficits is real, and they possess the latent skills they need. Given time and a little guidance, they'll impress you. If this is someone already in your life, it could be a friend of a loved one who is finally ready to take action and looking to you perhaps for some sort of support. If it is a new person arriving in your work or love sphere, there is more to them than what appears on the surface. You might find yourself in a mentoring relationship, or dating a person significantly younger than you. If you're cool with a bit of an expert—the novice dynamic—you've got yourself a solid collaborator.

Maybe you are the Page of Pentacles. If so, it is time to stop daydreaming and start doing. Perhaps you've always wanted to learn a certain trade, or take up an interesting hobby, or figure out a way to monetize a hobby you're proficient at. The Page is telling you it's time to take those crucial first steps—join a class, order supplies, build your website. Reach out to people who might be able to mentor you; take them out for coffee and see if they have any wisdom they're willing to share. If the Page is arising in a romantic scenario, you might find yourself in a bit over your head. Maybe you are in your first significant relationship, or dating someone older than you whose experience is intimidating. With the Page, you learn by doing and prove yourself by your dedication to acquiring knowledge. In relationships especially, people learn by experience—how to communicate, how to be a good partner. Pay attention and learn from your mistakes. If your lover is worldly, don't be too proud to learn from them.

If the Page of Pentacles represents a situation, it is an opportunity that is being offered to you or one you've already pounced on. You are only at the beginning of finding your way through this new world, so be humble and diligent. If you apply yourself, you will impress others, and this opportunity will lead to many others. What is being offered to you is nothing short of the full potential of the suit of Pentacles; sure, there is failure in the suit (and in our lives), but there is also tons of abundance and potential to go far and become a respected master of your craft, whatever that may be.

Be the Page of Pentacles

I recently moved to Los Angeles with the intention of getting good at writing for television and film. Though I've got a dozen books under my belt, this sort of writing is *very* different, and a challenge to a writer, like myself, who's prone to tangents and doesn't think much about structure. Entertainment writing is *all*

structure. I come to it as the Page of Pentacles, knowing that all sorts of glory is possible if I work hard and learn the ropes. And we all know this town is filled with people whose dreams leapt to their deaths from the Hollywood sign, so I'm quite aware of the potential for failure the Pentacles also hold.

- To channel the positive qualities of the Page of Pentacles, I got my hands on a lovely chunk of raw honey citrine. There are many kinds of citrine, and they are all wonderful for different things. For hard work, focus, dedication, and the unflagging energy such an effort requires, honey citrine is the best. There is another citrine that is also a great work crystal—orange citrine. The primary difference between the two is that orange helps with money; it's an abundance crystal.

  Why, when I am working to make my living doing this writing, wouldn't I get the orange crystal, you ask? In keeping with the focus of the Page of Pentacles, the emphasis is on learning, applying myself, working hard. Everyone always wants money—I'm sure everyone reading this right now wouldn't mind a bump in their income. But to focus on that at a point when I'm trying to learn the craft would mix up all the energies. To keep the focus streamlined and pure, snag a honey citrine, sit with it, dedicate it to helping you work hard and accumulate knowledge and mastery, and keep it beside you or on your person as you take on your tasks.

- Here's a nice spell to harness Page of Pentacles energy. Get yourself some soil, a pot, and flower seeds. Go for something easy to grow, unless you're an expert gardener—then you can do whatever you want. Write down what it is you want to master. Really get into it—imagine yourself living your ideal. What would it feel like to succeed at this? Start from the beginning

and write out how you imagine the process going, taking you from beginner, through initial achievements, to mastery.

Fold the paper up and put it at the bottom of the planter. Place the soil on top, plant the seeds, and begin taking care of your plant. As it slowly grows, so will your skills sharpen and deepen. Let this plant be your vegetable familiar; move it to a bigger pot when necessary, or even out of a container and into the earth itself.

The Knight of Pentacles

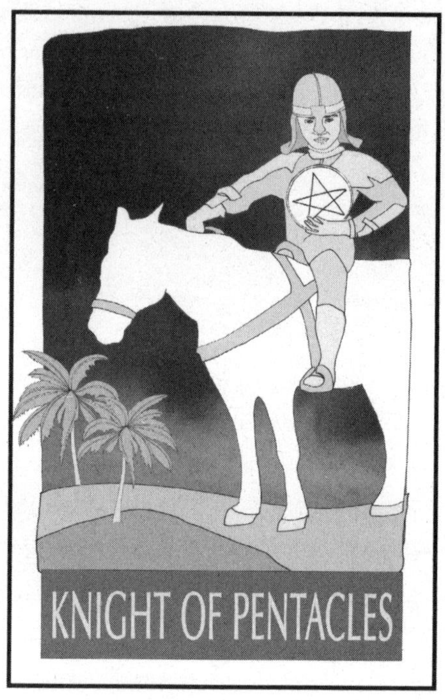

The Knight of Pentacles is significant for being the only horse with all four hooves on the ground. To say that this Knight is *grounded* would be the understatement of the eon. There will be no leaping forward, no dashing into the winds, no trotting gallantly forward. This Knight, for better or for worse, is sticking with where he's at. And where he's at almost certainly revolves around tasks, duties, work, and responsibility. For all things there is a time, and there is a time for the Knight of Pentacles. It's just not, like, the funnest time in the Tarot.

If the Knight of Pentacles is a person, he's probably someone you know because you work alongside him or he is helping you out somehow. For sure the work this individual carries out is impeccable. They're a total perfectionist, and if they show up in your work life as a boss or superior, that probably sucks. If you're working beneath the Knight, there is probably nothing you can do to match his work ethic and standard of perfection. If you do match up, buy yourself a round of drinks—you're brilliant. The rest of us will toil under this humorless taskmaster, wondering if they have *anything else* happening in their lives but this j-o-b. Nope. They don't. These workhorses are probably workaholics. They are wired to get a job done. If you're on the same team, they might raise the bar of what is expected, so better get busy. If they are working for you, you're psyched. They are going to quickly become indispensable. They probably won't gun for your position either; the Knight of Pentacles isn't particularly ambitious, he's just a hard worker who wants to deliver what is expected of him as perfectly as possible.

If the Knight has popped up as a possible romantic option, know that this person probably will show their love for you by vacuuming the house. They just might buy you the house too; the Knight likes practical, stable things and will work until he gets what he wants. If you're not interested, let them know ASAP because they will stubbornly pursue you until you spell it out for them. Then they will go away and you'll probably never see them again. If you're looking for a date who brings you on exciting vacations or surprises you with gifts and nights on the town, this is not that person. They can be a little on the dull side, but they are loyal and sincere and will pledge their hearts to you. If you're cool with supplying the fireworks, the Knight will make sure the ground is clear and all safety precautions have been met before you bring the sparkle.

If you are the Knight of Pentacles, it means you are being called to work, work, *work*. All work and no play makes Jack a dull boy? Oh well. That's just how it's going to be right now. Put your nose down and dedicate yourself to the task at hand. You are invested enough in whatever it is to want it to be successful, and its success is pretty much in your hands. You have the ability to build something stable and lasting, but you are going to have to buckle down and apply yourself. No slacking off, no cutting corners. Your standards should be high; you can meet them. Hopefully, none of this is a big deal—you're the Knight of Pentacles after all, you're wired for this! But in case your resolve is slipping, or you're feeling whiny or wanting to take a break, this card is here to give you a firm *no*. Your work is not done yet, and you can't stop until it is complete.

The Knight of Pentacles can also represent a situation that is sort of dull and tedious but has to get done. It could be something as banal as running errands, or a higher-stress task like doing your taxes. (Says the freelancer who just filed joint taxes with her wife for the first time. *Sheeeesh.*) Maybe it's a more massive project, like renovating a house, or even building one from the ground up. It's going to require your dedication and commitment for the long haul. If you don't value what's on the other side of all that toil, don't do it. It's going to be hard work, so make sure you have a meaningful connection to it to get you through the back-breaking days.

Be the Knight of Pentacles

- If you need to channel some of the Knight of Pentacles's hard-working diligence, bring some rosemary into your life. The herb promotes accuracy and learning; it's a hard worker that brings the alertness needed to do a good job and stick with a task. Get your hands on some rosemary oil and daub it on your temples before getting to work. Take a sniff when you feel yourself lagging, or use it in a diffuser to spread the scent around your workplace. The vibrations will keep you focused and committed.
- If you are suffering from a bout of serious laziness and procrastination, I have a soup spell to get you off your ass. Of course, you *do* have to get off your butt to make the potion in the first place. So. Ask the Universe for the willingness to help yourself and gather these ingredients: three cloves of garlic, minced; one onion, diced; an inch or so of fresh, grated ginger; some astragalus root; and as many shitake and reishi mushrooms as you like. The main player in this spell is the astragalus, known in Chinese medicine as Huang Qi. It brings energy and will protect you from the evil force of sloth.

  Sauté the garlic (good for keeping your willpower powerful) and onion (brings endurance) in some olive oil. Add a couple of cups of vegetable broth, the astragalus, and the mushrooms. Add salt (purification), black pepper (courage), and some cayenne (banishes negativity and will help the spell act faster). Stir this concoction nine times counterclockwise, saying, *Knight of Pentacles, hear my plea, take this laziness away from me.* Simmer until it's ready to be eaten, about 20 minutes, and enjoy. Repeat as necessary—it's good for you!

The King of Pentacles

When the King of Pentacles comes calling, I hear the Jay-Z lyric, *I'm not a businessman, I'm a business, man!* in my head. In fact, all the top rappers of our culture flood my brain when this comfortable ruler arrives. The King of Pentacles has it all. He's worked for it all and has become an authority on what it takes to rise to the top. This King is not afraid to claim all the power and all the knowledge, because he knows that he's earned it. He's not lord-

ing it over anyone else, not really; he's just jubilantly accepting his mega-fortunate destiny. This King likes the best things life has to offer and doesn't sweat laying out the cash for it. They're also in the position to be very generous, and here I think about the many family members, chosen and otherwise, supported by rappers who make it big. In the hands of this King, hard work, massive payoff, community support, and generosity are all one thing. Think about Jay-Z and Beyoncé donating over $1 million to the Black Lives Matter movement. Think about the dapper YA king Daniel Handler, also known as Lemony Snickett, and his wife the artist Lisa Brown donating $1 million to Planned Parenthood. The King of Pentacles urges us to unabashedly enjoy the fruits of our labor, to splurge on a luxury or two if we're able, and to throw some cash at the segments of our community in need of it.

If the King of Pentacles has come into your life as a person, they are deeply trustworthy and hardworking. Don't hold any surface-level pomp or visible wealth against them; they come by it honestly, and there is more to them than what's in their wallet. Any time you spend with them, whether in the workplace, the social sphere, or—lucky you—the dating landscape, will soon have you convinced that the only thing more solid than their bank account is their character. So go ahead, trust in this person, collaborate with them, hire them, marry them! It's a delight to be so close to such generosity of spirit.

If you are the King of Pentacles, something is being asked of you. Maybe it is actual money; if you've got it, you shouldn't hesitate to help out. Your time or your energy might be requested, and if so, find the time in your calendar to participate. You are probably being asked to lead in some way, and before you get annoyed or flabbergasted or overwhelmed, take a moment to ask—why you? You clearly have a certain standing in your community. You have something others don't, and someone believes it might be helpful. As long as the cause checks out, go for it. Also, if you were thinking of starting any type of charitable organization, or hosting a benefit, or somehow spearheading activity that will benefit your community, this card says, *Go!*

If the King of Pentacles represents a situation, it's a rich one, one that will be deeply fulfilling in most if not all ways—financially, spiritually, socially, emotionally, mentally. Sort of a perfect opportunity. Say yes to it! If the only thing holding you back is a bit of embarrassment at your literal embarrassment of riches, don't fret. Just do what you can to bring the opportunity to others like yourself. Spread the wealth and enjoy it.

Be the King of Pentacles

- One of the most kingly crystals around is lapis lazuli, a gorgeous, deep blue stone that was found all over King Tut's tomb. Carry it to enhance your sense of your own royalty, to accrue honor and power, to help protect you from the envious evil eye, and to generally increase your success. Consecrate it before a white, black, or green candle, and as you ask it to bestow these gifts upon you, pledge your commitment to the surrounding communities to share your success and power with others. Carry the stone with you everywhere and sleep with it under your pillow.

The Queen of Pentacles

First, let me point out that the Queen of Pentacles's cape descends from her *head*, where it is tucked beneath her *crown*. There is no symbolic meaning in this; it's just awesome. And taking a moment to enjoy the simple, beautiful things in life is totally this Queen's style, so I thought it appropriate to begin by admiring her.

The Queen of Pentacles is a self-made woman. Sure, she might have had a little help from a parent or the King, but she put it to wise use, not frivolously burning through any theoretical trust fund but using it sensibly to build a simple yet beautiful life for herself. She probably tithes 10 percent of it to a charity because she's a generous sort. She has enough to be generous, you might point out, but one of the messages of the Queen of Pentacles is that we all do. We are all rich, and we all have enough to be generous. If this depiction of mellow lushness isn't resonating with you, perhaps it is time to look around your life and simplify. One reason the Queen of Pentacles has time to stop and smell the roses (and plant the roses, and tend the roses) is that she keeps her life very simple. No outrageous scheming, planning, or brainstorming for this one. She doesn't much see the point of most things and would rather sink her energy into, like, making a really killer soup stock.

If the Queen of Pentacles has come up in your life, lucky you. This person is super-nurturing and backs up her caretaking energy with solid skills. If she tends to you while you're sick, she isn't going to sit on her ass watching *Broad City* and passing you a pill every three hours; she's going to whip you up a nutritional stew, and she probably raided her home apothecary for some (homemade) tinctures and balms too. She's got a motherly vibe, and if she's your actual mother, then lucky you times a million. Chances are she's just a maternal person, of any age, though she very well might work with children or have a brood (or dreams of a brood) of her own. This person is beyond reliable. They're super-practical and handy, and in addition to cooking you stew and delivering your medication in a timely manner she also might fix your printer, stop that leak in your sink, and sew a button back onto your coat before she leaves. By keeping her life simple, the Queen of Pentacles has omitted the distractions that prevent so many of us from being present in the moment. She is super-present. Make sure you rise to her standards while you're hanging out; the least you can do with this super-helper is share your presence and appreciation. And if this is a love situation, I hope you like old-fashioned mix CDs, homemade bread, and cohabitation in a wonderful, homey environment, because that's where you're headed.

If the Queen of Pentacles represents a situation, it's one that is very good for you, one that will materially benefit you, one you've probably been working hard to get, or working hard to be fit for. This card has *yes* all over it, so do avail yourself of whatever opportunity it's suggesting. If you find yourself with some extra cash, be frugal with it but not miserly. Throw a dinner party with all the finest ingredients, then toss the rest in an IRA. Investing in a home—either buying your own or investing money to beautify what you already have—is also a good use of funds under the Queen of Pentacles. If she's up for you, chances are you are doing well financially; if this isn't true, she might represent a situation or a person who could help you improve your economic situation. This isn't a get-rich-quick scheme; the Queen is a hard worker. She wants to have enough to be comfortable, and she wants you to want to be comfortable too. She doesn't see any valor in poverty and hopes that you don't either. Neither does she think money should be lavished on senseless luxury. She is the financial middle path, enjoying what she has in a modest yet passionate way, acting generously, and saving for the future.

If you are the Queen of Pentacles, how lovely! It might mean that your powers of nurturance are in demand. If you're being

called to take care of someone, never fear—you have the energy and are even likely to enjoy it. If no one's asking for your chicken soup, why not throw a dinner party for some friends to show off new recipes and bask in mutual affection. In addition to being nurturing, the Queen of Pentacles is a super-capable hard worker, so if you're running her energy right now, it might mean that a lot is being expected of you at work—or you might be expecting a lot of yourself. Knowing this Queen, it could be both—clocking in eight hours on the job, then coming home to work on your DIY kitchen reno. If you were under the influence of any other queen, I might be worried, but this one will make sure there's a food delivery app on your phone, Epsom salts in your post-reno bath, and eight hours of sleep at the end of it all. She works hard and self-cares hard, so if you're being asked to put the pedal to the metal, make sure (a) it's a temporary situation, and (b) you're able to be extra nice to yourself while you're working. The Queen of Pentacles would also totally up her probiotics and vitamin C during such a moment, so why don't you too? Manage your money like a boss, work like a horse, entertain like Martha, and indulge like a hedonist. That's the Queen of Pentacles way.

Be the Queen of Pentacles

- Throw a Queen of Pentacles dinner party, serving all charmed food. Many herbs and spices do double duty as dinner ingredients *and* magic ingredients, so all you need to elevate a normal

dinner party to an elaborate spell is intention. Here's a short list of magical ingredients that are pretty commonly used in cooking: allspice (healing), almond (to overcome difficulties), bananas (prosperity), blackberry (healing), cabbage (money magic), cayenne (to dispel negativity), dill (protection), endive (sex magic), fennel (to banish drama), galangal (hex breaker), garlic (purification), hibiscus (love), lavender (peace), leeks (protection), lemon (remove negativity), lettuce (sex magic), mace (reunions), nettle (to banish negativity from the home), olive (matchmaking), papaya (love), quince (protection), radish (lust), saffron (more lust), tamarind (love), tangerine (high energy), vanilla (mental abilities), vinegar (to banish evil), walnuts (to make wishes come true), yucca (purification)—I could go on and on. It seems like anything you can put in your body has some type of magical use ascribed to it. And if it doesn't, put your own on it.

To enchant your dinner party, spread candles throughout the area where you will cook and entertain. Select significant flowers and other decor. While you prepare the food, stay focused on what your intention is for each dish—to bring love, healing, reunion, protection, prosperity, sex, whatever you like. You *might* want to tell your guests that your food is enchanted; I think it's bad manners to cast spells on people without telling them. But if you've done your work, the magical aromas will be working on your guests from the moment they walk through the door. Who would refuse you? Make sure to infuse your beverages with magic too, even the water you serve. Put a little plate aside as an offering to the goddess. Bon appétit.

- Get yourself a pot of lavender. Like real, living lavender, with roots and dirt, not just decorative stalks or tips. (Although I did have a witchy friend who made herself an eye pillow of nothing

but loose lavender and it remains one of the best things I've ever smelled!) With your focused intention, you will dedicate this plant to the Queen of Pentacles, who is basically a manifestation of an earth goddess. By caring for this plant—whose magical properties include love, protection, healing, peace, sleep, purification, and relief from sorrow and mental angst—you will be invoking the powers of the Queen of Pentacles, asking for her energies to be present in your day, asking for her qualities of prosperity, generosity, wisdom, and nurturance to grow inside you.

Feel free to harvest the lavender as it comes, using it in cooking or teas, as a sleep aid or, most especially, as a gift to others.